15⁰⁰

About Coach Bagonzi

I have known Dr. John Bagonzi for over 30 years and have consulted with him count-less times — working with him during the summers while in high school and college, through my professional pitching career and while a professional pitching coach myself, Coach Bagonzi has been an invaluable resource for me. His tremendous knowledge of the science of kinesiology, and how it is applied to proper pitching mechanics, combined with a lifetime of playing and coaching baseball puts him in an elite group as far as I am concerned. His passion for learning and teaching coupled with a great sense of humor results in a truly unique person. John is someone I feel most fortunate to have been able to call coach as well as *my* good friend. *He is a genius in pitching.*

> **— Rich Gale, Major League pitcher Kansas City Royals
> pitching coach, Boston Red Sox**
> Nineteen years in pro-ball.

The best pitching coach in the east; a pro's pro — very intelligent about pitching con-cepts- great overhand curve(a thing of beauty) — the best I've ever seen — I chased him all over the continent trying to sign him. Had all the goods. Once saw him pitch both ends of a doubleheader with a no-hitter in the second game.

> **— Lennie Merullo, Major League shortstop Chicago Cubs
> former director Major League Scouting Bureau
> Presently with the New England Division**

Mechanics are essential in becoming a good pitcher. Although mine have been refined throughout the years, it all started with Coach Bagonzi.

> **— Chad Paronto, Major League pitcher
> Cleveland Indians**

No one knows more about pitching than John Bagonzi. He works with all our pitch-ers — I wouldn't have anybody else.

> **— Tom Underwood, longtime coach
> Plymouth Area High School**

John Bagonzi has been a frequent contributor to Coaching Management Magazine, *a publication for high school and college coaches. His articles always provide insight into the game and hands-on advice for old and new. He always appears in our yearly baseball edition.*

> **— Eleanor Frankel, editor-in-chief
> Momentum Media Sports**

John is undoubtedly the best-ever coach in New Hampshire. His teams were abso-lutely prepared, and played with class and precision; they were great to play against. His pitchers always had great curveballs. Though they always beat you — you never would have known after the game — they won with class.

> **— Bob Savage, Major League pitcher
> Philadelphia Athletics**

—continued

I like Dr. Bagonzi's theories and agree completely with him on the push-off concept.
— **Bob Feller, Cleveland Indians Great**
and Major League Hall of Famer

John is far and away the best coach ever in NH. He turned our baseball program around instantly and we've been going strong since. He knows pitching better than anyone I know of.
— **John Clark, Athletic Director and**
vice president Plymouth State College

He made me ready for pro ball when I was 17 and everything he taught me I used — I won 4 of my first 6 games at the Class A level — he is an incredible motivator.
— **Steve Blood, Minnesota Twins**
(won 50 games in pitching Woodsville High School to three state championships)

Bags and I were experimenting with all types of pitches long before people knew about them. John was always ahead of his time on development of certain pitches.
— **Bob Smith, Major League pitcher, Boston Red Sox,**
Detroit Tigers, and Pittsburgh Pirates

Coach Bagonzi is a perfectionist. He made me understand spins so well that I had two quality pitches when I went to Class A ball and won six of my first seven games. As a coach, John Bagonzi always pushed us beyond what we thought were our limits. As athletes, we would do anything he asked of us, out of respect for him. The lessons he taught me on the court and on the field are still with me now — in how I deal with life, work, and the problems that come up. He shaped players' characters to believe they could do anything they wanted, as long as they were willing to work hard. My opportunity to play professional baseball was largely due to John teaching me how to throw a curveball.
— **Jim MacDonald, Major League pitcher,**
Houston Astros

John and I played together years ago with the Corning Red Sox — he had a great curve. I agree with him totally on the drive-off the back leg concept. I also share his thoughts on throwing inside and using a two-seamer and four-seamer in the North/South style of pitching. He's a great pitching technician.
— **Bill Monbouquette, Major League pitcher**
and pitching coach, Boston Red Sox Hall of Fame
Currently coaching in Detroit Tiger's system.

Dr. Bagonzi's articles are highly received in Collegiate Baseball Magazine. *His vast experience and technical expertise makes him greatly appreciated by our readership. We are indebted and grateful for his superb writing skill and style and are pleased to have his contributions.*
— **Lou Pavlovich, Jr., editor *Collegiate Baseball***

The Act of Pitching

by Dr. John Bagonzi
edited by Alex Levin

Published by Pitching Professor Publications
Woodsville, New Hampshire

Fifth Printing

Published by Pitching Professor Publications
19 Pine Street, Woodsville, NH 03785

Principal photography by Alex Levin
Illustrations by Bryan Steward
Design and layout by Pat Goodwin

www.pitchingprofessor.com

Printed in the U.S.A.

ISBN 978-0-9778250-0-4
ISBN 0-9778250-0-0

Dedication

I dedicate this book to the most important person in my life, my wife Dreamer Deese Bagonzi. She hails from Winnsboro, Olympia, Columbia area of South Carolina, and is truly a southern belle who has become a bona fide Yankee. And I mean Yankee only in the regional sense, as in her uncompromising devotion she has taken even my Red Sox to heart.

This remarkable person has been the muse for all of my projects and has caused me to soar to levels I probably would not have reached without her support. She is my partner for life, and has encouraged me in my endeavors without fail. The completion of this book is as much a tribute to her perseverance as to my own and I hope that she receives the same satisfaction as I have in the completion of this work. Thank you, Dreamer, for all that you do, for the family and home that you have blessed me with, for your constant support, for your always honest opinion, and most of all, for who you are. I know it may sound clichéd — but I couldn't have done any of it without you.

Acknowledgments

This page is intended to extend appreciation to all the pitching models who appear in this book for their diligence and cooperation.

To my typists — Brian Ross, Kimberly Roy, Roxana Morrill, and to my proofreaders — Cecilia Guecia and Corinne Cothern, for your promptness and excellence, I commend and thank you. To Steve Ross of Ross Business Center who weathered through so many copies of work and quickly rendered material essential for the grist of the book, I give my thanks.

My sincere appreciation goes out to all the great students and players who have made my life so interesting and rewarding, and to all the coaches who have shared in my curiosity and exploration. With a special thanks to Tom Underwood. To John Clark, Director of Administrative Services at Plymouth State, I must express how valuable your friendship and support has been. To the many participants whose grasp of technical instruction and resulting advancement has given me great satisfaction, I appreciate your commitment and applaud your development. And finally to all those pitchers who have made it into professional baseball and ultimately the Major Leagues, I extend my utmost congratulations and wish you the very best in your careers.

I want to extend further appreciation to Jim Deaderick and the Hedgehog*hill* Group for their continued support, without which this project would never have been started.

Also to my daughter Teresa Godoy for her assistance in photos and Bill McLane, Amy Wright, Dana Paronto, Wayne and Mary Beth Dickey for contributing essential photos, my sincere appreciation.

Author's Word Regarding Editor

There can be a unique relationship between an author and his editor. They share common highs and lows. They weather rough spots together. I feel I've achieved this very close relationship with Alex Levin, the editor of *The Act of Pitching*. Being the baseball person Alex is, has certainly allowed for a common understanding of many of the technical aspects of this writing. Being able to brainstorm areas that are controversial has enabled us to link into strong viewpoints in subjects that are often avoided.

I have a high regard for his editorial expertise, his quest for excellence and his pursuit of accuracy. I also like him as a person, a humanitarian, and a friend. It is with these thoughts that I thank and commend Alex Levin for his diligence in seeing this project through and bringing *The Act of Pitching* to fruition.

EDITOR'S PROLOGUE

SOME THINGS ARE JUST TOO GOOD TO KEEP UNDER YOUR HAT.

My son Marcus started off his season in our Cal Ripken twelve and under league by pitching a complete game no-hitter with fifteen strikeouts and just one walk. He mixed it up all afternoon with a high and tight four-seam fastball, a two-seamer that zipped across the bottom of the strikezone, elusive as a stealth bomber and a palm ball change-up that even one of the umpires described as *nasty*. Now halfway through the season, he's allowed a total of five hitters to reach base and none of them have crossed the plate.

Marcus is one of the models featured throughout this book. Another pitcher featured in the book is Chad Paronto. Like Marcus, Chad was born and raised in New Hampshire. Chad was called up by the Baltimore Orioles this spring and has been pitching some pretty good ball in a relief role. He has a 93 + mph fastball, but even more importantly, a sinking fastball that breaks bats and induces groundouts. Aside from their state of origin, Marcus and Chad have something else in common. Marcus is not what I would call a *natural,* although he is so smooth and graceful with his delivery, he looks as if he was born to pitch. Even the casual observer finds it a pleasure to watch Marcus work. So too is the case with Chad who is able to unite all the strength of his 240-pound body with great and often flawless mechanics.

The common denominator for this five-foot tall sixth grader and this six-foot-four Major Leaguer is that they both credit Coach John Bagonzi, the *Pitching Professor,* for giving them the kind of mechanics that is allowing each of them to have his day in the sun. Lenny Merullo, the one time director of the Major League Scouting Bureau, refers to Coach Bagonzi as "the best pitching instructor in the east, a pro's pro."

From what I understand about the Paronto family, the path that Marcus is now walking is fairly similar to that of Chad's. Both have fathers who preached fundamentals from day one. Chad wasn't a standout pitcher from the start, but adhering to the belief that great mechanics leads to good pitching, he just kept getting better and better until he started passing by all those hotshots who had previously held the spotlight.

Marcus is now in his fourth season of pitching competitively and though he has always won more than he has lost, during most of his first three years, he was never the first choice to start a big game. Coaches felt Marcus just didn't have enough juice on his fastball to take on the better hitters.

In an effort to help get my son over that hump, I bought just about every pitching book on the market and a few videotapes as well. Some of the information I garnered from these resources helped a bit. But all the information seemed piecemeal and in the end I still didn't have a clear understanding of how I should go about in helping Marcus become a better pitcher. I tried searching the Internet and discovered that for every suggestion offered, one could find a dozen countering views, plus countless arguments that seemed to be more about ego than anything else.

Then early spring of last year I brought Marcus to an all-day pitching clinic put on by Coach Bagonzi at the local high school. From the time that Coach starts talking, it takes all of about thirty seconds to realize that this guy is the real thing, and you don't have to be a baseball person to realize this. One highbrow individual who lumps baseball in with mud wrestling and demolition derbies, said on meeting Coach Bagonzi, "You can tell right off he's one of the good guys."

And that might just be the most perfect description of Coach. No *BS*, no insatiable ego, Coach is a person who cares. He tends not to care about what other people think of him, nor does he care about getting rich or famous. What he cares about is making each pitcher he encounters into a better pitcher.

Coach is a rare blend of artist and technician, teacher and student, old-school gruffness and compassionate sensitivity. And, though there may not be anyone on this planet who is more knowledgeable about pitching, he approaches each day looking to learn a little more, he approaches each clinic looking to discover new ways to make pitchers understand the information he wishes to impart.

At Coach's clinics (and I've been to several now) you might find college pitchers or high school pitchers or Little League pitchers. Sometimes you will find them all mixed into one group, but no matter what the age, what the level, every pitcher and would-be pitcher knows that Coach is talking directly to him. If this is the age of the hyperactive, undisciplined child, you wouldn't know it by observing one of Coach's clinics. Everyone pays attention: one, because Coach expects you to, and secondly, because what he says is understandable and very relevant to what each participant is trying to accomplish.

Before coming to the clinic, I knew that getting rotation on the ball was important but I didn't know how to make it happen consistently. I knew the basic differences between a four-seam and two-seam fastball, but had only a vague sense of how to grip the ball. By the end of the clinic I knew all that and more. Through the course of the day Coach also discovered that Marcus was losing power off his fastball primarily because he wasn't reaching back far enough to maximize the power of the pitching circle.

Probably the most valuable thing we learned that day, was a series of drills that were simple enough to take home with us. One such drill dramatically improves rotation. And the Stride Drill — which by itself is worth the price of admission — gave us a systematic way to develop, monitor, refine and correct mechanics.

Sometimes when you try a different approach, you have to look real hard to see if it makes a difference. And sometimes you're not sure if you're actually seeing improvement or just your hopeful projections. That's not the way it is after working with Coach B. The improvements are very evident and very real and they often show up in the following day's boxscore.

When you spend time with Coach, what you learn goes way beyond technique. You come to learn that while good pitching mechanics might take some time to bear fruit, it's important for each pitcher to live in the present rather than always be dreaming about that big Major League career. A player's *day in the sun* might take place in the pros, but could very well happen in college or in high school or even in Little League. We owe it to each player to give him the tools that will help him realize his best potential at any given moment. The lessons about winning and losing learned in Little League, the attitudes and approaches formulated in high school, obstacles overcome at any age, courage enacted on any stage will shape a character and prepare one to deal well with anything that life dishes out.

Another big lesson learned from working with Coach is the concept of believing in ourselves enough that we will let ourselves get good. Such a lesson was very applicable to the creation of this book. We always had an eye on making this the best pitching book ever — the most complete, the most systematic, and the most readable. When topics came up that were shrouded in vagueness, when techniques were encountered that seemed unexplainable, we worked and worked them until they were no longer vague or confusing. Like with great mechanics, no shortcuts were taken in this book. We shot over 7,000 photos and browsed another 2,000 to get the 400 in this book. We made this book for all levels, for all kinds of students. And unlike any other book of its kind, we took the painstaking effort to lay it out so that the reader will never have to flip a page to get to a referenced picture.

By reading just the bolded print and looking at the pictures, one will come away with more valuable information than is found in most pitching books. But those who wish to achieve the ranks of pitching's inner sanctum will want to read the whole book from cover to cover because it's all here for anyone who is willing to give himself permission to get good.

When you're really good at what you do, Coach's philosophy is that you shouldn't brag but rather keep it under your hat. In this introduction from beginning to end, I've violated that principle and I apologize, but our first imperative as Coach says is to help pitchers realize their full potential.

CONTENTS

INTRODUCTION
PITCHING IS AN ACT

As humans, we fill our lives with activities. Many we partake in by the mere consequence of being alive. We eat, we sleep, we breath, not because we think to, but because we feel compelled to. . . So too without conscious reason or intent, we may feel compelled to pick up a rock and toss it across a field — sometimes having a target in mind, other times not. But to be human also means we have the opportunity to consciously involve ourselves with this world. We have the chance not just to react to our world but to act upon it with full participation.

Pitching a baseball in a competitive arena is an act and like any other act, it has a reason behind it and an intent in front of it.

To the spectator it may seem like the pitcher on the mound is involved in the simple action of trying to throw a ball past a batter. It may seem like a one-dimensional mechanical performance (geniuses in any art make their acts seem simple, even effortless), but each throw, each pitch holds a full story with a past and a present. And when it is filled with artistry and craftsmanship, it becomes a beautiful story.

Every pitch is a biomechanical happening. It is also an artistic event with the talent of athleticism (agility, strength, rhythm) on display. It is a celebration of craftsmanship: the search for perfection and refinement that is forever ongoing.

Searching for that refined combination of art and technique is the hallmark of the master craftsman. It may be an eternal and sometimes elusive search, but if we are true to our intentions — even if we never achieve perfection — along the way we will achieve more rarified levels of craft. It is that pursuit — the time and effort spent in learning and mastering technique and athletic expression — which is present and intelligent that makes one a craftsman, and the display of his or her talents an act.

To all the great pitchers of the past and those today committed to the development of your craft, thank you for your model of excellence. The new ones strive to emulate your craftsmanship.

I was asked to do a book on pitching a long time ago. Being essentially a traditionalist and pitching in the era of ironclad tenets, I had quickly evolved as a technician, which was helping me develop a vocabulary and a language to communicate ideas and fix flaws. But even though I had plenty of information and ideas, I still didn't think I'd be able to accurately present my views.

I'm glad that I waited. Because doing something well is one thing — it only requires you to know how to make something work for yourself — but to teach something, to coach something, requires that you know that something inside out, and that you have some ideas about the way people learn.

I love pitching — and I believe you can get very good at it, if you do enough right things. . . .

Coaching for many years at the high school and college level, and doing pitching clinics for many years has put me in touch with pitching and pitchers just about every day for the past four decades. In the beginning, I realized I had plenty to say, but needed to live my pitching career through my subjects still further in order to fortify and embellish my existing beliefs so that they could apply to everyone, and not just to me.

Now the time has arrived to create a work that communicates in a way people will be able to understand and find useful, so that those wanting to be pitchers and those wishing to help pitchers can have an aid that is complete, sequential, and sensible.

Having an unfulfilled professional pitching career has actually given me the impetus to pursue questionable areas and to learn as much as I can. I cherish the accomplishments of pitchers working under my teaching and supervision. Each aspirant with whom I have been privileged to work has provided me with one more opportunity to pursue pitching excellence.

There are no experts on pitching. No one ever reaches the point of knowing all there is to know. Although, there are some who believe they do. . . . Good pitching instructors always leave the door open to new ideas, and their search for excellence is eternal. I like to consider myself one of those. I want young pitchers to improve. *Each one is me pitching all over again.*

This book is based on a pitcher's experiences, a coach's ardor, a clinician's practicality and a teacher's expertise. . . .

It is with these traits that this book will attempt to give a strong definition to the truth of pitching as a process — fortified by the author's love of teaching, particularly to those motivated aspirants who strive to be the best they can. They are the ones who make the work worthwhile. First and foremost good coaches teach to improve. Adhering to fundamentals, and good technique — and making corrections where applicable; this causes winning to follow.

Do pitching coaches pitch through their students?

...The good ones do.

Coaching has put me in touch with many hundreds and hundreds of young pitchers and given me a study in endless varieties of pitching forms and styles, as well as an appreciation of different anatomies and body shapes. My subjects have ranged from the nine-year-old aspirant to the twenty-three year-old still attempting to be a pro, as well as the established pro looking for another pitch. All along the way, a plethora of questions regarding the pitching process have been brought forth, by teacher as well as by student. Many of these questions still remain unanswered. Thank heavens many have been answered, and there has been a great satisfaction in developing a rather strong philosophy on pitching mechanics and technique. But even that is not equal to the satisfaction one achieves in watching the artistic expression of the pitching performance where the whole becomes something far more beautiful than the sum of the parts.

ANALYZE BUT DON'T OVER-ANALYZE

In this age of communication, we've seen an awful lot of so-called experts on pitching come onto the scene. They seem to have a fetish for propounding great solutions to mechanical flaws and will offer solutions on the fly through Internet pitching forums, often giving us the over-analysis of an obvious glitch. They also have a tendency towards the attitude that the human body can be programmed like a robot. Well-intentioned as they may be, I wonder if such analysts can actually throw a ball and often I discover in my conversations with them, that they cannot. Over-analysis can be an exercise in useless prattle, but because intelligent people are involved, one can get deceived as to its validity. The improvement of pitching technique is open-ended, but one can get close to the truth without getting lost in a myriad of technical *how about's* along the way.

Don't fix things that aren't broken! Learn where things aren't broken and leave well enough alone.

BACK OFF AND SEE THE PARTS

One must take care to not objectify mechanics so much that the *forest is missed for the trees.* The sum total of technical steps should reveal an integration of leverage systems that produces a smooth flow of events and an end result that is at least as strong as its parts combined. When this does not happen, it deems well for the observer to consider the artistic and rhythmic quality of the process. Sometimes the problem lies not in the bone and sinew and neurons, but in the soul and spirit of the matter. Always the bottom line is the throwing of the ball. If the pitcher is doing everything as he should and the result is not what is hoped for, at some point we have to stop expecting that we will find a solution through

tinkering. We should instead try to encourage the artist to emerge, the one who takes pride in his craft, the one who has accepted his mission and is driven to complete it.

To a certain extent, the craft of pitching means connecting the dots. Once the picture is drawn, it must still be colored in by the individual in his own style with his own strokes. When this happens, don't be afraid to stand back and just admire. Better to lose yourself in the beauty of the act, instead of in a jumble of technical terms.

Always remain true to the idea of having the pitch flow naturally, and not be forced.

THE FALLACY OF THE KISS PRINCIPLE

To say that everything is simple is to perhaps mislead, because in over-simplifying one may miss the nuances and subtleties that need to be encountered. The KISS (keep it simple, stupid) principle may have some validity, but simplicity should be achieved at the end of the journey. Exploration and confirmation are vital factors in the successful refinement of the pitching process. Before simplicity is arrived at, one must first journey into the realm of unanswered questions. There are many little subtleties, which, if learned, will allow the marginal player to cross over that line into effectiveness.

The super-talented pitcher may ignore these hidden edges. But such athletes are rare. Those careers based solely on raw talent are often the shortest. Most of us can't afford to ignore explorations of the minute. That is often what it takes to experience the exhilaration of excellence.

MY FIRST CURVE

My father was a bowling alley proprietor and a prominent bowler in his own right who refined bowling to an artistic expression — smooth, stylish, efficient, accurate, and masterful. We never talked about it. My mother, I suspect, never wanted me to be a bowler. My father bet on bowling matches, and while he won much of the time, my mother probably emphasized the losses more. Don't get the wrong idea — I loved my mother dearly and she loved and supported my baseball career immensely.

At any rate, my father never attempted to encourage me to be a bowler, and certainly never taught me its intricacies. However, whenever it was made known that he was bowling, either in a match or just for fun and practice, you could be sure I would be in the front row. I watched him like a hawk. I was always trying to decipher what it was that made him such a portrait of grace and mechanical efficiency. I suspect he knew he was good because he was a very proud man. However, he was extremely humble, and never flaunted his skill.

Occasionally, as I got older, we would bowl together just for fun and, while I'm sure he wasn't trying to embarrass me (I surely was a good bowler), typically the score was lopsided in his favor. Once I saw him get a spare by standing on the left side of the alley (he was right-handed), and rolling a big curve, he picked off the corner pin. I was completely amazed; I thought it was magic and wanted to capture it for myself. I snuck down on Sunday morning and practiced the big hook over and over again until someone heard me (we lived over the bowling alley) and put a stop to it. On another occasion, with a single pin on the right side of the alley, he rolled a reverse curve the equal of the big hook and picked off the pin. I again was so shocked that I vowed I had to also learn this reverse curve — which I proceeded to do on Sunday mornings. I eventually got quite capable of accomplishing these two types of curves. My father told me subsequently that there was more to bowling than rolling curveballs.

I suspect I inherited my fascination for making balls do magical things from my father, but just as importantly, from those early days I developed the belief that such magic was a learnable skill. That with enough dedicated practice and proper focus, fueled by desire and curiosity, the artistry would come. And while I was left to my own devices to develop the skills my father so dramatically revealed, over the years I've come to believe that proper teaching has a place in the equation. Ultimately, one has to have that hunger for perfection — no amount of teaching can ever compensate for that. But there is a place for teaching. Through my father, I learned the importance of having a role model, of having an ideal to aspire toward. So to that end I have continually attempted to refine my own ability as an example to those I would teach. But also through my own hunger I've learned that there is a place for teaching that goes beyond modeling. My own coaching tenures and my pitching clinics have been a living testimony to that and with this book I hope to continue such a tradition.

The models I have used in this book are pitchers of all levels who have achieved various degrees of success in the act of pitching, including myself. Like my father, they are all models that one can learn from. But unlike my father, I have no ambivalence towards the achievement of pitching excellence for those who would desire it and so have sought though my instruction, through my words to impart the lessons that years of experience have taught me. Indeed there is no replacement for experience. One ultimately learns to pitch from a mound, not from a book. But proper instruction can reinforce and set one on the proper road.

MY STYLE OF PITCHING

I was a North/South type of pitcher (see Approaches to Effective Pitching). I've encouraged many of my subjects to use this approach, however I'm very aware that other approaches might be more effective for other pitchers. As a collegiate and a pro in Canadian Leagues, I was very much an overpowering, overhand type of thrower, employing a fastball with a sharp curve and constantly attempting to deceive by changing the batter's eye levels. I was surely a blue-collar pitcher. Pitching over 200 innings a season was my usual. Going nine innings and more was routine. I once pitched a doubleheader against the University of Rhode Island (2-0 and 4-0, the second game being a no-hitter). Sixteen Major League scouts watching in the stands each offered me a bonus contract to sign. This approach

to pitching was very effective in college where my five no-hitters still remain a record at the University of New Hampshire.

Upon entering the Red Sox organization — while this approach was successful to a satisfactory extent — a more refined technique or style was in order. It is with that in mind that this text is written. My career was culminated at age 29 (voluntarily) and I had 117 career wins at all levels by then. I continued to pitch informally while coaching, so experimentation progressed.

DO WHAT WORKS

One of the beautiful things about staying on the *cutting edge* is that one gets to see old truths born and reborn. Yesteryear's adages have a way of coming back to reaffirm themselves as the correct way. However, not all of them get reconfirmed; some get outright overruled! But the quest for melding the best of the old with the best of the new goes on. The *truth* or *close to the truth* lies in this range.

The game is infinite like anything else, and it's a shame that there are those that don't like innovation, because this is an ongoing and evolving event like education, medicine, science etc. Baseball has had much improvement to it, and that is not to say that the game in the past was lacking, but there is a *state of the art* in everything. I revel in it even after many years. It is beautiful. What is happening today is tremendous; however, because my background is traditional, I also respect the artisans of the past with great fervor.

The evolution of the pitching process requires the awareness of new ideas and the changing of ideas that may prove less functional as the game goes on. However, there are ironclad tenets, which rule the process and likely will never change. We should be suspicious where some of these absolutes get tampered with, especially where they interfere with the prime directive.

I'm grateful for the Mike Marshall's of the world who are so thoroughly versed in the scientific aspects of athletic performance that their proclamations have a finality to them. Because they also speak from the voice of experience, their views are worth their weight in gold when one is attempting to clear up a controversial area in technique. They speak with substance, both with regard to athletic performance, and the laws of physics and biology. But the Marshall's of this world are few and far between. And for every Marshall, one can find a hundred would-be experts.

One of the great dangers that occurs in a field where so many *experts* abound, is that people will sometimes be guided or misguided by that would-be expert needing to make his mark. This sometime results in change occurring for change's sake, and the acceptance of concepts that are long in logic, but short in truth.

Physical laws are unalterable and final. They have the handwriting of god on them; they are not the invention of any individual but are the discoveries of such geniuses as Newton and Magnus. In pitching a baseball, these laws come dramatically into action, and to suggest that the act of pitching a baseball is not subject to them is to revoke them, which I for one don't feel authorized to do.

Some areas of question exist that fall into the realm of honest controversy. These might include the advantages of the power slider versus the power curve, the use of weights to develop arm strength, the value of the high hard one versus the low hard one. But to argue some others is to make argument against the design of our universe. The ability of a fastball to rise is one such discussion where the participants sometimes choose to ignore the laws of physics. Discussion about pushing off the rubber also falls squarely into that category.

Even if we ignore the physical evidence and keep our discussion on a more earthly plane, to say that pushing-off is a fallacy is to call to task some, if not all, of the greatest pitchers who have taken the mound. We're talking about pitchers who have won a lot of games, pitched a ton of innings, lasted a long while, were relatively free of serious arm trouble, and made handsome livings at their craft. These magnificent hurlers either pushed off, (or thought they did), tried to push off, or created the impression they did, and would have been most skeptical if you tried convincing them that they would have been better pitchers if they hadn't tried to push off.

Bob Feller called me a while back to assert his view on the push-off. Ted Williams — among many others, myself included — believe that Feller is perhaps the greatest righthanded pitcher of all time. Without question, he generated as much power as any pitcher in the game. His fastball was recorded at 107 mph (albeit with photoelectric cells). Bob expressed in no uncertain, but quite colorful terms, his thought that pushing off the rubber is especially important when it comes to throwing the ball hard. For me the opinion of Bob Feller in this area is quite enough. And when you couple his authority with Newton's concept *that for every action there is opposed an equal reaction,* I don't think there's much room left for reasonable argument.

In this book's chapter on mechanics, I address still further the issue of the push-off, and while I believe without doubt that one pushes off, I'm sure there are quite reputable individuals who have convinced themselves otherwise. And that's okay with me. If a pitching aspirant wants to believe such, and gets great results believing that he doesn't push off, I'm not going to jump all over him. In my world there is room for differences in approach and perception both. Variety is part of the human condition. To not accept variety is to ignore the human element of the great game of baseball.

As long as baseball is played by human beings, it will evolve haphazardly by happenstance, no matter how much order we attempt to impose. Great Mechanics is all about the beauty of bringing order to chaos — about overpowering randomness with planning and execution. It is awesome to watch a pitcher working with perfect balance and rhythm. At such times his performance is not only effective, but it appears to be effortless. To witness it is to get a glimpse of our harmony with the order of nature. Like the work of any great artist in any field, it can restore our faith in the divinity and purpose of the human experience. And as awe-inspiring as it is to watch, to get a chance to function in that sphere — even for a short while is even more exhilarating. Great Mechanics gives a pitcher the chance to achieve such a state — his humanness will determine whether he takes full advantage of that chance.

Some people would reduce baseball to a game of stats, one set of stats matched against another, but baseball is a game played by humans. All the dramas of being human are played out between the white lines. Courage and heartbreak, will and weakness, strength and cleverness all make appearances in most every game. And the Act of Pitching plays itself out center stage from the first pitch to the last.

PLEASE TAKE NOTE

IF YOU PLAN TO PRACTICE ANY OF THE TECHNIQUES IN THIS BOOK, DO SO WITH MINDFULNESS AND UNDER THE GUIDANCE OF A GOOD COACH.

Some guidelines:

◆ Always warm up your body. Start with rotational stretches, moving all your joints within their range of motion: shoulders, wrists, knees, etc. This lubricates the joints to prepare them for activity. Deep muscle stretching should only be undertaken after you've warmed up your body with light running, light throwing, bike work, or calisthenics. Stretching is also a good time to take an inventory of your body, to get in touch with any stiffness or discomfort while it is whispering, instead of waiting until it screams at you with pain.

◆ You don't have to learn your limitations the hard way. Listen to your body; it will tell you with fatigue when it is getting tired; it will tell you with discomfort and pain if you are abusing it.

◆ Curveballs don't hurt arms, but bad mechanics and foolishness do. Any pitch incorrectly thrown can hurt your arm. Good mechanics provides a safety net and a litmus test for any experimentation you do. Never compromise good mechanics.

◆ Never forget the importance of deceleration after the release point. Stopping the arm abruptly is a surefire path to injury.

◆ Don't overthrow: that means too hard or for too long. No matter where you fall along the speed spectrum of fastballers, you should be throwing a couple mph below your maximum speed. At your max speed you will not be able to control the ball, and sooner or later you will push the envelope an inch too far and do damage.

◆ Giving a100% effort does not mean throwing hard enough to rip your arm out of its socket; it does not mean ignoring pain; it does not mean hiding an injury. It means getting the maximum out of your ability through good training and gamesmanship.

Use your body wisely; it's the only one you will have.

IN PURSUIT OF THE HOLY GRAIL
A FASTBALL CAN BE TAUGHT

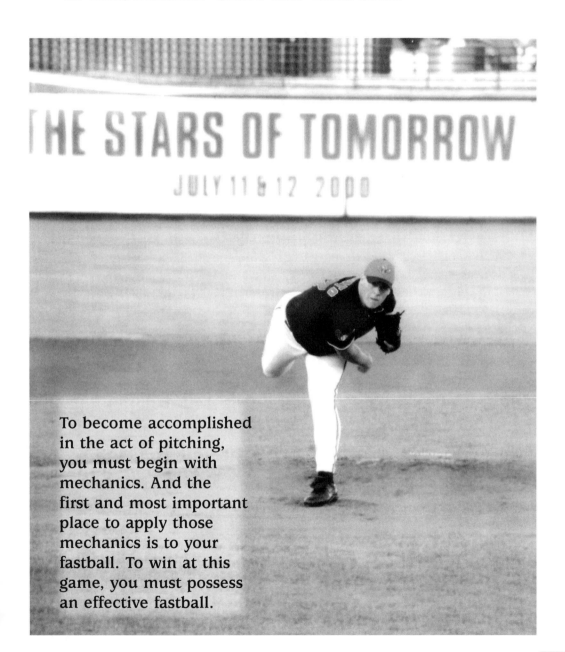

THE STARS OF TOMORROW

JULY 11 & 12 2000

To become accomplished in the act of pitching, you must begin with mechanics. And the first and most important place to apply those mechanics is to your fastball. To win at this game, you must possess an effective fastball.

1

In every sport, from day one, some Holy Grail is always sought after. . . some magic chalice, which will imbue its bearer with infinite, immortal, unstoppable power. In baseball pitching circles that Holy Grail is the fastball — not just any fastball, but the supreme fastball that cuts the air like a laser, the heard but unseen fastball that shatters bats and reduces the best of hitters to desperate flailing.

Today, as in yesteryear, aspiring pitchers are constantly on the prowl for that perfect fastball. It's the trademark of the pitcher birthmarked for success, and it's what separates prospects from rejects when professional and college scouts are scrutinizing the wares of potential luminaries.

CONTRARY TO COMMON BELIEF, THE FASTBALL IS NOT A GIFT FROM THE GODS, GIVEN TO JUST THE ANOINTED FEW.

In fact, if we are going to get down to the work of making pitchers out of throwers, we should get off the kick that the fastball is always a genetically-endowed phenomenon. I've observed many *manufactured* fastballs; I've seen many a pitcher go from having no fastball to having a fine one, and it doesn't happen overnight with the visitation of an angel. Having spent a lifetime in a *pursuit mode* on pitching excellence, I'm totally convinced a fastball can be taught and can be learned!

RESIDING IN EVERY PITCHER IS A FASTBALL WAITING TO BE DISCOVERED AND DEVELOPED.

1985 — One Ugly Fastball...

...but what a personality. On the last day of the 1985 season, Phil Neikro won his 300th game as a member of the Yankees. When people think of Neikro, they think knuckleball, but even a knuckleballer can't survive on one pitch alone; even a knuckleballer has to have a fastball. To prove the point in that history-making game, Neikro didn't throw a single knuckleball until he faced the final hitter of the game. With a fastball that supposedly had no pop and a breaking pitch that didn't break, all he did, at the age of 46, was hurl a five hit shutout. Location, movement, change of timing — if you can master those three things, even a jalopy of a fastball can be effective, even one thrown by a gray-haired baseball senior citizen.

WHAT IS AN EFFECTIVE FASTBALL?

Some concessions need to be made. A 71 mph fastball may never become a 90 + mph fastball, but it most certainly can move into the 80 + range. There may be a genetic ceiling for most when it comes to pure raw velocity, but any pitcher in honest pursuit of excellence is shortchanging himself if a fastball is not a principal part of his repertoire.

The *supreme* fastball or *tall-order* fastball comes in all sorts, but generally has the following eight characteristics, only one of which can be measured by a radar gun.

1. High velocity (mph)
2. Veer or movement (tail)
3. Character (pop)
4. Second stage velocity
   (action in the strikezone)
5. High degree of rotation (alive)
6. Location
7. Deliverable on demand and
   without stress
8. Deception

The lore of the good fastball has probably been with us since before the wheel. It no doubt was part of the caveman's survival kit. The better throwers of rocks or spears probably had more meat to eat, lived longer, and produced more descendants.

Pursuing the Holy Grail can be a lifetime affair, and one shouldn't give in to the notion that *you either have it or you don't.* This age-old adage may be true if you are looking to achieve that most exquisite Nolan Ryan type fastball. However, I submit that constant pursuit of an *ultimate* fastball leads the chaser into developing a *better than before* type of fastball, which very well may be quite adequate for his developing repertoire. And an adequate fastball is an essential element of any pitcher's repertoire. By adequate I mean an effective fastball — one that is thrown with enough speed to contrast your other pitches, one that possesses enough speed or movement to challenge a hitter's reflexes, one that the batter knows you can throw for strikes.

Ultimately, the fastball like any other pitch is subordinate to good technique, technique that can be improved upon piece by piece.

Rare are those young pitchers who get the most out of their body in pursuit of the ultimate fastball. Finding that fastball hiding in one's body requires adherence to the principles of mechanics and having an eye toward detail. Getting the hip properly loaded and finding the stride length can each add a mile or two or three.

Absolutes exist in the realm of pitching, especially with regard to the fastball. Without pushing off the rubber, any quest for the Holy Grail of pitching is futile from the outset.

Failure to get one's chest over the wall can rob a pitcher of another five miles.

Coaching TIP Good players practice what they are weak on. Great players look to make their weaknesses into strengths.

AREAS FOR TECHNICAL IMPROVEMENT OF THE FASTBALL

- ◆ Amount of rotation and type of rotation
- ◆ Arm speed (including wrist speed) and arm strength
- ◆ Launch phase excellence
- ◆ Mechanical dexterity and rhythm
- ◆ Balance
- ◆ Development of the off-arm

In this chapter we will concentrate on the first two items from the above list. An in-depth discussion of the remainder of the list will follow in the next chapter on mechanics.

GREAT ROTATION CAN BE FELT!

No one is doomed to mediocrity because of a humble fastball. Even a weak fastball can be juiced up. By *doctoring* — giving different types of spins to the fastball, one may create different forms of effectiveness. A fastball with sinking action may be quite a bit more effective than a higher velocity fastball that is straight. Pure velocity by itself has to be quite high (high enough to challenge bat speed and reduce decision time) to be effective.

Perhaps the greatest identifiable element in a high quality fastball is *tight rotation*. Tight rotation here infers fast rotation (the number of turns the ball makes over a given distance).

> **Tight rotation** does not refer to how the ball should be held; if tightness of grip has any relation on spin, it's a negative one. Overall, it is far better to **think in terms of a loose grip.**

Great rotation is largely a measure of the mind. It is the desire of the hurler to implement a large amount of spin to the baseball. Most people can improve rotation by paying attention to certain factors, among them grip, finger pressure, hand speed, angle of release and wrist development.

INFINITE GRIPS

Fundamentally, most fastball grips can be considered as either four-seam, or two-seam. This leads many to the false conclusion that only two types of fastballs exist. The difference between the two is often described as being dependent on where your fingers are placed in relation to the seams of the ball. Your fingers run across the seams with a four-seam fastball, and they line up with the seams on a two-seamer. Hence a four-seamer is sometimes referred to as wide or across the seams, while a two-seamer is referred to as narrow or along the seams. But in this simplified view of the fastball, some valuable information and valid alternatives are let go by the wayside. In actuality, if we were to define our fastballs by how they connect to the fingers, there are also one-seam, three-seam, and for that matter no-seam fastballs.

FOUR-SEAM FASTBALL

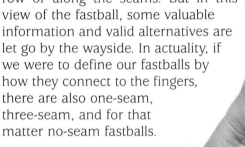

TWO-SEAM FASTBALL

What makes better sense is if we differentiate a two-seam from a four-seam fastball by the number of horizontal seams that cut the air during the rotation of the ball in flight. When one looks at it that way, it becomes very clear why there is more movement on a two-seam fastball and more velocity with a four-seamer.

 Pick up a ball, if you would. (My guess is that if you're serious enough about the art of pitching to be reading this book, like myself, you probably have one within arm's reach at any given moment.)

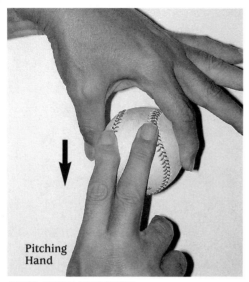

Create an imaginary axis for the ball to spin on by holding it between your thumb and your index finger, with the pad of your thumb directly in the center of the widest spot in the middle of one of the horseshoes. Place the pad of your index finger in the center of the horse-shoe on the opposite side and spin the ball on that imaginary axis. That will give you the basic rotation of a two-seam fastball. As the ball revolves, you will see the seams appear in a pattern that is far from symmetrical, with the two horizontal seams bunched up together. This causes the air to cut across the ball in a most erratic fashion, which gives the ball its movement.

Pitching
Hand

TWO-SEAM FASTBALL
(Ball traveling away from pitcher.)

To get a feel for the rotation of a four-seam fastball, create your imaginary axis by placing the thumb between where the seams come closest to meeting. When you put the pad of the index finger opposite the thumb at the other end of the axis, the pad of that finger will end up on the other spot where the seams are closest. Spin the ball now between your fingers and you will discover that each revolution causes four-seams to cut across the air at consistent intervals which creates a greater air flow across the ball, so that its flight will be quicker and less erratic than that of the two-seamer.

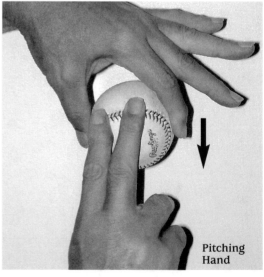

Pitching
Hand

FOUR-SEAM FASTBALL *(Ball traveling away from pitcher.)*

To get variations on movement and velocity, we can tip the axis on both balls as much as sixty degrees in either direction. Even tipped the full sixty, we can see that either two or four-seams can be seen spinning on the horizontal axis.

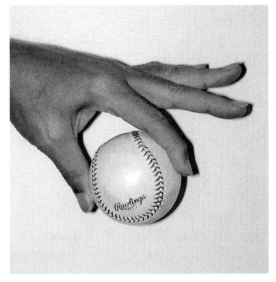

TWO-SEAM TILT

TWO-SEAM TILT

FOUR-SEAM TILT

FOUR-SEAM TILT

It makes sense to talk about two-seam and four-seam in **relation to rotation,** as our prime directive isn't to grip the ball, but to **achieve proper rotation** with its consequent movement.

If pitches are classified by the grips rather than by rotation, then how one holds the ball will become the prime directive. Grip is important, but only in relationship to how a certain grip makes the ball behave once it leaves your hand.

In studying the act of pitching, your goal should not be to make your grip look like that of baseball's great pitchers. Sure, emulate the way they hold the ball, but fixate instead on how you must doctor the grip to make the ball move the way their balls move.

HORSESHOE DOWN **HORSESHOE UP** **HORSESHOE LEFT** **HORSESHOE RIGHT**

As a rule, a two-seam fastball will have less velocity but more movement than a four-seam fastball.

To further understand grips on the ball, we can also orient our grips in relation to the four horseshoe patterns that the seams express. Horseshoe down, horseshoe up, horseshoe left, horseshoe right are the terms that I employ.

Any one of these variations can alter the rotation of the ball, not only in amount but also in direction. And every pitcher has to discover, through hours of *conscious* practice, which grip creates what effect coming from his particular hand, and what differences are made by even the tiniest adjustments of the fingers. This is obviously due to anatomical differences in the length and straightness of people's fingers and thumbs, the flexed and relaxed span of one's hand, palm size, and even fleshiness of the hand. These differences can enhance or detract from pressure points and will directly effect amount and direction of spin.

Harder throwers will have more of a tendency to throw a four-seam fastball, but if you don't have the kind of velocity that will truly compromise a batter's reaction time, you are probably better off throwing a two-seamer. Nowadays most professional pitchers will throw a variety of two and four-seam fastballs, although most will have a favorite. Whereas a Randy Johnson can depend on a four-seam fastball traveling just short of a 100 mph as his bread and butter, a Greg Maddux is more apt to rely on the late-break action of his two-seamer.

PRESSURE POINTS

Too much pressure from the middle finger, or a middle finger that lingers on the ball at the time of release, can cause a *cut fastball*. Unless this is a carefully manufactured *cutter*, it will most likely detract from the action of the ball. A true *cutter* is a special pitch with a lot of possibility to it (see Chapter Five to learn how to throw a cutter with a purpose), but an accidental cutter weakens the kick of the ball and causes it to fade — generally into the batter's *sweet zone*. Many young pitchers will throw this sort of cutter, but when their fingers are properly retrained they may suddenly discover another five mph on their fastball.

For a strong fastball, the index finger should be the one of emphasis and pressure. This can be achieved in the following way:

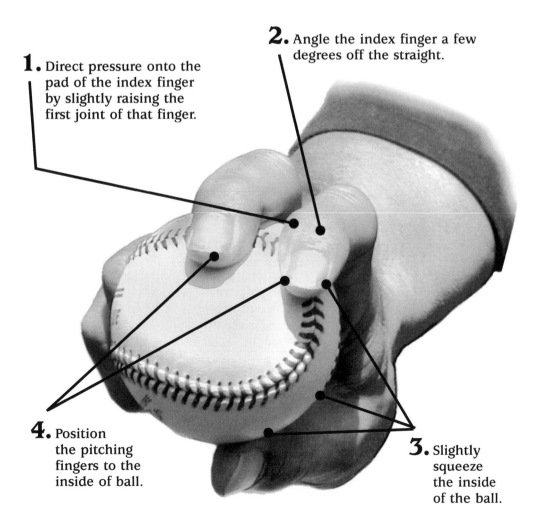

2. Angle the index finger a few degrees off the straight.

1. Direct pressure onto the pad of the index finger by slightly raising the first joint of that finger.

4. Position the pitching fingers to the inside of ball.

3. Slightly squeeze the inside of the ball.

LEARNING TO READ THE BALL
A WORD ABOUT HOW WE DEFINE ROTATION

Somewhere in the pitcher's learning process — high school, college, pitching camp, minor league — he should be exposed to the different kinds of rotation (spin) that can be placed on the baseball. Whether they admit to it or not, realize it or not, all good hitters are adept at reading the ball. Through years of experience they might have come to instinctively learn that when the ball's seams are seen spinning a certain way, a slider is the pitch, or when they perceive a red dot, a curve is what they must contend with. In the fraction of a second that is allowed, developed reflex must take over: the read must occur and the swing must be adjusted in accordance with that read.

A pitcher doesn't have the luxury of instinct in the reading of a ball. In order for a pitcher to master his craft, he must be well aware of the impact various spins have on the ball and have the ability to assess whether such a spin has been achieved. Two variables need to be utilized in the reading of a ball, the spin of the seams and the red dot. Every pitch that rotates will display one or the other, or both. Fastballs are primarily read by the spinning of the seams and breaking pitches more so by the red dot. The red dot is more or less an illusion. It is the center of the spinning ball's axis. Being in the center it moves at a much slower speed than the rest of the ball and consequently, borrowing color from the red seams, it appears as a still, red dot. A classic slider probably presents the most blatant example. With the well thrown slider spiraling like a football in flight, the red dot appears exactly in the center of the ball. The easiest spin to read is probably that of the straight fastball. This ball spins from bottom to top as if on an axis running exactly parallel to the ground.

THE CLOCK

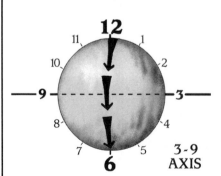

3-9 AXIS

Numbers can be assigned to give us a common language when describing the spin of a ball. Utilizing the face of a clock sitting perpendicular to the earth as our reference, we can then label the spin using the clock's numbers as our coordinates. For the purpose of this book our viewpoint will always reside with the pitcher rather than the hitter. Consequently that flat fastball will have an axis that runs three to nine and the spin of the ball will be noted as 12/6 starting with the bottom number first to indicate the backspin of a fastball. A straight drop curve, which would have top spin, would be a 6/12.

A PURE 12/6 ROTATION ON A 3 TO 9 AXIS can result in a fast pitch, but quite straight. The red dot will not be discernible on this pitch. These numbers on this particular fastball hold true left or right.

Compromising the central rotation with a little veer to the right or left gives the fastball its character.

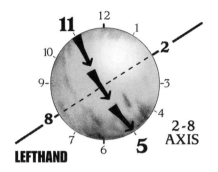

LEFTHAND

2-8 AXIS

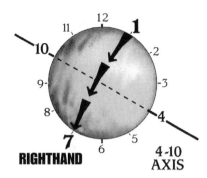

RIGHTHAND

4-10 AXIS

With some exceptions, the desired type of rotation on the fastball in flight is Eleven *to Five* (11/5) for a lefty and *One to Seven* (1/7) for a righty.

Further examples of reading the ball can be found in Chapter Five on curveballs.

All diagrams are from the pitcher's viewpoint.

THE SAIN SPINNER

Developed by the legendary pitching coach, the John Sain spinner is a great tool in understanding the axes of various pitches. Not only will it help our eyes in reading the ball, but it will also help our fingers get a feel for what certain rotations should feel like coming off the fingertips. For absolute clarity, two spinners can be utilized, one for the two-seamer and a second for the four-seamer.

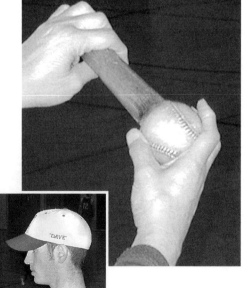

ELEMENT OF VEER

In the pursuit of the ultimate fastball, when one recognizes the *tail* or *veer* of the pitch, he is started on the trail of the best pitch in baseball. It can truly be a work of art. It is a pure pleasure to watch a pitcher who has diligently and consciously doctored his fastball. Natural movement is rare and is reserved for those few individuals who by the nature of their anatomy and delivery can make a ball move or veer with little or no effort.

Unfortunately, most pitchers — especially righthanders — don't have good natural movement on their fastballs. For whatever reason, lefties seem to have a greater natural capacity to make the ball veer off-center. (Perhaps this is a by-product of constantly having to adjust to a righthanded world: having to twist their wrists to use righthanded scissors, having to drag their pen across the paper with hand bent so they can see what they have just written). Whatever the reason, the fact is that lefties have more natural movement on their pitches. This is too bad because a lot more righthanded pitchers would be outstanding if they could make their fastball move.

It is necessary to do everything possible to get some action or movement on the fastball, especially that second stage movement in the strikezone. Many fastballs are devoid of any late stage movement and lack the activity in the strikezone to be effective. Consequently, these fastballs cannot exist by themselves. To cloak a deficient fastball, one should fortify his survival kit with curves, sliders, splitters and change-ups.

A fastball that is totally straight and around 90 mph can be somewhat difficult to hit. In effect, it reduces the batter's decision time. However, if the velocity goes much below 90 mph and travels a straight line, it becomes relatively easy pickings for college and professional hitters. But when you give that 86, 87 or 88 mph fastball some late movement, it can become a first class pitch. Give it impact and character (pop) at the end, and you have yourself a fastball you can live by.

Remember, not all fastballs are genetically endowed! Some are manufactured. Ample and exact rotation can give a *dull* fastball a new existence. All measures should be taken if your fastball is missing the *life* necessary to put the batters on *red alert*.

Often times a good high school pitcher will delude himself into thinking he has a Grade A fastball. At the scholastic level if one has good control, even a sub 80 mph fastball can get a pitcher by in most situations. Consequently, a pitcher who is having success racking up strikeouts with the mediocre fastball is in for a rude awakening when he moves up to the next level.

Often times a high school pitcher with that sort of mediocre fastball will cruise through a season only to get crushed in the playoffs when he comes up against some better bats. When this occurs, it's easy to blame the thumping on a bad day or bad luck, rather than on the exposure of a weakness. However, the pitcher who wants to move up to the next level had better take a hard honest look at what he is doing and then put in the extra work, so that come the following season, the whole scenario of *getting close, but falling short* doesn't replay itself.

FEEL THE BURN, HEAR THE WHIR

You know that you are starting to maximize rotation when you can feel a slight burn on the fingertips with release of the ball. Another telltale mark is that zipping or whirring sound a rotating ball will make in flight. Good fastballs can be heard as they travel through the air.

No matter how strong a thrower you are, the fastball will begin to decelerate very shortly after release. However a fastball with good movement will appear to retain its velocity or even speed-up as it crosses the plate and will hit the catcher's mitt with pop. When that happens you'll know it, and so too will the hitter and the fans.

There are many drills that effectively enhance the mechanics necessary to improve a fastball, but to improve wrist or hand speed, the Wrist Drill as explained in Chapter Thirteen is a must.

ANGLE OF RELEASE

The angle of release often impacts the veer of a fastball. With a righthanded thrower, if the hand and wrist are turned to the right and a three-quarter arm delivery is utilized, the ball will tail. If a 2/8 rotation is achieved, you will have a sinking fastball, which is a very effective pitch. For a lefty, a 10/4 rotation must be employed with the hand and wrist turning to the left.

For sheer velocity, overhand or three-quarter overhand probably works best. It is with these angles in mind that the pressure point concept is maximized.

For a full discussion of arm angles, see the chapter on mechanics.

A GLOSSARY OF FASTBALLS
TWO-SEAM VARIETIES

ACROSS TWO-SEAMS

This one seems to move a little faster with good movement that gives it some tailing action. It's thrown with a 12/6 rotation, but you may get a little more movement with 1/7.

RIGHTHAND

LEFTHAND

ALONG TWO-SEAMS

This might give the ball more tailing action, but slightly less velocity than with an across the seams grip. If you can accomplish a 2/8 spin, it will also give you some sinking action and might even behave like a cutter. Many pitchers will refer to this as their sinking fastball. There's some flexibility in how high one should grip those two lateral seams. In some cases the thumb might be the rule of thumb. Most who have had success with the pitch will adjust the ball so that the thumb can best grip the bottom seam. Another thing that comes into play is that resting the fingers where the seams grow wide will still give the pitch decent lateral movement, but probably won't sink as much.

RIGHTHAND

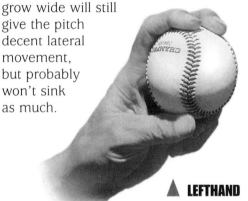

Notice the ▶ slight tilt of the hand. This helps create a 1/7 or, better yet, a 2/8 rotation.

▲ **LEFTHAND**

TWO-SEAM HORSESHOE UP, ON ONE SEAM

This grip which doesn't receive enough attention is one of my favorites. When thrown with a 1/7 rotation and enough velocity this pitch will give you late movement. The two fingers pulling across that seam can give the ball great rotation. I tend to keep my thumb off the bottom seam, but nothing says some people won't get better action by pulling on the seam.

RIGHTHAND

▼ **LEFTHAND**

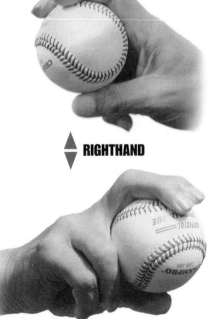

TWO-SEAMER, NO-SEAM

This is the fastball I threw most often when I was throwing my best and one that I encourage everyone to give a shot. It has to have 1/7 rotation, 11/5 lefty. Thrown at 12/6, it's very straight and very hittable. Use the index finger to create a little extra pressure. When thrown well, the ball will have a little run on it. This pitch can serve nicely as a complementary fastball for a person with a good curve — as those with supple wrists will have an easier time getting the proper spin. The no-seamer was utilized by Mickey Lolich and as was the case with Lolich, when thrown with good velocity, it can rack up some K's.

RIGHTHAND

▲ **LEFTHAND**

SPLITSEAM FASTBALL

The splitseam fastball is not one of my favorites. I think there are more effective ways to throw a sinker. The thumb needs to be on the bottom seam. Rotation is helped along by the middle finger. It's not an easy pitch to stay on top of and if the thumb doesn't do its work, the pitch will tumble out of the hand and behave like a bad cutter. It's rotation should be off-center, with a spin somewhat in-between a four and two-seam fastball, but closer to the two-seamer.

Rotating the ▶ seam up from the thumb will give the pitch sinking action.

RIGHTHAND

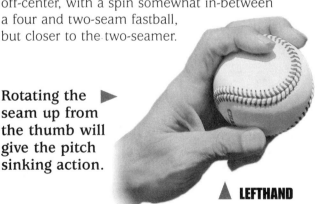

▲ **LEFTHAND**

FOUR-SEAM VARIETIES

When it comes to four-seam fastballs, in terms of grips there is no where near the variety as with 2-seamers. The four-seam pitch is probably the first fastball the Little Leaguer should learn, as 4-seamers don't move as much and hence can be easier to throw for strikes.

For the more mature pitcher, a four-seamer is not the pitch of choice unless the ball can be thrown at least hard and probably very hard. Bob Feller used this grip, as did many other hard throwers. The mythical rising fastball is a four-seamer. As will be explained in Chapter Ten, the ball doesn't truly rise; it just doesn't drop as fast as the eye anticipates. A good four-seamer will also look smaller to the batter than the two-seamer.

Most typically, a righthander would throw a horseshoe right four-seam fastball (lefthander, horseshoe left). In some rare instances a pitcher may try to get movement by reversing the horseshoe.

LEFTHAND

RIGHTHAND

CLASSIC FOUR-SEAM OR RISING FASTBALL

It's not unusual for this pitch to be thrown with a straight 12/6 rotation. But no pitcher can exist feeding hitters an exclusive diet of four-seamers with 12/6 rotation. Eventually the hitters will dial up their bats. You have to mix in something that moves and a change of pace pitch — preferably both. I try to encourage pitchers to develop a 1/7 or 11/5 rotation with this pitch. This can be accomplished by getting inside of the ball, adding a little extra pressure with the index finger and by moving the index finger slightly inward. One should note that the more the pitch moves off the 12/6 rotation, the less rise it will appear to have.

The difference between the average and quality four-seamer is often defined by one's ability to add strong wrist movement on the release of the pitch. A fluid whip-like snap of the wrist is absolutely essential. Practicing the Wrist Drill with a weighted ball will help greatly towards this end.
(See Chapter Thirteen on Drills)

No rule says that you have to throw the four-seamer exactly the same way every time out or for that matter with every pitch. Eventually a good pitcher will develop an intuitive feel for what might be effective in a given situation. Such a pitcher might factor in weather and the condition of one's fingers, as well as the variables of the game scenario. That kind of flexibility will make a big difference in how easily the hitters adjust that third and fourth time through the line-up.

FOUR-SEAMER INSIDE

Not typically one's primary fastball, but a good pitch for one who has a high velocity four-seamer. Doctoring this pitch with the fingers off-center will give the ball some movement. Thrown at 1/7 by a righthander, it will veer in on the right-hand batter.

TWO-SEAM CUTTER

FOUR-SEAM CUTTER

While the cutter is a hybrid, which can be considered a breaking pitch or a fastball – just like with the fastball, a two-seam cutter will have more movement than a four-seamer. While the four-seamer above can be utilized, I believe the one shown to the left (horseshoe left for a rhp) will have better movement away. One reason I encourage a horseshoe right fastball is that horseshoe left can more easily produce that accidental cutter.

CUT FASTBALL

When throwing a fastball, one's grip should be firm but never tight enough to give resistance. In an effort to keep the grip soft, some pitchers fail to get the ball as far back as they should. There should be very little space if any between the ball and the arch formed by the thumb and index finger. That space is one of the characteristics of a cut fastball, talked about in-depth in the breaking pitch chapter.

There is nothing wrong with using a cutter. In fact, it's a pitch I would utilize, were I pitching today, to keep hitters from sitting on my fastball. Unlike most fastballs, the cutter will fade away from the hitter. However, poor grips will often lead to that unintentional cutter that when delivered without proper angle (the top of the ball turning slightly outward) neither moves with speed nor fades. The two-seam cutter must be off-center with close to an 11/5 rotation, which explains the fade.

A few pitchers have the power to throw a four-seam cut fastball which seems to fade while allowing the hitter minimal reaction time. It's a great pitch for a closer as it is almost impossible for the hitter to adjust to it over the course of a single at-bat, especially if the pitcher also has a change-up he can depend upon. This pitch too should be thrown off-center. With both two and four-seam cutters the thumb should be pulled in to the hand a little more than with a typical fastball.

For more detailed instruction on throwing a cutter see the chapter on breaking pitches.

INCREASE YOUR VELOCITY AND DEVELOP YOUR ARM (AT THE SAME TIME)

We need to recognize that arm strength and arm speed do not always correlate. Possessing a big strong arm does not guarantee the necessary arm speed important to deliver a high-speed pitch. Increasing arm speed may increase arm strength, but the reverse of this is not necessarily true.

I've done numerous studies on this — including my doctoral thesis — and am able to substantiate the fact that moderate overload training, particularly in a simulative (pitching motion) type exercise, will increase pitching velocity. I do not believe in heavy weights when it comes to simulative exercise. The act of throwing requires a complex interplay of muscles for both acceleration and deceleration of the arm, involving some relatively delicate structures, especially the shoulder. There is no one specific weight training exercise that will get all those muscles firing in the proper proportion required to throw a baseball. Heavy lifting, while it might improve overall explosiveness, will do more harm than good as it puts wear on the joints and can stimulate excessive growth in certain muscles that will prove a hindrance to a live arm.

Making your pitching arm strong and developing a fastball do go hand in hand. A good fastball is almost totally dependent on good arm speed. And while DNA certainly plays a role, there are numerous ways a pitcher can maximize arm strength.

PRESCRIPTION FOR A STRONG ARM:
CONSISTENT THROWING, WEIGHTED BASEBALLS, AND LONG TOSS

No exercise replicates the throwing of a baseball as much as throwing a baseball. This may seem like an obvious statement, but the fact of the matter is that overall, developing pitchers just don't throw enough baseballs.

Back a generation or two ago, kids played an awful lot of baseball, a lot more than they play today. For many kids, it was their sole activity, weather permitting. Sandlot and pick-up games today are not a regular occurrence and the Little Leaguer rarely gets to throw more than twice a week over the course of a few months. The same is often true for high school players as well, unless an interested adult encourages more practice.

The fact is that unless a developing pitcher gets involved in a program of consistent throwing, he will not develop the arm strength, the arm speed and arm endurance to throw competitive baseball in an effective manner without risk of injury. Throwing from the mound, throwing from the practice mound, throwing from the flat with regard to mechanics, throwing long toss, need to become a year-round ritual. And not mindless throwing either, but rather giving attention to spin and location with every pitch.

There are no shortcuts when it comes to developing velocity. The closest thing to a quick fix when it comes to developing velocity is the weighted ball. When it comes to overload training there is no better tool. I've seen youngsters and young men add five mph to their fastballs after twenty minutes of weighted ball work.

Developing arm strength that translates into arm speed is a tricky business. One tool that may help is the elastic cord, which can provide resistance in simulative throwing exercises.

Anatomically the fastball is a *constructive* pitch — curves, sliders, knuckleballs are not necessarily destructive pitches, but they surely do not develop the arm. Used judiciously, breaking pitches enhance one's repertoire, and if not overused do not deteriorate arm power. However, overuse of the breaking pitches can result in diminished arm speed. In other words, when throwing, at least three quarters of the time, you need to be throwing a fastball. And the younger you are, the more fastballs you ought to be throwing.

When playing at long toss, it's essential to employ excellent mechanics.

POWER ORIGINATES WITH THE LEGS

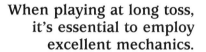

I suggest that the transfer of energy from the bottom part of the body to the arm and ultimately to the fingers is where the Art of Pitching resides. One must pitch with the legs. One thing most every power pitcher has in common is strong legs. To watch a Nolan Ryan, Tom Seaver or Roger Clemens throw you can't help but recognize that their fastballs originate in those tree-trunk thick thighs and tremendous calves.

As I stated in the introduction, I am of a strong mind when it comes to the notion of the pitcher pushing off the rubber. To my way of thinking there is no mid-

ground. Newton's Law holds that *for every action there is always opposed an equal reaction.* The rubber is not just a marking point; like the bases it serves a functional purpose. That function is to provide pitchers with a way to push off into their delivery.

A great fastball requires a commitment from the pitcher to get everything out of his body that he can.

To negate the use of the rubber would be like saying a sprinter doesn't push off the blocks. (How explosive of a start would they get without those blocks?) To say that it's foolish and a waste of energy is like arguing that a pogo stick doesn't need to go down before it goes up, that potential energy isn't stored up by pushing a spring to the ground. If you don't push off the rubber I will contend that you are doing yourself an injustice!

> Do everything you can to make your legs strong. And by all means, **push off that rubber!**

Watching kids standing atop the rubber makes me realize that many pitchers from the word *go* are being deprived of a chance to throw their strongest. Lift heavy with your legs! Run! And then make that hard work pay off by driving off that rubber.

FLEXIBILITY

Maximizing flexibility is another way for pitchers to get the edge that takes them closer to the inner sanctum of superior pitching. Any tightness will rob you of arm speed and limit your capacity for leverage. The more flexible your wrist the better able you are to snap it on release. The looser your arm, the more likely you will be able to extend it to the ideal leverage point.

Make stretching part of your daily ritual and practice your focus by concentrating on the muscles you are attempting to elongate. One note of caution is that people with a more rangy type of build will be more susceptible to looser and actually less stable joints. Be aware that this is not always indicated by loose muscles. Quite the contrary, a taller person could be tightly muscled but still have stretchy joints. To avoid joint problems, use good form while exercising and be careful to not exceed a normal range of motion, especially with regard to hyperextension of the joints.

YOU WILL FIND NUMEROUS EXERCISES employing weighted balls in later chapters. You will also find descriptions of long toss, of in-season and off-season throwing programs, as well as specific weight bearing and resistance exercises, including use of rubber tubing in Chapter Twelve.

THE SECOND STAGE FASTBALL

A fastball that veers or sinks in that last instant as it approaches the plate is the devil's pitch. Getting the main action of your fastball to take place in the business zone, to get it to dodge, dart, drop or fade as it crosses through the strikezone is to achieve the golden crown of pitching excellence. Of course that goes for other pitches as well. Late breaking sliders, cutters, and curves, albeit slower in velocity, are equally devastating.

VEERING ACTION (rhp) comes from a 1/7 ROTATION. SINKING ACTION (rhp) comes from a 2/8 ROTATION.

Achieving second stage action on your fastball is all about great rotation. While no pitch accelerates like a long distance runner who sprints to the finish line, that delayed movement which destroys the batter's reaction time is very real. One could speculate that there is an ideal amount of rotation that creates the greatest movement. Those with lesser rotation will waste that movement before the strikezone, and those very rare individuals with too much rotation will never have the ball decelerate enough to achieve that action — but those who can get a pitch vigorously rotating *just right* will see the ball decelerate to that magic instant where the ideal speed of rotation will cause the greatest imbalance of air pressure, creating the greatest movement just as the ball crosses the plate.

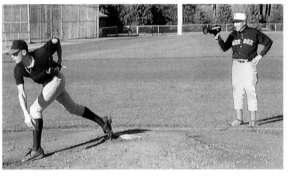

Your best fastball doesn't have to be overpowering to have a second stage to it. It does however need to have great rotation. It behooves all pitchers — but especially those with sub-par velocity fastballs — to increase rotation to the maximum of their ability. This should be an on-going daily effort. In all of one's throwing practice — in long toss, in the Wrist Drill, in warm-ups — great concentration must be put on getting just the right finger pressure and alignment necessary for good rotation. Fingertip sensation will reveal if sufficient rotation is being employed.

VELOCITY HAPPENS IF YOU DO ENOUGH CORRECT THINGS

The ability to get good movement on a baseball is one of the most precious qualities a pitcher can have. It needs to be alive! Even if one throws a fastball with little velocity to it, with crisp rotation and good location, it can still have some character. Getting good rotation doesn't preclude one from achieving greater velocity. Just remember that good intentions are never enough and while it's important to read about this stuff, the knowledge you gain is worthless without diligent practice. It's funny how those successful searches for *Holy Grails* always end up by searching within one's self. Every pitcher has a fastball inside of him waiting to come out.

THE LIVE BALL FACTOR
SPEED DOES NOT EQUAL EFFECTIVENESS

To help further emphasize the importance of a pitcher's movement, we've created this subjective formula. The subjectivity comes in because one of the factors — action of the pitch — has so many variables it's virtually unrecordable, and its effect can only be measured by the hitter's resulting success or befuddlement.

ACTION is the amount of movement, veer, sinking, fading of the pitch particularly in the second stage. What might also be called *character*. It is measured on a scale of 0.8 (no movement, virtually impossible) to 1.5 (excellent movement). 1.2 would be considered as okay or average movement.

SPEED is the measurement of a pitch in miles per hour.

- Major League pitch must have LBF over 90-95
- High school over 75-80
- Little League pitch must be over 50-55

ACTION x SPEED = LIVE BALL FACTOR (LBF)

- Major League pitch must have LBF over 90-95
- High school over 75-80
- Little League pitch must be over 50-55

FOR EXAMPLE, AT THE PROFESSIONAL LEVEL —

A 60 mph pitch must move like a bumblebee. (1.5 action x 60 mph = 90 LBF) Any pitch, even a knuckleball, thrown under 60 is going to eventually be punished.

$.9 \times 90 = 81$ (a totally flat fastball)

$1.2 \times 90 = 108$ (good velocity slider with decent movement)

$1.5 \times 76 = 114$ (a Koufax type curveball with great movement)

$1.1 \times 97 = 107$ (a fearsome Randy Johnson type fastball)

$1.3 \times 78 = 101$ (a Tom Glavine change-up)

Even the pitcher with a 92 mph fastball is going to have trouble if he doesn't have any movement on the pitch. He may blow it by the hitters for a little while, but by the second time through the order, professional hitters will tee off on it — that's what they get paid for. Any pitcher who keeps his live ball factor up over a hundred is going to be a consistent winner at any level.

MECHANICS ARE EVERYTHING!

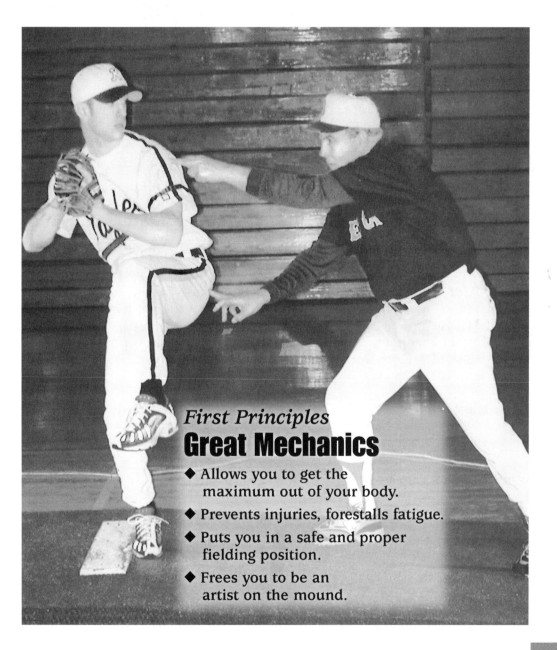

First Principles
Great Mechanics

◆ Allows you to get the maximum out of your body.

◆ Prevents injuries, forestalls fatigue.

◆ Puts you in a safe and proper fielding position.

◆ Frees you to be an artist on the mound.

PART I

IT DOESN'T JUST HAPPEN IN LITTLE LEAGUE:

After a few innings of successful work, suddenly the kid is having difficulty getting the ball across the plate, and when he does, he is pounced on by bats that he easily tamed just an inning or two earlier. His pitch count isn't high and the radar gun has picked up no appreciable difference. The pitching coach makes his way out to the mound. Forlorn but expectant, the kid awaits a few words of wisdom. The coach looks the kid squarely in the eyes and says; "Keep the ball down. Throw strikes." The young pitcher nods his head and waits for more. The coach senses this and as he turns to walk away, he again says, "Throw strikes," but this time adding another little piece of genius, he tells the kid, "Throw hard. . . ".

Don't let up, don't give in are the usual words shouted out to the pitcher who is in the midst of trying to keep a bad situation from becoming desperate. And certainly at times, those aren't bad pieces of advice, but when the kid has every intention in the world to throw a strike and it just isn't happening, then a little more help is in order, a little more brainwork; a little more coaching is required.

If you're a coach or a pitcher and you do not have an exceptionally strong understanding of mechanics, you will be left to fix problems by trial and error or even by way of superstition. But if you do have a deep respect for mechanics, your day in the sun will be longer than most and rarely obscured by clouds; you will have the opportunity to harness your natural abilities and master your full potential.

One must remember that **great mechanics** are not about being robotic. In fact, great mechanics allow for **freedom.**

Great mechanics allow the career pitcher to make adjustments in consideration of a forever changing body. They're what allow a pitcher to have faith enough to throw his third best pitch in a full-count situation.

Great mechanics require an incredible consciousness of body without allowing self-consciousness to creep in. The body is the pitcher's tool, the *ball in motion* its product. To achieve a successful end, a pitcher must allow himself to be objective in scrutinizing mechanics; he must be an outside observer. Baseball has enough chance built into it already (that is why even great teams lose a third of their games). With great mechanics the pitcher knows that he is going to do everything possible to deliver a good pitch. Once the ball is out of his hands, chance may have its say, but through consistent attention to mechanics, the pitcher can limit elements of chance to his favor.

The visual artist who has a depth of knowledge about his paints and has the fundamental ability to create various strokes strongly imbedded in his muscle memory is free to attack the canvas thinking only about what he desires to express. So too the pitcher who is a master of mechanics can concentrate on willing victory and dealing with the nuances of the game, if his fundamentals are solid and dependable. A writer can recognize a bad sentence by ear — *it just doesn't sound right,* but unless that writer has a grasp of proper grammar, fixing the problem will be a matter of trial and error. So too is it true of the pitcher; when something feels like it's wrong, a sense of mechanics will allow one to see the problem with clarity and the solution will become obvious.

IMPROVE YOUR MECHANICS

When elements of baseball pitching are discussed, the focal point invariably comes to "How can the ball be thrown harder?" As a pitching coach, my answer to that is, "IMPROVE YOUR MECHANICS!"

With some pitchers this improvement can be monumental, particularly those who possess good arms. There are some pitchers whose mechanics are solid, who are getting all they can out of what they have, but who still don't throw hard. With these individuals an effort needs to be made to increase arm speed and improve rotation to make their pitches livelier if not faster as was talked about in the last chapter.

Coaching **TIP**
You can do everything right and still fail, but it is less likely.

TEN STEPS IN FULL MECHANICS

STEP ONE: THE PURCHASE

A pitcher has some latitude in how he starts. Referred to as the *purchase* or *ready position,* this is where the pitcher addresses the batter and the situation with his attention and takes a sign from the catcher. All movement is born from stillness and it is in that first instant of stillness that the pitcher exerts his authority. The hitter will often try to seize the initiative by stepping out of the box or will attempt to be distracting with the swinging of his bat, but once the pitcher takes the purchase, a shifting of gears must occur. In fact the taking of the purchase should be the trigger that begins the pitcher's playback of muscle memory.

Find a purchase that works best for you and stick with it. Three are shown below.

This is my preferred purchase.

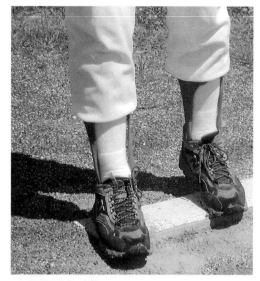

The feet should be parallel and on the rubber, standing off-center to your pitching side. Some pitchers will vary where they stand, but one should build from the orthodox. Don't cover hitches in your mechanics by moving about on the rubber. Chances are that if your pitches are consistently off to one side or the other, there is a problem in your body alignment or release that may cause further problems, including physical ones, down the road.

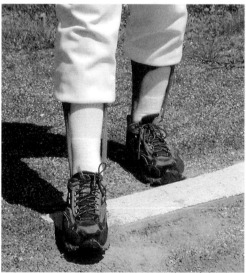

The toes of the feet may be even or those of the throwing side might be back a few inches to a full foot length with the feet flat or the back heel lifted slightly. The toes may point out some to the power side. Allow your knees to bend slightly, let your center of gravity drop into a sense of solidness. One should always start with a sense of balance, strength and a solid root.

Coaching **TIP**

There are two major problems that every pitcher falls prey to at some point...

1.) Rushing

2.) Flying open on the front side

STEP TWO: GRIPPING THE BALL

The plan moves into action with the gripping of the ball deep in the web of the glove. Some prefer to take their purchase from this position as well. Be sure to shield the ball from the hitter's view. Here the weight may begin to shift to the rear leg. The shift is a mental thing at first. When practicing, focus on emptying the weight of the front leg before you begin to move it. If you are rushing, you will end up lifting a heavy leg and balance will be more difficult.

In Step Two the ball can be held at varying heights from below the belt to above the head. Ideally, I like to see it held somewhere between the belt and the chest. In the set position you will see a great variety (see Chapter Seven) You should be in a balanced position to quickly be able to execute a throw to an occupied base, and your vision should never be blocked. The distinct pause required to avoid a balk is also easier if the hands are held in a comfortable position. If you are uncomfortable, there will be a tendency to rush.

STEP THREE: LIFTING THE ARMS

This is a preferred but optional step. Some will utilize a more compact motion, managing to build enough energy and tension as they move directly from Step Two into Step Four. Keep the back of the glove to the hitter. Keep the shoulders relaxed, the elbows bent. Allowing your arms to stray too far from your body, can cause your center of balance to creep upward. The hands can go back behind the head if flexibility permits, just as long as the ball remains hidden.

STEP FOUR: PIVOT

Pivot on the power foot by lifting your heel and turning on the ball of the foot so that the toe is directed towards third base (first base for the lefty). Keep the heel up and the knees flexible. Drop the glove down to above the shoulders. If you go any lower, you will begin to forfeit power. Continue to keep the ball hidden. Maintain the chin and eyes on the target. Close the lead shoulder so that it too begins to point towards the plate. Past this juncture you must be fully committed to pitching the ball.

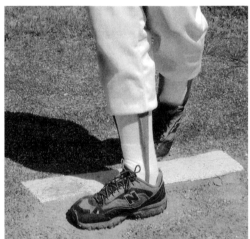

RIGHTHANDER

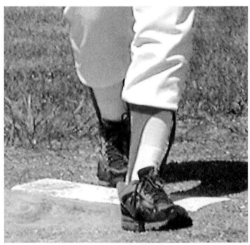

LEFTHANDER

STEP FIVE: LOADING THE HIP

This is the halfway point, where the hips and torso become fully loaded, and the step that determines whether you will be solely dependent on your arm for power, or whether you will fully involve your entire body in the act of pitching. You must be willing to stretch your body's limit at this point.

Leading with your knee, lift your leg as you rotate the hips fully to the power side. Many hurlers will stop the knee just as it breaks the horizontal plane — even with the belt. Make a conscious effort to break through that plane and lift the knee towards the rear shoulder. The amount of load one can achieve at this point is seemingly infinite. Don't sacrifice balance or posture. Keep the power leg bent with the back straight and the chin, shoulder, and lead hip all pointed to the target. (see the use of imaginary eyeballs in the chapter on control). The button of the cap should be directly over the ball of the back foot. Keeping the knee of the power leg flexible and your posture aligned will keep your center of balance from rising excessively with the knee.

When lifting the leg, think about leading with the knee, rather than lifting the foot. Also, don't allow the foot to fly out front (although plenty do), as this will detract from balance and power. The toe of the lifting leg should be level or pointed down slightly. This will put the tension in the hip rather than the leg and will encourage you to land on the ball of the foot rather than the heel when you step into throwing position.

Don't let foot swing out!

Don't stop here!

STEP SIX: HAND BREAK

As the knee comes down, the hands break apart, with the thumbs of both hands pointing down. Here the ball can be glimpsed by the batter for the first time; you can make it harder for him by keeping the hands on the same line, obscuring his view with the glove.

The pitching hand reaches down and back, with the flexible wrist snapping the hand around so the ball faces behind. The shoulders and hips remain in a closed position. The back leg begins to spring straight and drive the body forward. A common problem is the tendency to break the hands too abruptly and not fully. A smooth full hand-break is another checkpoint to avoid rushing. The stored energy of the bent knee and the coiled upper body are now beginning to release.

A second almost distinct action occurs in Step Six after the hand-break. This is where the pitcher must extend back with his throwing arm, the ball facing to center-field, to maximize the pitching circle.

STEP SEVEN: THE MAGIC MOMENT

This is the dramatic moment we envision when thinking about the act of pitching. The front leg lands on the ball of the foot and the arm is in a launch position with hand above the head at about ten or two o'clock.

The elbow is even with or higher than the shoulder — with fingers on top of ball. This step is the most important part of the mechanical process; the energy of movement and the release of potential energy come together at this critical time. It is for this reason that you need to be correct and technically sound at this juncture.

Some minor variations will be found at this level. The throwing arm can be held in a high-cock position. Ideally one should cover the box with the lead arm extended for as long as possible, but having the arm folded-in is acceptable too, just as long as the elbow has not started to pull back prematurely.

It is also important to not step too wide or too narrow.

STAYING ON TOP

HIGH-COCK POSITION

Those who have the habit of throwing inside may be guilty of stepping too wide. However, if you step too narrow, you will not be able to fully open the hips. During Step Eight, the hips should end up square to the plate, but this will not happen without the proper stride at this point. A great deal of attention should be given to the Stride Drill, which you will find is the cornerstone of our chapter on drills.

NOTE WELL:
To maximize power, the shoulders and hip should open a fraction of an instant after the foot touches down **and not before!**

STEP EIGHT: REACHING FOR THE RELEASE POINT

It's important to visualize the release point well past the actual release — which occurs above the bill of the hat — so as to get the full acceleration of the arm into the pitch. As the hand passes the ear, the thumb turns forward. You reach the position of the torso going over an imaginary wall with the hips and shoulders fully rotating open, the back foot pushing off, and the elbow of the glove-hand pulling back.

By going over the wall, I mean that the torso leans forward as if throwing over a wall. Power pitchers like Roger Clemens and Pedro Martinez will go over the wall to the extreme that their chests are parallel to the thighs of their lead legs, with very little space between the chest and the knee.

GOING OVER THE WALL

STEP NINE: BURY THE SHOULDER

The finishing of the pitch cannot be rushed either. After the pitching hand has passed through the release point, the shoulder should be fully buried before the rear leg comes forward. Pitchers will often times make the mistake of bringing the leg forward and burying the shoulder at the same time, which does not allow for the arm to fully decelerate or for hip action to be completed. Also, when the back leg rushes ahead, the pitcher will tend to stumble forward which can leave him in poor fielding position.

At the end of the movement, you can imagine your pitching hand dipping into a bucket no higher than the knees.

BURY SHOULDER INTO BUCKET

Too often the follow-through does not receive proper attention. Just like every other part of a pitcher's motion, it should be practiced until the timing of the shoulder and leg is smooth.

STEP TEN: REAR LEG RELEASE

The completion of the hip rotation at the end of the throwing motion pulls the back leg off the ground and forward. You can think of it as stepping over a log or a bucket (a different bucket than in Step Nine) with the back leg. The toes of the rear foot should point down as the foot lifts. Your landing of the rear foot should be gentle like an airplane touching down. It can end up even with or a bit ahead of the stride foot. This position has a lot of variation to it. Tolerance for slight differences on the ending should be allowed. However, there should be a distinct ending of the pitch. The ending is your signature, and like signatures, there are all kinds, but without it the transaction hasn't been closed.

REAR LEG RELEASE

THE LANDING

You can think of it as stepping over a log or a bucket (a different bucket than in Step Nine) with the back leg.

Coaching TIP Teaching should be one idea at a time.

Zeroing In On Position Seven —
THE MAGIC MOMENT

Hiding in most young pitchers' bodies is a latent fastball — one that hasn't been realized yet.

There are several athletic pursuits in which propulsion — the ability to propel an object with force and accuracy — is a vital factor. The degree to which one can unite parts of the body so that potential (stored) energy is rapidly converted to kinetic (motion) energy often dictates the level of success. Athletic skills such as throwing a shot, hurling a javelin, slapping a puck, hitting a baseball, or driving a golf ball all require a timing and a union of forces at an optimum instant to achieve top performance.

Nowhere is this more obvious than with a pitcher throwing a baseball. Done correctly, there is a surge of power and an acceleration of the throwing process (arm speed) which in turn increases velocity. I refer to this optimum instant as The Magic Moment, which occurs as we enter Position Seven, The Launch Phase.

During The Magic Moment, the four parts of the body utilized in pitching:

1) The pitching arm
2) The back leg
3) The off or lead arm and
4) The lead leg

are synchronistically united to generate a single action. It is rare in a young pitcher that you find a smooth integration of these four body parts in motion.

Ultimately, when a pitcher is able to synchronize these four parts of the body in a smooth, harmonious manner, mechanical efficiency follows. And when integrated with the inertia already created by initial coiling events (rotation of hips and thrust from back leg) a surge of power occurs and a newly improved fastball often times emerges. And while this sudden increase in power might seem like magic, it is simply the product of doing enough right things with enough effort in their proper order.

As already mentioned, the most beneficial exercise towards achieving this unified flow is the Stride Drill. By eliminating the movement of the front leg and the most challenging aspect of balance, the drill focuses on synchronizing the other three parts. The developing pitcher should spend a significant amount of time practicing this all-important drill as explained in Chapter Thirteen. The Stride Drill satisfies a large part of pitching absolutes and when attended to with proper effort and attitude, is essentially self-correcting.

KEY POINTS IN GREAT MECHANICS

CERTAIN ABSOLUTES in pitching are critical to the balance and leverage systems necessary to launch a baseball with velocity, movement, and control.

These certain identifiable essentials are recognizable in the mechanics of all successful pitchers and are as follows:

1. A focused preliminary stance (purchase).
2. A fluid windup that overcomes inertia and generates momentum.
3. Continuous alignment between the target and key body parts, each in its turn, including knee, hip, shoulder and head.
4. Wrist movement that gets one on top of the ball immediately following a fluid, never-hurried hand-break.
5. An effective natural stride that places the slightly closed toe just to the glove side of center — with center defined as an imaginary line going from the middle of the pitcher's plate to the middle of home.
6. The unification of power through launch, made possible by leading with the hip.
7. An emphatic triggering of the hips, accompanied by a rolling of the buttocks to activate leg drive.
8. A strong pivot initiated by the hips on opening and carried out on the balls of the feet.
9. The discipline to keep the hips and shoulder from opening early.
10. An opening of the hips upon touch down of the front foot which immediately triggers an opening of the shoulders.
11. Covering of the box with glove-hand, right up until arm acceleration.
12. Great arm acceleration several inches before passing the ear, up through the release point.
13. Elbow kept high through acceleration phase with the arm in the power release position (the wrist and hand turned out sixty degrees from center) with powerful wrist release.
14. Arm acceleration aided with a strong pulling back of the off-arm at the instant the box is uncovered.

15. Extension of the arm and torso through the release point, bringing the chest over the wall.

16. A hard driving of the shoulder downward after release so that it is fully buried with the completion of the torso going over the wall.

17. An uninterrupted completion of the pitching circle so that the hand reaches several inches below and to the outside of the lead knee before the rear leg comes forward with pitching shoulder pointing at the target.

18. Continued focus on the target for a count of two after release.

19. A continually balanced center of gravity that is not compromised by wandering limbs or by some body parts getting ahead of others.

This list of key points could easily be expanded beyond the nineteen mentioned, but I feel that these nineteen provide as good a checklist as any when it comes to the development of a rhythmically efficient delivery. Some of the nineteen are self-explanatory, others could use some elaboration which we will achieve over the next few pages.

KEY POINTS

KEY POINT 3
DIRECTING THE SHOULDER TO THE TARGET

A bead should be taken with the shoulder of the off-arm towards the target. A similar bead should be taken with the buttocks of the same side, as the pitcher rolls his hips and takes a full pivot position. It appears to line up the body well with the target in drawing these two beads and serves as a reminder to the pitcher to retain the closed posture initiated by the outward pivot of the back leg. Sometimes it helps if the pitcher imagines an eyeball on his off shoulder looking to home plate, and then subsequently an eyeball on the lead hip looking to the plate as well. The idea of using eyeballs is fully covered in Chapter Three.

KEY POINT 4
GETTING ON TOP OF THE BALL

Top of the ball doesn't mean throwing directly over-hand. It signifies the position of the fingers on the ball. To *get on top* means leading rather than push-ing the ball to the top of an imaginary circle where forces come together to accelerate the speed of the throwing arm and consequently impart motion and energy into the ball. *Staying on top* means keeping the fingers atop the ball right through release.

Getting on top of the ball starts early in the delivery. As soon as the hand breaks from the glove, the ball is held earthward as the pitcher reaches back. Then he pulls the ball up to the point where the thumb points toward second base or cen-terfield, with the back of the hand facing toward the head.

The arm attains a position that is more vertical than horizontal to create a poten-tial for leverage advantageous to velocity. If the fingers are below the ball, they defeat the whole process by pushing the ball to the top of the circle. So that rather than releasing the ball with the fluid, uncoiling energy of the entire body that culminates with the whip-like snap of the wrist, the ball is dragged and stiffly cat-apulted forward on the strength of the arm alone.

In many cases, the pitcher will fail to reach back far enough. This is one culprit to look for when a pitcher suf-fers a sudden drop in velocity.

It's not unusual for a young or very inexperienced pitcher to miss the first wrist break and end up hold-ing the ball skyward, so that he approaches the launch phase as if he were getting ready to throw a pie rather than the ball. This approach cuts leverage and does not allow a full transfer of energy into the snapping of the wrist. ▶

LOW-COCK TO HIGH-COCK

A subtle but essential bit of timing occurs after the hand break.

Rushing can occur in either of two ways: the foot prematurely planting as the hand pulls back into low-cock, or the arm short-circuiting the pitching circle and pulling directly into the high-cock, making the foot plant a split second too late.

Some individual pitchers get away with variances, but to maximize power and assure that one gets on top of the ball, this timing should be developed. Preceding the high-cock position with the low-cock is mandatory for the power pitcher so as to coordinate rotational forces and the strength of the lower body to create the explosion of energy that is then transmitted to the arm, wrist, hand, and ultimately the ball. This is truly the *Magic Moment.*

LOW-COCK

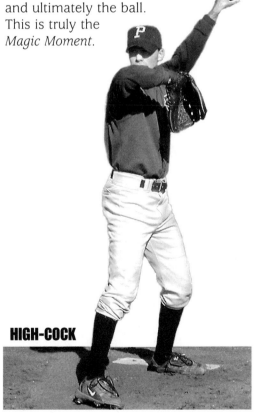

HIGH-COCK

PRE-LAUNCH POSITION

As the arm pulls back into the low-cock position, the ball of the lead foot should just be starting to touch down with all the weight still on the back leg.

LAUNCH POSITION

Just as the hand travels through the pitching circle and reaches the high-cock position, the foot is firmly planted with the weight beginning to move forward.

Whether the pitcher cocks in a higher or somewhat lower arm position, he must complete the pitching circle, going up and over to make the most of his leverage.

KEY POINT 5
STEPPING TO THE CENTER LINE

When striding forward, you should land on the ball of the foot slightly to the outside of that imaginary center line running from the middle of the pitcher's plate to home. The toes should be straight or turned in a few degrees across the centerline — which I prefer — but never outward. The knee must be bent forward and remain flexible so that it can absorb the impact of the landing and aid with balance as the pitching side of the body comes through.

KEY POINT 6 & 7
LEADING WITH THE LOADED HIP

No matter how precise and fluid your mechanics may be, all the energy stored through the windup, leg lift and hand-break is almost completely wasted if you fail to properly load and lead with your hip.

> Many otherwise fundamentally sound pitchers cause an awful lot of **problems** for themselves, including loss of velocity, by **failing to load** and **lead with the hip.**

In approaching the Magic Moment — as the front foot lands and the money arm moves into launch position, hand above the hat and held back — the torso should remain closed, with the front hip still loaded and the front shoulder still pointing at the target. Having the hip open at this point would put it too far ahead of the accelerating arm and result in a gross forfeiture of stored energy. Quite often the failure to lead with the hip can be traced back to an improper loading.

Failing to fully load the hip not only takes away from the potential power of the hips, but without the proper tension that comes from being fully loaded, the hip is apt to drift and open early. This is a common cause of rushing.

LEADING WITH THE LOADED HIP

ARE YOU PLACING FALSE LIMITS ON YOUR HIP LOAD?

Pitchers will often sell themselves short when it comes to achieving their maximum capacity for hip loading. A fear of falling is usually the culprit rather than a limited range of motion. To discover how much more you can load that hip, try the following experiment.

Place the foot of the lead leg on the seat of a chair. Hold your position and have someone bring the chair back and in towards your rear shoulder. To feel the hips load still further, raise the heel of the foot so that the toe points down. For taller and more flexible folks, a glove or two can be stacked on the chair. In all likelihood, with the fear of losing your balance negated, you will discover that you have a greater range of motion than previously experienced, and accordingly, a greater capacity for hip loading.

Make a mental note of how your hip feels when it is fully loaded with the support of the chair. Attempt to replicate that feeling in the hips when you are practicing your delivery. Don't allow the loading to be compromised by a lack of balance. If you practice it often enough, the balance issue will quickly resolve itself.

the six alarm
ANOTHER NUMBERS GAME

In an effort to create a common language of numbers, the baseball is looked at as being divided into thirds. With the top third being referred to as ONE, the middle being referred to as TWO, and the bottom third referred to as THREE.

1. Top
The only part the hitter should see.

2. Middle
Last part you want them to hit.

3. Bottom
The part the hitter should never see.

When the sweet spot (the middle of the fat part) of the bat meets the middle third of the ball with vigor, the result is what is called a #6 type hit. This is the best a hitter can hit the ball. Obviously pitchers want to avoid very many #6's. Some of these are hit right at fielders and are caught. But anytime a pitcher begins to surrender a rash of #6's — whether they are dropping or not — it's time to put the bullpen on alert.

Coaching **TIP** Rushing results in throwing uphill!

KEY POINT 8
PIVOT STRONG ON THE BALLS OF THE FEET

PIVOT DRILL —This simple but excellent exercise teaches the pivot necessary to align the legs with the plate as the hip opens. Don't start the movement with the feet, instead initiate the turn with a sharp and powerful hip twist, lifting the heels enough to allow the pivot to occur on the balls of the feet. Leading the pivot with the hip will prevent any lag time and loss of energy that would occur if the feet were to lead.

PIVOT DRILL

If you study the basic mechanics of pitching, you will ultimately realize that if you key both your arm and leg motion off the action of the hips, the upper and lower halves of your body will work in unison. This principle holds true in most athletic ventures. The boxer who fires his hip will step and punch at the same time, making him much quicker than the boxer who steps and then punches.

KEY POINT 9 & 10
KEEP THE HIP AND SHOULDER FROM OPENING EARLY

1.

Many pitchers suffer from early torso rotation and still throw the ball effectively, but it's likely they give away some velocity. Timely trunk rotation brings on the union of hips and shoulders to assist the rapidly accelerating arm. It is important to master this particular concept in both a full wind-up and stretch position.

When the pitcher lands with the hip open as in the first picture, the hips will no longer be fully available to help accelerate the arm.

2.

3.

When the foot lands with the hip not yet open, as in the second picture (above), the subsequent release of its stored energy will kick the arm into turbo-drive (3).

With the opening of the hips, the feet pivot to unify the upper body with the driving rear leg, adding still more power to the accelerating arm.

A moment of truth occurs in that instant when the foot touches down. If there is not a powerful release of hips and shoulder, then the four quarters of the body are not working harmoniously, and appreciable power is lost.

The shoulder and hip must be closed at this critical time before opening, and I cannot emphasize this enough. Even if the pitcher were to close more than shown in the above photo, it wouldn't become a problem. The only time a problem could occur with too much closure would be if energy were expended towards second base and not home plate. Absolute cocking of the hips must occur if the lower part of the body is to be a factor in velocity.

PROPER TIMING is a beautiful display of the precision required to be technically sound in the pitching process. Those who master it are true artists.

KEY POINT 11
COVERING THE BOX

When the pitching arm reaches launch position, close to the top of the pitching circle at around ten o'clock — the batter has a chance to finally get a good look at the pitcher's hand. Good hitters focus on this point, which is usually visualized as a seven-inch square box surrounding the pitcher's hand.

By raising his lead arm and dropping the glove palm down across the batters line of sight, he can effectively *cover the box* and obscure the batter's read of the grip. It also means that the hitter is going to have to pick up the ball much later and with regard to reaction time, a tenth of a second delay is like adding another ten mph to the pitch. Even though the pitch isn't moving that fast it seems to get there in a bit more of a hurry than expected.

Pitchers who are especially good at covering the box are sometimes referred to as *sneaky quick*. This type of pitcher — usually a veteran — seems able to find little extra ways to deprive the batter of already precious reaction time. One thing they all do is cover the box.

← THE BOX

Incorporating Cover The Box with a Knee Drill will allow pitchers to focus on getting the ball in the right spot. Height of the pitcher will be a factor in determining where to hold the glove.

If some inexperienced pitcher is breaking the upper eighties with a lively fastball. I'm not inclined to mess with his delivery unless he's doing something that's going to hurt his body down the road. But for those prospects with borderline fastballs, finding ways to steal reaction time is a must. All youngsters learning proper mechanics would do well to incorporate this covering of the box from the start. Buying into its importance will help the potential pitcher realize that the difference between being a winner and being a loser can be measured in tenths of a second and tenths of a second can be bought with diligent effort.

KEY POINT 12 & 13
POWER POSITION OF THE PITCHING ARM and ACCELERATION

The speed at which the hand and forearm come through the power position is essentially the speed at which the ball will move when it is released.

Here it should be noted that velocity and acceleration are two different things. Velocity is simply the amount of distance covered over a given time. Acceleration is a far more complex thing. Two items making impact with a target at exactly the same velocity will not necessarily have the same impact. If one is accelerating and the other decelerating, the accelerating object will have greater potential energy and because of that, will hit with greater impact.

The greater the acceleration of the arm in that Magic Moment, the more potential energy there will be stored in the ball and the less deceleration it will experience over the course of its path from mound to plate. (All pitched balls have begun to decelerate long before they reach the plate) But the most significant factor in determining the rate of deceleration is the tightness and direction of rotation.

The elbow is up when the ball is at the top of the pitching circle and it should remain up, right through release. As the arm approaches and then passes the ear, the forearm will

naturally turn the ball forward. The wrist here needs to be supple and flexed, with the hand angled back so that upon release sudden acceleration occurs with a very powerful snap of the wrist.

It is in that instant when the ball is unveiled that all energy must be brought to bear. It is in that instant that you will often times hear a powerful pitcher grunt or let out a burst of breath. The ball may only be five and a fraction ounces, but the effort required to propel it is no less than what goes into electrifying the neural system and firing all the muscles of the arms, back, and chest when pressing a huge weight, or when pushing a car, or when turning the lid on a jar that just won't give. The push-off, the rotation of the hips and shoulders, the forward movement of the arm, the snapping of the wrist must all culminate in a tremendous explosion of energy that is the act of pitching.

KEY POINT 14
THE SECRET OF THE OFF-ARM

In watching a baseball game, even the novice fan will notice a difference in the gracefulness of execution from one hurler to the next. One pitcher's delivery might remind us of finely tooled precision machinery, while another might call to mind a collection of spare parts hastily strung together. And while any of a few dozen things may add or detract from this impression of gracefulness, it's how a pitcher makes use of his off-arm that determines whether his delivery is more akin to a Rolls or a jalopy.

With some pitchers, the off-arm seems to know its purpose and have a place; with others, it seems to be just hanging on for the ride and would surely fling off into the stands were it not well-attached. Whether we call it the lead arm, the glove arm, the front arm, the directional arm, or the off-side, it is the arm that doesn't sign the contract, doesn't get babied and rarely gets its due. But its value goes beyond being a tendon donor for Tommy John surgery and serving as a place to hang one's glove.

Many pitchers have had highly successful careers despite consistently poor utilization of the off-arm. You can also find another group of pitchers who control the off-arm to their benefit for the delivery of a fastball, but then completely ignore its use when throwing a breaking pitch. And then there are still others who will practice with great form, but come game day, fail to pitch what they practice.

Coaching **TIP**   Basics of the game are the same at all levels.

THE OFF-ARM SERVES AS A SUPER-CHARGER

The off-arm makes up half of what the old school used to call the *Captain's Wheel*. The Captain's Wheel is best viewed from above.

Looking directly down on a pitcher as he delivers the ball, what we'll see is the whole shoulder process, from right to left, turn rather sharply like the middle of a big steering wheel. With the striding leg, and the rolling hips focusing power to the pitching side of the wheel, it becomes apparent that there is a tendency for the action on the wheel to be a little lopsided. However, with the well-schooled pitcher, you'll see that action on the thrusting side being balanced by the action of the off-arm. When the off-arm is pulled back with proper timing and in the proper direction, it balances out the forces on the wheel, while providing an extra boost to the centrifugal energy which is the primary source of power for the pitching arm.

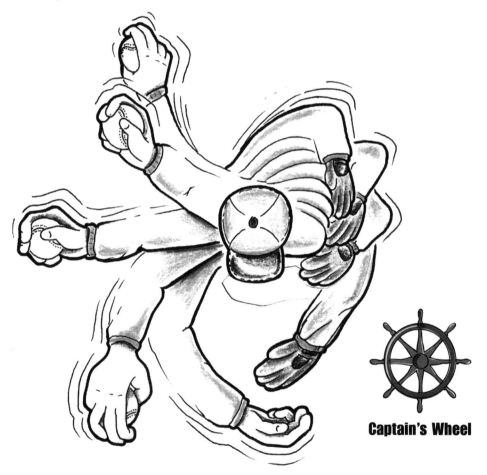

Captain's Wheel

Using the off-arm may not be necessary for generating power, but that second hand on the wheel certainly makes the job easier.

If you're not convinced that the off-arm is integral to the pitching process, try this little exercise. Tuck your off-hand in the same side hip pocket. Now leaving it there, go through the motion of throwing and see just how much power you actually have. . . . end of discussion.

As the pitching hand passes the ear and the thumb comes to the front, with the elbow high and leading, the glove-side at this time should be starting from the position of *cover the box* as talked about previously. As the throwing arm, forearm and wrist rapidly accelerate, exploding to release, the significance of the off-arm begins to manifest, pulling back with great vigor, the glove naturally rotating palm upward. The stronger the arm is pulled back, within the limits of control — the greater the transference of energy to the turning torso, the pitching arm, and ultimately the ball.

The glove can come to rest on the hip, up under the armpit, or swing free in the back. I prefer the first two positions as this leaves the pitcher more prepared to start his work as the fifth infielder. The third position, as exemplified here by Dizzy Dean, (middle picture) was far more popular two or three generations ago and made for a more suitable ending to the highly dramatic big windups that were once part of baseball.

In the past, the traditionalist coach instructing on mechanics often overlooked or minimized this source of power, but in studying old clips and photos, despite a lack of instruction, there wasn't a single hard thrower who didn't make use of the off-arm one way or another. Back then it wasn't unusual for a pitcher to have more than one off-arm finish. One can find pictures of Dean finishing a pitch with his glove tucked tightly to his side.

One way to visualize the proper and crisp movement of the off-arm is to imagine your elbow firing backwards like a piston, with enough strength to punch a hole in the belly of anyone foolish enough to be standing behind you.

THE BALANCING FACTOR

In our discussion of the off-arm, I would be remiss to leave you with the impression that its only duty during delivery is to provide power. In addition to assisting the pitching arm with acceleration, the off-arm helps stabilize the rotating forces (hips and shoulders) and with its tight purposeful movement also increases the stability of balance, so essential to effective performance.

Floppy or sideward movement on the part of the off-arm seems to cause mechanical problems that consequently cause control problems. (Remember that every inch we are off in our delivery translates to a seven inch difference at the plate.) These problems can prove fatal to a pitching career by robbing one of control or even worse by causing injury. There are no extraneous parts to the body when it comes to efficient pitching. Every inch and every pound of your body must be used purposefully and efficiently. It is the only tool that the pitcher has. And any part of your body that is not used consistently or efficiently is going to create problems.

> The act of pitching is already subject to enough random factors that can compromise the achievement of a desired result. So why allow the use of the off-arm to become one more?

Take the time to analyze the action of the off-arm in your own delivery or in the delivery of those you work with. Ideally its proper usage should be embedded as muscle memory early on in a pitcher's development. But this doesn't mean that the seasoned pitcher is doomed to be a slave to bad habits. If you believe change is impossible then it will be. If you're like most people, you probably believe that other people's problems are way easier to solve than your own. Well you'd best get over it. Give yourself permission to learn, permission to get better. Whenever we practice, we are teaching ourselves whether we realize it or not. Once we recognize that, we can see just how easy it is to teach ourselves something wrong. All we have to do is keep practicing without being conscious in our effort. But as humans we're built with the capacity to make some choices. And whenever we practice, we have to remember to teach ourselves the right way rather than the wrong way, which of course assumes that we have to care enough to know the difference.

MIND FIRST, THEN MUSCLE, AND THEN SPIRIT

The above is a Chinese saying and to my opinion it's the way to approach almost anything, including our physical development and even when it comes to dealing with bad habits.

Recognizing a problem for what it is, has got to happen first off. Recognizing the problem and then recognizing that something can be done is an act of the mind. Actively looking for a better way and then practicing it and fine-tuning it is what comes next and that requires the full participation of the body, the full willingness of the muscles to try on something new. When this occurs with enough repetition, the new habit replaces the old and becomes part of one's nature. And then it's up to spirit to breathe life into this new habit and allow its full expression.

Each seemingly *little thing* that one does may not seem like much. But when you start picking up a mile an hour here and there with going over the wall, covering the box, using the off-arm. . . that unacceptable 75 mph fastball is suddenly in the mid-eighties. On any level the difference between a great fastball and a mediocre one is less than ten miles an hour.

KEY POINT 15
CUTTING THROUGH THE RELEASE POINT and GOING OVER THE WALL

If the Commissioner of Major League Baseball proposed that the distance from the pitching plate to home plate be lessened by six inches, *just so it would be an even sixty feet,* there would be screams of outrage from every hitter across the land. "You'll turn us all into a bunch of hitless wonders," they would scream. "You'll be giving those prima donnas on the mound one more unfair advantage." And if it were to happen, we pitchers would all be walking around wearing *cat who ate the canary grins.* Of course it isn't going to happen — unless maybe you happen to play in Dodger stadium.

But the fact of the matter is that a lot of pitchers could gain six inches or even a foot on home plate, if their deliveries included what I call, *going over the wall.*

Going over the wall has nothing to do with prison breaks but has everything in the world to do with giving yourself the best break the rules and your craft will allow. By imagining that you are passing your torso over a wall, running perpendicular to your lead knee and just a few inches higher, not only will you bring your release point closer to the plate but you will also improve the quality of your pitch.

A pitcher should recognize that going forward is absolutely essential to arriving at a consistent release point and also paramount in determining a proper downward delivery angle, which enhances the pitcher's effectiveness by improving action and augmenting deception. As we spoke about earlier, while the ideal release point is actually just below the hat, it's advisable to imagine it as being significantly lower.

By imagining ourselves releasing on full extension we tend to find our natural release point with great consistency without any disruption to arm speed. You will also find that your follow-through will become remarkably smoother by throwing through the actual release point.

Very seldom are kids in Little League taught and encouraged to go over the wall. This is unfortunate as at that age pitcher's bodies are much more pliable and their capacity for getting over the wall is far greater than after their bodies mature. And while those at more advanced levels are more apt to bring their bodies forward on delivery, few are those who take full advantage of this technique.

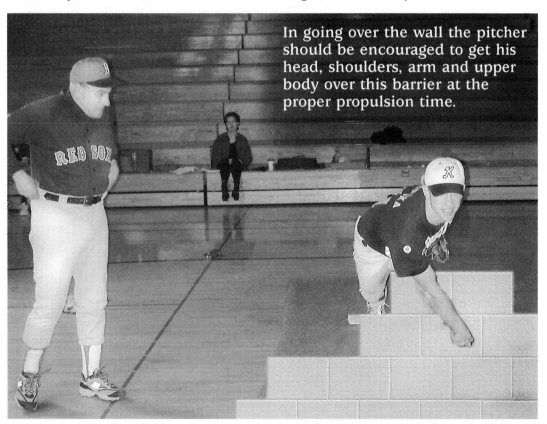

In going over the wall the pitcher should be encouraged to get his head, shoulders, arm and upper body over this barrier at the proper propulsion time.

Visualizing a wall or using an actual thigh high barrier when practicing slowly helps to reinforce this crucial part of the delivery. Setting a rope or string across the mound at thigh level is a good substitute for the wall as it will not interfere much with stride and follow-through.

When this visualization is used repeatedly, the image itself can serve the pitcher well during the later innings of a game. As fatigue sets in, mechanics change and the action of going over the wall becomes less and less. Because of this, a pitcher's release point will begin to rise as will the ball in the strikezone. If the pitcher has spent many hours working his release and has the idea of going over the wall strongly imprinted in his visualization of perfect mechanics, all it takes is a simple reminder. The coach can save himself from a trip out to the mound by simply shouting to the pitcher, "Go over the wall," and the pitcher will have an instant understanding of what is going awry and how it can be fixed.

SEE THE NUMBER!
The upper back should pass over to the extent that the pitcher's number (on his back) can be seen by someone looking straight at the hurler.

Don't confuse your body by developing two sets of habits. All drills incorporating release should be practiced utilizing the principle of going over the wall.

KEY POINT 16 & 17
BURYING THE SHOULDER, FINISHING THE CIRCLE, and PREPARING TO FIELD

It's especially hard to impress upon young people, and for that matter anyone not versed in pitching theory, that anything a pitcher does after release can have an impact on the flight of a ball. Ultimately quantum mechanics may prove to us that the future does influence the past in ways we cannot as of yet comprehend. And I am a firm believer that the mind is an amazing thing and that the energy of thought can effect things beyond our physical reach.

The relationship between hitter and batter is unlike anything else in sports, the two are united in a complimentary activity that has a greater relationship to dueling than it does to sport. It involves thirty seconds — in its approach to readiness — of mental and physical preparation to engage in a joint activity lasting no more than four to five-tenths of a second.

Saddaharu Oh, the greatest Japanese slugger, came into his own when he recognized that there was a relationship and a play of minds between hitter and pitcher that went far beyond the concept of intimidation. It was more like one of partners dancing together. He saw the pitcher's movements and delivery as every much a part of himself as his swing.

In the act of pitching, that relationship between hitter and pitcher doesn't end with the release of the ball, any more than it starts for the batter with the pitcher's movement forward. The dance continues as the ball is in flight. To opt out at this point is to leave all in the hands of the batter. To be successful, to give a complete and full effort in the achievement of our envisioned success, we must stay with the act of pitching to its conclusion. Mind alert and focused, body poised and in balance.

Besides influencing the outcome, two more things must be accomplished in one's finish. We must deal with insult and assault. The arm must be protected from injury and we must ready ourselves to deal with the ball put in play.

Coaching TIP

In order to make it in the world of competitive sports, you have to believe that effort is a renewable resource.

The throwing side of the chest should try to touch the lead knee as the pitcher accelerates through the release point. If this is done well, the pitcher's right shoulder should be properly buried, and he will be able to extend his arm to the bottom of the circle.

The image of the pitcher finishing up by swinging his throwing arm around and into a bucket is very useful here. This will remove stress from the arm. After the

throwing arm has come full circle, the power leg will swing forward to prepare one to field the ball. Remember that this foot must touch down lightly like the landing of a jet.

All of this must be practiced to the point of being instinctive, as the pitcher should continue to place all of his conscious focus on the flight of the ball and its interaction with the hitter.

Like pitching the ball through the catcher's mitt, like reaching for a release point beyond the actual release, so too we must cast our focus beyond the ball's physical release for our focus to be its most powerful on release. A simple way to practice this extension of concentration is to maintain one's focus for a count of two or for an entire out-breath and the beginning of an in-breath after the back foot touches down

Coaching TIP

Proper conditioning can actually overcome bad mechanics for a while – but every pitcher with bad mechanics will face a turning point.

Use a chair to accustom the pitcher to having his rear leg come off the ground before it comes forward rather than dragging it towards the front. If the leg does not come up the weight will not transfer fully forward. Take the pitcher and elevate the leg just a little beyond his comfort zone and then have him come forward to the landing. Don't replace the Stepping Over the Bucket Drill, as explained earlier in the chapter, but alternate their use.

PRACTICING ON THE FLAT

While it's a good idea to get plenty of practice throwing from the mound, it's advantageous to spend some time practicing your full mechanics on flat ground. It's especially useful when trying to work out of a poor habit. On the flat, one doesn't have to worry about balance and better focus can be placed on the torso and arms. Also any awkwardness can't be blamed on the incline of the mound. If you can get good trajectory and movement while throwing from the flat, chances are this will be enhanced throwing on the mound.

KEY POINT 19
THE ESSENCE OF BALANCE IN PITCHING

In any sport, the ingredient of balance is integral to high performance. In baseball, only those pitchers who achieve the highest level of balance maintain a consistent level of success over a long period of time.

Performers such as Roger Clemens, Nolan Ryan, Steve Carlton, Don Sutton and Warren Spahn, all Hall of Famers (or about to be), who have been outstanding performers over a span of twenty years or longer, have always exhibited great balance in their mechanics. Their respective styles have flourished and, in turn, enhanced their longevity. The common denominator in their styles has always been balance.

JUST WHAT IS BALANCE?

It surely is an absolute in pitching. We can explain it as the ability to first unite the forces of acceleration to achieve the utmost propulsion in pitching, and then unite the forces of deceleration when the body is recoiling in the aftermath of release. It is the latter effort that diffuses the violence of the pitching act upon the body, eliminating wear and tear and promoting longevity.

Many pitchers may utilize appropriate balancing techniques in the beginning of their mechanics, but fail to decelerate properly because of poor balance and therefore achieve a mediocre ending (or even a very poor ending) to what might have been potentially a great pitch!

Good mechanics keys good balance. They almost always go hand-in-hand. Reaching the mid-point of the mechanical process in a balanced condition almost always guarantees a sound delivery.

It seems that if the latter essentials are cheated upon, there is a gradual decay backward, until the entire pitching process is interrupted. It is important therefore that a proper ending be emphasized, implemented, and maintained.

If one is conscious of maintaining a fluidity of motion, the possibility of forces coming together at the proper time with acceleration is not dependent on coincidence.

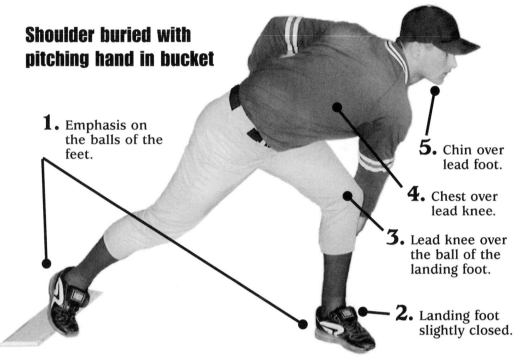

Shoulder buried with pitching hand in bucket

1. Emphasis on the balls of the feet.

5. Chin over lead foot.

4. Chest over lead knee.

3. Lead knee over the ball of the landing foot.

2. Landing foot slightly closed.

If we get to this place with a sense of balance and still have a fastball that's lacking, we have to conclude that somewhere along the way we are failing to generate and/or release power, because balance isn't the problem; in fact, it's unlikely that mechanics in general is the problem.

ESSENTIAL ASPECTS OF BALANCE

If we take our inventory of balance at this point, when the pitching arm speaks its final lines in the act of pitching, as shown in the picture above, we should end up with a pretty good assessment of the quality of our balance. We could not have gotten to that point unless we expended our energy with balance. And that balanced expenditure would not have occurred unless all four pieces of our pitching machine were properly working.

Conversely, if we are not achieving that ending balance, we may well have to go back half a dozen steps, or even more, to discover where it is we are getting off-track. *For example:*

If we land with our weight on the heel of the front foot rather than the ball, it might mean we are simply stepping with too straight a leg, or it might be we are not keeping our toe down. And we are not keeping our toe down, either because we are simply being lazy with it, or because we have to flex our foot to regain balance. That being because our one-legged stance is unsteady, either because we just haven't attended to it enough or maybe because we failed to properly turn our foot in the moves following our purchase. And that failure to turn our foot might be because we haven't practiced it enough, or perhaps because we were distracted when on taking the signal we held our glove in such a way that it interfered with our vision.

> Mechanics may be a series of movements but remember when the **balance is fluid** and the details are well-attended from beginning to middle to end, it is merely one long continuous action of **coiling, compression,** and **release.**

The truth of the matter is that one never really achieves balance, but rather one is always working towards maintaining it.

The above statement is an important psychological distinction to make for those who feel they have trouble with balance. Usually we only think of balance as the ability to stand on one leg like a crane. Once we recognize that balance is a continuous effort rather than a state of being we plateau upon, we become less intimidated by our own adventures with it.

Also, recognize that balance in stillness is never nearly as strong as balance in motion. Anyone who has ridden a two-wheeler can tell you that much. Pitchers should be encouraged to look for balance in motion. When we come up on one leg, we should think in terms of bringing our balance up with us from the ground. It makes all the difference when we think of balance as something we are bringing along with the motion, rather than something we need to achieve at the height of our leg kick.

One big difference between the American and the Japanese way of pitching is that the Japanese tend to come to a very distinct pause as the knee of the kicking leg reaches its apex. The Japanese belief is that the pitcher must achieve perfect balance in stillness before proceeding. The American view tends to believe that this pause should be minimized, as any kind of pregnant pause challenges the rhythm of pitching, and also allows base runners an extra jump.

The Stride Drill and Long Toss are great exercises to work with the balance of your motion.

PART III

THE MATTER OF ARM ANGLES

In discussing the relationship between mechanics and velocity, the one factor that often gets overlooked is arm angle. Throwing from the correct arm slot can often mean increases in velocity and movement, and improvement in control, particularly for someone who has his mechanics reasonably well developed.

We identify arm angles by considering our pitching arm to be like the hour hand of a clock. While facing that clock, hold either the right or left arm straight up, fingers pointed to the sky, and you would be throwing from the twelve o'clock slot (a very unlikely prospect). Extend the right arm perpendicular to your body and you will be throwing from the three o'clock slot. For you southpaws, hold the left arm perpendicular to the body and you will be throwing from the nine o'clock slot. As you can obviously figure, lefties throw from between six and twelve o'clock, whereas righties are slotted on the right side of the dial between twelve and six o'clock.

STANDARD OVERHAND

It is next to impossible to throw from a true twelve o'clock position, although some pitchers manage to come just a few minutes shy. One o'clock for righties and eleven for lefties would then be the standard overhand slot.

TEN O'CLOCK

TWO O'CLOCK

3/4 RELEASE

A two o'clock or ten o'clock slot would be a three-quarter release. Anything below the sidearm slots of three and nine o'clock and you would be underhand.

SIDEARM

Most pitchers don't throw right on the hour. Often they are a little short or a little beyond one hour or the next. To differentiate we can use the terms plus and minus, so that a right-hand pitcher throwing between one and twelve would be throwing over-hand plus. For a lefty, throwing between eleven and twelve would be overhand plus.

Overhand minus or three-quarter plus would be between one o'clock and two o'clock for a righty. Between eleven and ten o'clock for a lefty.

FOR MY MONEY, THREE-QUARTER PLUS FOR BOTH RIGHTY AND LEFTY IS THE BEST ARM SLOT.

It has the leverage, the greatest potential for downward trajectory, and therefore positively effects velocity and movement on both fastballs and breaking pitches. Obviously though, cases can be made for other angles, with Hall of Fame portfolios to back them up. But, If I'm your coach, and you are not especially effective throwing at what I might consider an eccentric angle, you are going to have a tough time convincing me that throwing the ball at any angle that's not around 3/4 plus makes sense for you.

DETERMINING YOUR STRONGEST ARM ANGLE

Nobody knows better than your body what your ideal throwing angle should be. I use the following exercise to allow the body to reveal its strength.

Line up about 5 baseballs on the ground in centerfield. Tell the pitcher that you are simply testing arm strength. To keep from tainting the experiment, don't mention anything about arm angles.

Have the pitcher take a short run to scoop up the first ball.

With a running step or crow-hop, have him throw to a catcher at home plate on the fly. Take note of the arm angle the pitcher uses to get his best throw. Repeat the throw four more times, all the while looking for noticeable patterns in your observations.

Another test with similar effect is to place five balls in the deep shortstop hole and have a runner at the plate ready to go on cue. Have the pitcher — the subject — scoop up a ball and throw to first to try and beat the runner. Again note the arm angle. With this drill make sure to have the balls situated to the pitchers off-hand side so that sidearm won't necessarily be the required angled.

Once properly fitted and established, your choice of arm angle should not be subject to fluctuation anymore than your hat size. Some slight changes may need to be made over the years, but certainly not between pitches. Mixing-up arm angles as a way to confound the hitter is master level stuff. Wandering around the clock à la El Duque, David Cone, or Louis Tiant is only reserved for the most seasoned of pitchers.

To establish a consistent arm angle for the fastball, curve (slider) and change-up is desirable so that the batter cannot detect differences in pitches due to different elevations. Good batters look for slight deviations in arm angles that are associated with variations in pitches and are quite adept at picking them up and adjusting quickly. Of course for almost every rule, you'll always find those who make the exception work. Steve Carlton, for example, was known to alter his arm angle rather than his grip to differentiate his slider from his curve. Of course having one of the all-time great sliders as well as a strong curve allows you to bend the rules some.

One needs to find out early where his best arm slot is and then work it into his system of refined mechanics. Fine-tuning with arm angles is an area where the pitching technicians need to observe carefully both pitching results and physiological implications as adjustments are made. A radar gun is the final arbiter in terms of velocity. And all things considered, it's probably in everyone's best interest to find the strongest arm angle and work from there. Rotation and mechanics are more easily taught than arm speed.

ACHIEVING A DOWNWARD PLANE

As pitchers, a large part of our work is to befuddle hitters. Most hitters are trying to achieve a flat plane in which to hit. Whether they swing up slightly (Ted Williams) or down slightly (Charlie Lau), the net effect is coming onto the middle third of the ball in as flat a plane as possible.

It is necessary for a pitcher to establish his own plane and stay away from the plane that will bring about #6 type hits (see previous box). The establishment of a downward plane is the result of throwing overhand or three-quarter overhand to create a trajectory that makes a level swing futile. This becomes even more pronounced when a breaking pitch, especially a curveball, is thrown from the correct trajectory.

The dilemma of dealing with pitches up and in, and down and away, is always a problem even to the good hitter. If a pitcher really wants to mess with the hitter's head, he can once in awhile throw a pitch with a flatter trajectory. Thus the hitter will have to make still another decision, "Do I want to adjust to his usual difficult trajectory or wait on the trajectory I prefer which might never come?"

Proper arm angles along with solid mechanics will allow the pitcher to consistently achieve the ideal release point and consequently, the ideal plane of delivery. As long as the pitcher operates on the advantage of his trajectory, he has an edge on the hitter.

THE IDEA OF UNDERHAND PITCHING
. . . AND THE CASE FOR IT

I almost always stop short of encouraging young pitching aspirants to throw sidearm or underhand.

Every now and again I will work with a young man who is totally convinced of the fact — even willing to bet me — that he throws faster from the sidearm slot. Perhaps it's the seemingly crisper delivery or the drop in trajectory or the surprise in a hitter's face when a pitcher drops down on him. I could have made a lot of money over the years if I'd ever taken them up on their bets. Usually, I'll let them persist for a few minutes, then out comes the radar gun, and bang. . . . Aren't they surprised to discover that invariably there is a drop of at least five and sometimes as much as ten mph going from a three quarter to a sidearm delivery?

Unless a pitching coach with considerable expertise can recognize that there is a significant advantage for a down south approach, I feel strongly that a young pitcher should keep his arm angle well north of three or nine o'clock.

Obviously baseball has always had its share of outstanding underhand/sidearmers: Dan Quisenberry, Kent Tekulve, Dick Hyde, Ted Abernathy, Dennis Eckersley, Ewell Blackwell, Carl Mays, and Eldon Auker to mention a few.

Few people know that immortal Walter Johnson, winner of over four hundred games, threw his blazing fastball from the sidearm slot.

Some of the pitchers I mentioned were truly genuine sidearm/underarm pitchers and others such as Eckersly gained some or more of their angle by bending their torsos to the side so that they actually threw from close to a 3/4 slot just laid on its side.

Coaching **TIP** Great pitchers sometimes teach us something new, but more often it's that they find new ways to bring forth the old principles.

THE BIRTH OF THE ART OF DECEPTION

In its infancy, baseball pitchers were required to deliver the ball with a straight arm with the release point at the hip or below, which essentially meant that the ball had to be thrown underhand. In 1872 the rules were adjusted so that the pitcher was allowed to jerk his arm, bend his elbow, and snap his wrist — providing his hand was still below his hip on release. This opened the door for sidearm pitchers, and with the sidearm delivery came the curveball, and also a change in attitude.

Up until that point in *base ball*, as it was referred to in the 1800's, the pitcher was supposed to accommodate the hitter, pitching the ball high or low as requested. The clear intention of the game had been to have the ball put into play. In 1872 that intention became a little murky. Pitching as an art of deception made its debut, although the rules were still such that umpires could keep a batter swinging until contact was made.

In 1884, the National League broke its last attitudinal ties to the gentlemanly English game of cricket by lifting all restrictions on arm location. Now with the American competitive spirit fully unfettered, embarrassing the hitter with a K was no longer considered bad sport. Pitchers began to throw overhand before the ink on the new rulebook was dry. Instantly run totals dropped, strikeouts became a phenomena, and the intimate relationship between pitcher and hitter moved to center stage as it shifted from one of cooperation to one of intense dramatic rivalry.

In today's game Steve Reed of the Indians, the White Sox's Kelly Wunsch, (possibly the first lefthanded submariner since the 1880's), Byun-Hyung Kim of the Diamondbacks and Scott Sullivan of the Reds exemplify a resurgence of the breed. Korean born Kim may be the most intriguing of the lot. With a delivery from between five and six o'clock, he has one of the nastiest late break sliders in baseball and a fastball in the low nineties which keeps hitters from sitting on the slider.

With a few exceptions, relief pitching is where most underarm/sidearmers have found their niche. Obviously, the introduction of a different trajectory late in a game will prove to be a dilemma for the batters. Fastballs that sink and curveballs that rise are pretty hard to adjust for in a single at-bat.

Until very recently, throwing from below the horizontal was considered more trickery than artistry — fairly odd considering that the art of pitching is all about the art of deception. I had to think twice myself, before deciding to give underarm/sidearmers some consideration in this book. Sidearmers have a history of being overlooked by the big leagues. Both Quisenberry and Tekulve went undrafted out of college.

Despite what would seem like a high level of stress on the elbow, sidearmers have racked up an awful lot of years with high workloads over the course of long careers. Eckersly and Tekulve are in the top five for all time pitching appearances. Tekulve had seven years where he made over 70 appearances including 90 at the age of forty. Wunsch and Sullivan both put up big appearance numbers in 2000.

WHAT GOES INTO THE THINKING THAT LEADS A PITCHER IN A SOUTHERN DIRECTION?

◆ Anatomy or injury inhibit some from being able to generate overhand arm speed. Numerous sidearmers were standard style throwers who rejuvenated their careers by dropping down while on injury rehab.

◆ Sidearmers and underhanders seem to have better control. Two of the stingiest pitchers of all time, Eckersly and Quisenberry both had seasons with walk totals that even *Three-finger* Brown could count on his two hands. Walter Johnson in his time exemplified great control, much to the relief of the hitters.

◆ Better movement seems to result from starting down low. From that angle, fastballs will run and curveballs appear to rise. People like Quisenberry, and back in his day, Carl Mays could make the ball move in ways that defied description while keeping in the strikezone. Throwing from three and nine o'clock or below certainly lends itself to keeping the ball low.

◆ For most of us, the sidearm pitch can feel more comfortable and compatible with the human body. The rotation of the hips and shoulders — the Captain's Wheel — feeds more directly into a sidearm than an overhand delivery.

But ultimately what should determine whether a pitcher drops down or not are the results he gets when he does. *Does he get the batters out?* is always the bottom-line question.

One of the challenges in teaching the sidearm and the underhand is that it's much harder to find reference points for the pitching circle. But whereas throwing sidearm is much more natural, the release point becomes self-evident.

The main **danger** of this style of pitching is that any ball that escapes upward feeds right into the typical **batter's Swing Plane.**

REQUIREMENTS FOR DROPPING DOWN

FASTBALL MUST RUN AND SINK If it does not, then there must be high velocity to the underhand fastball. Quisenberry rarely broke 80 mph with his fastball, but great sinking movement within the strikezone resulted in groundball after harmless groundball. Inevitably, if you can't get good velocity or good movement/location on your fastball, your career will be a short one, no matter what the angle. Although Quisenberry didn't depend on speed, his effectiveness took a nosedive when he lost a few mph and with it, probably a little rotation off his pitch.

If you have a strong curveball with great finger action, adjusting it to a down-under trajectory can be readily accomplished with little tinkering.

CURVE OR SLIDER MUST RISE OR APPEAR TO RISE

This phenomenon is probably due to the low release point and is magnified by the contrasting sinking motion of the fastball. In all likelihood this is an illusion, as the ball simply does not drop as much as the brain calculates it should. However, for a pitcher like Kim who throws from the near bottom of the clock, there may indeed be some significant upward movement. When his slider is working, it supposedly breaks a good foot across the strikezone, creating an up and away angle that is unique to the game. However, even in Kim's case the slider, and for that matter, the curve will not be effective if it wanders high enough to allow the batter to see more than the top third of the ball.

MECHANICS MUST BE STRESS FREE A trade-off occurs when a pitcher drops down. If thrown properly there should be less wear on the shoulder but possibly more on the elbow. Side-slingers seem to have less arm trouble than overhand pitchers, although until a study is done to prove this, I wouldn't bet the farm on this idea.

Many pitching coaches don't understand about mechanics from below the perpendicular, which is probably why we don't see more of these stylists. To throw from the bottom of the clock, numerous adjustments must be made. The hand is not going to end up in the bucket with follow-through. One is going to have reach out more so than reach back at pre-launch. Ultimately, the basic truths will still hold: leading with the hip, landing on the ball of the foot, reaching for the release point, finding a path of deceleration. Adhering to them should be your litmus test in the restructuring of mechanics.

MY OWN CHOICE

While in college at the beginning of one season during our exhibition games, I'd been experiencing some discomfort with my shoulder. Not wanting to miss my turn taking the ball, I experimented with an underhand delivery and discovered that if I dropped down low, I experienced no pain at all.

You can't survive throwing underhand without great control and without having at least one pitch with strong movement. Not many can throw a slider from below the perpendicular with any consistency, but with the proper upward trajectory and great rotation, it will look like it's going to be rising right up into the wheelhouse and then rip right down across the knees.

I pitched that entire game underhand, mixing fastballs and curveballs. The result was a six inning two-hit shutout. Fly balls off the curve and ground balls off the fastball — which did sink some — made this an intriguing way of pitching. However I did not follow up on this, and I remained a standard overhand pitcher throughout my career.

Looking back, I now recognize that back in those days, there was some stigma attached to throwing underhand, especially for a starter. Part of that dated back to Carl Mays, the less than personable submariner who killed popular Cleveland shortstop, Rex Chapman with a pitched ball (the only occurrence of its kind in the majors). Even though the game originated with underhanded pitching, as we moved into the twentieth century, throwing underhand became regarded as trickery and somewhat less than manly. When we refer to someone as being underhanded, it's not exactly a compliment.

In 1967, underhander Ted Abernathy pitched 106 innings of relief, leading the National League in appearances and saves with a 1.27 ERA, numbers that would make him a Cy Young candidate were he pitching today. Abernathy never even got selected as an All-Star. Back not long ago, if a coach suggested to a pitcher that he drop his delivery down, it was a definite insult to the ego. Dabbling with underhand pitching as I did for that brief moment gave me an appreciation of its effectiveness. And while I would still hesitate to call myself a booster of throwing underhand/sidearm, I do recognize and appreciate its potential.

PART IV

THE BEGINNING, MIDDLE, & END

When a pitcher lifts his craft to art, every pitch tells a story.

And every story told has a beginning and a middle, followed by an end. And while it is the ending that we may remember best, a good ending doesn't mean much without a captivating start and a fluid middle.

THE START *WHAT HAPPENS BETWEEN THE LINES IS MY RESPONSIBILITY.*

If one starts with a very purposeful approach (the purchase), the trend toward effectiveness is initiated and the stage is set for a series of positive events to take place. I've always held the idea that starting off with the right attitude means believing that pitching isn't fifty or eighty percent of the game as some say, but rather that up to ninety-eight percent of the game is mine to control, with luck — good or bad — accounting for the other two percent. This puts responsibility for the outcome squarely in my hands.

Emanating a positive, aggressive impression from the outset is absolutely essential. You are the overlord and any claims the hitter makes to the contrary is irrelevant. You control the pace of the game, you initiate all action; your choices dictate the hitter's response, and no matter how capable, no matter how hot, that hitter can never take charge unless you allow him. This is an edge allowed you and you must take any edge that can be had in the battle between pitcher and hitter that is the heart of the game.

No matter how many times a batter steps out of the box or commits other actions to disrupt your rhythm, to your mind he is no more than the sentenced man, coming up with trivial distractions while walking his last mile.

Your projected attitude is paramount. Once the batter sees that there is no fear in your eyes and nothing to be gained by attempts at intimidation, your authority is established, and backed by good execution, it will be maintained throughout the game.

Everyone has heard the adage, "It's not how you start that matters, but how you finish." And there is some truth to that, but when dealing with pitching, if you use it as an excuse for sloppy mechanics, you're making your job harder, not easier.

To be wishy-washy or defensive in one's approach bodes well for defeat. As long as the pitcher is positive and forceful in implementing his mound presence, as long as he is confident in his ability to execute, as long as he knows that his survival kit is well stocked to forestall and survive emergencies — as long as he is rooted, balanced, and clearheaded — the beginning of his delivery will become the physical manifestation of his mental approach.

THE MIDDLE (POSTING) LOADED AND READY

In a ten-step delivery approach, the middle or posting position comes with the loading of the hip in Step Five. This is the halfway mark. If everything has been fluid and balanced up to this point, the stage should be set for the Magic Moment. The target, long decided, is completely fixed upon with every inch of one's being and purpose. This is the state of concentration without elimination. Breath is under control and the mind is completely focused on the task at hand, so much so that you can be aware of everything going on around you without breaking your focus. Reaching this point comfortably with poise and balance should enhance the remaining steps in the delivery. Here the pitcher, like the archer with his bow fully pulled, is prepared to release all his energy into the unified act of pitching the baseball.

THE FINISH GIVE IT AN ENDING

After arm angles have been established and the anatomy of a pitch has been developed, then a proper ending needs to be addressed. How one ends does indeed matter, but one mustn't forget that the ending occurs through and beyond the point of release.

When each pitch is considered a masterpiece with no room for mediocrity — and this should be the mindset — then the end of the pitch should be its final artistic touch. To allow for an improper or hurried ending is to allow erosion or regression to take place.

> ## Exploding with vigor and rushing
> are two different things. Rushing pulls the energy forward often ahead of its base. He who rushes to the finish misses the point, much like the young orchestra member who proudly declares that not only did he finish the piece, but he finished it first.

GIVE THE PITCH AN EXCLAMATION MARK!

On a change of pace pitch, the ending may be the all-important ingredient. Pitchers who have great change-ups invariably have great finishes, usually better even than their fastball finish.

On a late breaking fastball, one with second stage action, the final acceleration and pronation of the wrist are what gives it character and definition.

On a curveball, the last development of the wrist on rotation may be the criterion for a great break. The same holds for a slider.

A lot can go wrong at the finish, but it's all correctable, providing recognition occurs.

A correct ending doesn't have to linger. It can be subtle and quick and not always blatantly noticeable. But it must be consistent and the forces of deceleration must be invoked. If the shoulder is buried and the arm comes through so that the hand goes into the bucket and the glove hand comes to its proper spot; if weight is transferred through the balls of the feet and the knees remain bent and flexible, then a good ending is probable.

If you are a pitcher, your delivery is your identity. As with any performance, there should be a precise ending, capturing the value and essence of the moment. This is your signature.

To begin correctly and to end correctly is to create a technical masterpiece and consequently an artistic happening. Striving for this everytime does not require special diligence or energy. It simply requires a thought process that includes doing things right and the striving for excellence.

Suddenly there is no consistent release point — the front shoulder flies open — the pitching elbow drops or lags behind — weak arm action takes place — rotation is choked on release.... Can all of these misadventures be happening because the pitcher failed to finish his pitch?

A baseball is more than just a thing of cork, yarn, and leather. Through your fingers on release it can sense the intent of your finish and will reward or punish you appropriately long after it's in the air and you think your relationship with it is ended.

THE ART OF ARTISTRY

We human beings don't program very well. Our downloading capability is far less than that of the machines we build. With the exception of a few rare geniuses, repetition must be part of any equation we design aimed at proficiency.

REPETITION x EFFORT = PROFICIENCY

And for mastery to be our result, we must bring significant consciousness to our effort and fortify that effort with endless amounts of practice.

REPETITION^3 x CONSCIOUS EFFORT = MASTERY

However, even when we adhere to such an equation, the closest we'll come to mastery is the occasional masterful pitch, inning, or game. Just like it is with balance, mastery is never achieved but must always be worked towards. Certainly, levels of expertise can be achieved, but to sit back and declare ourselves to be masters complete is an open invitation for disaster. God lets some venal sins go unpunished, but when it comes to pridefulness, he makes quick work of us mortals.

But just because we can't achieve perfection, that's no excuse to keep from working towards it. We should never settle for anything less than that which our best effort can accomplish. *Good enough* is the battle cry of the mediocre and it's a phrase we should throw on the trash heap, along with the other lies we tell ourselves such as *I can't do it* and *I don't have a choice*.

I'm of the old school that believes that you can accomplish anything as long as you choose to do so. And that anything you do, you might as well do well. As a coach and a player, it's been my experience that if you're putting the time into learning something, then it doesn't really take that much longer to learn it well.

If you're going to deprive yourself of the opportunity of getting good, because you don't want to put in the extra time, then you might as well stop now, because no one stays just where they are at. Without making a continual effort to get better, you will get worse. Going the extra mile will surprise you with rewards not even imagined. Often that extra time spent proves interesting and challenging and can be loaded with many unique opportunities. It's the time where craftsmanship begins and art develops.

In this concept of always giving the finishing touch to a project, we establish a higher level of achievement and refinement that moves us away from the overcrowded ghetto of *good enough* and into the exclusive neighborhood of excellence. If a pitcher continually attempts to give his pitch an expression, an identity of sorts, a personal quality (signature), then it is likely that style and substance will become one and a superior performance will emerge.

A FINAL WORD ON MECHANICS

TO PUSH OR NOT TO PUSH...
That is NOT the question.

To get into an argument over pushing or not pushing-off with the back foot may be a futile exercise. I favor the push-off concept strongly — but the other school, the Tall and Fall people, may have something to contribute to the discussion as well. To completely negate either concept is to be ignorant of the mechanics of throwing a baseball. Whereas the Tall and Fall people downplay the value of the back leg in pushing off the rubber, the push-off folks believe it to be paramount in developing thrust. Other than that, both sides concur on most points with regard to how a body generates power.

The more one studies any particular way, the more one comes to realize that the *Law of Individual Differences* exists everywhere, and the pitching of a baseball provides no exception. To be astute and functional in the technical approach to pitching, one may need to heed the variances among anatomies and leverage systems. Therefore no ironclad *push-off* or *no push-off* rule should properly exist if one is to take the marginal pitcher over the hump. Such dogmatism just gets in the way.

In the world of the technician, traditionalist viewpoints are sometimes unfairly quashed.

To make ourselves feel secure in a world that provides more questions than answers, we humans feel compelled to slap definitive labels on just about everything we can, including pitching coaches. Either you're a technician or a traditionalist — as if the two could be mutually exclusive.

Why in fact argue the value of the technician versus the value of the traditionalist? In reality, the best one could hope for in a coach is to find a traditionalist who seeks technical understanding or a technician who has a healthy respect for the past.

I've been around long enough to know that when a new and revolutionary concept is sprung on the world of pitching, that some consideration has to be given as to the motivation of those doing the springing. Are these people seeking to add something of quality to an already established science or are they simply looking for a way to serve their egos?

In the world of baseball there are a lot of well-intentioned and very sincere folks who are constantly on the prowl for any truth or magic formula that will give themselves, their children or their students a leg up on the competition. A whole industry — some parts more legitimate than others has come into existence to meet their needs. Being sincere people, they expect sincerity in others and are especially susceptible to any would-be guru who guarantees a quick fix. And when this guru exaggerates his claims and plays the guilt card — *have you really done all that you can for your child?* — we end up with a Pied Piper scenario, as well-intentioned people, uncomfortable with their uncertainty, flock to the one who may not possess, but is quick to express certainty.

I believe in change, I believe in new concepts, and though many of my fundamental ideas have remained the same over the years, many of the fine points and the ways I teach have changed considerably. However, whatever changes I have made are ones that have been thoroughly tested in the real world pitching lab. I wish it were so that all people who love this game would rigorously scrutinize the validity of untested new viewpoints before buying in hook, line, and sinker.

Old truths do need to be reexamined from time to time and occasionally room must be made for the new. New concepts undoubtedly invigorate the scene and vitalize the profession, but a novelty concept with limited proof — particularly one that claims to have all the answers — should be approached with caution.

Pitching coaches are constantly in search of the ideal combination of events that will produce a strong fastball. I am among them. And as a pitching technician, I'm particularly sensitive to teaching mechanics that will enhance arm speed. Through the years there have been disagreements on things other than push-off. The use of the middle versus the index finger, the height of leg kick, late closure or not. And for the most part I have great respect for folks who have argued one way or the other about the aforementioned. But when it comes to push off or not, I think some folks are trying to sell us a better mousetrap that only catches invisible mice.

And while I have respect for the thinking behind Tall and Fall, I'm not convinced that the Tall and Fallers don't push off as well. The Tall/Faller's main concern is that if one drops the post leg too much, one's weight will become centered in the heel rather than the ball of the foot, draining power back off into the earth. They are also concerned that by bending the back knee and becoming shorter, one begins to lose the advantage of downward trajectory that the mound offers. But they do recognize the posting knee must bend some and that the back leg must push forward to release. For some pitchers, Tom Seaver's drop and drive does work. You certainly can't argue with Seaver's results. But I agree with the Tall/Fall folks, that for most pitchers, if one begins to bend the knee after posting, one will quickly reach a point of diminishing returns.

Basically, what it comes down to is finding the proper coil and launch for any individual's particular body type. And thus it becomes a matter of degree. But what burns me are those folks who take the idea of Tall and Fall and attempt to convince us that any pitching coach who is encouraging a pitcher to get thrust out of his back leg is perpetrating a cruel coax that will rob that youngster of the opportunity for a career.

To suppose that one doesn't use the rubber to drive off from is ridiculous. Outfielders will undoubtedly tell you that to make the strongest throws, one has to drive off the back foot. Newton's third law *For every action there is always opposed an equal reaction* seems to be quite applicable here. Telling kids not to push off the rubber is like a telling a sprinter that if he pushes off the block he'll be sending his energy in the wrong direction.

When power from the rotation of the hips and shoulders is transferred to the arm and ultimately to the fingers, we have a union of forces designed by trial and error that produce a flow of energy optimal to the creation of a fastball. All measures should be taken to help this critical timing take place.

As the front foot touches down and the torso is still closed with all this potential energy ready to explode — I firmly believe the post foot will push or drive off. The back leg helps trigger the hips which work uniformly with the shoulders to produce trunk rotation, hopefully quite late, so that this energy goes into and with the inertial forces already in action and then transfers this energy to the arm, wrist, and ultimately to the fingertips and the ball itself.

Therefore if I am to believe that one truly does not push-off, I'll have to see quite a lot more in the way of hard proof and not just theory or speculation or even subjective observation before I discard the likes of a Bob Feller, a Tom Seaver and another hundred pitchers who got to the Hall of Fame believing that they pushed off the rubber. People remember what they want to remember and they see what they want to see. Call it the Placebo Effect if you want. Two people of honest intention can look at a pitcher and one will swear he's pushing off, while another will swear he isn't, What they see is much more related to whatever bill of goods they've been sold rather than what actually occurs.

THE ACT OF PITCHING
PORTRAIT OF A POWER PITCHER
A tribute to the absolutes of pitching

An act is an action and the act of pitching starts with a decision, requires a risk and offers a result. It is also an enacted drama and as a drama, the Act of Pitching involves preparation and performance.

PREPARATION

Like an actor preparing for the stage, a pitcher's performance is only a small part of his effort. Every pitch thrown in competition is representative of ten thousand thrown in practice.

His craft must be so developed that every move is buried deep in his muscle memory. Come game time, the mechanics of his craft is the responsibility of his body; when this happens fully, his mind can lift him to that next level, to that zone where true competitors engage in contest and true artists engage in the act of creation.

Even his game face must be practiced with diligence.

THE INTRODUCTION

When the pitcher takes the mound, he is no longer the clubhouse cut-up, the nice guy, the teddy-bear, or for that matter the psycho or the wild-man. As with the professional actor, his first step onto the stage completes his transformation. By his mere presence, he must let those who stand behind him— as well as those who would stand before him — know that he is the overlord on this *field of dreams.*

He makes the mound his own.

When he connects with his catcher and places his foot on the rubber, there can be no mercy in his eyes, no anger — just fire — in his heart. His gaze is strong and sure and beyond the touch of insult or intimidation. He fixes his grip in the privacy of his glove, not allowing the batter to focus on the ball, but only on the language of his body which speaks of strength, power and purpose.

THE BUILDING OF TENSION

His persona introduced, his character developed, he begins his story with the wind-up.

As he lifts his arms, he engages with the very laws that govern the universe.

He is an instrument now of physics. *To every action there is always opposed an equal reaction,* so he loads his body in perfect balance, every movement storing energy in his torso, his legs, his hips.

His hands break and he reaches back to store even more potential energy in his body.

THE ACT

Energy is further gathered with the continuation of the arm through the pitching circle, as the lower half of the body begins to prepare for the *reaction.* The stored energy is held, with the hips and the shoulder still closed. The hand breaking away goes to low-cock first and then rises into the high-cock.

The lead shoulder, the lead hip, the chin are all focused on the plate. The glove is continually positioned to conceal the ball from the hitter, who experiences an eternity's worth of waiting contained in but a fraction of a second.

THE CLIMAX

The pitcher's foot sets down and the story explodes to its climax. The ball of the lead foot touches first and with it all the forces unite. The feet pivot; the rear leg drives forward; the hips and shoulder snap open. The elbow of the off-arm thrusts back. The throwing arm travels from high-cock and up over the top of the pitching circle.

The elbow of the throwing arm drives to the batter like the head of a spear.

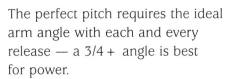

All energy unites to accelerate the arm. With regard to speed, the math is simple: the ball moves as fast as the arm.

The perfect pitch requires the ideal arm angle with each and every release — a 3/4 + angle is best for power.

Bending his torso over the wall, the pitcher must imagine the release point beyond where it truly occurs in order to place maximum energy and control on the pitch. It's a trick one has to play on the brain every time a ball is thrown. Perhaps this is a mechanism to teach us to follow-through, as the pitcher's arm will not survive such violence for long, if we do not properly decelerate it.

But there is so much more to a pitch than its speed. GREAT ROTATION is what gives the ball its life. Great rotation is what it takes to become a pitcher with stuff.

DÉNOUEMENT

In a drama it is the resolution that follows the story's climax. With pitching it is the follow-through. Every pitch has got to have an ending and it must be finished with the same focus with which it was started.

The lead shoulder is buried, the pitching hand swings around to the side. The back leg lifts up and comes forward. Balance is maintained; it is never gained nor lost. In harmony with the demands and capacities of his body, the pitcher never attempts a violation of the laws of physics. His root stays connected through the balls of his feet. His thoughts are not clouded by doubt.

He leaves the mound as he had entered, still a competitor no matter the turn of events. He has survived to leave on his own accord and if he is to return, he must maintain himself mentally through the course of the next half-inning, so that if it is possible, he will face the next three batters with even greater resolution than those he just faced.

THE MECHANICS OF THE 95 MPH FASTBALL

While size, which is a factor in throwing a baseball hard, is often regarded as the prime requisite, it may actually be secondary to great mechanics. However when the two conditions are united, you have the perfect matrix for a 95 mph fastball. This is not to ignore Pedro's great 95 + mph delivery at 170 lbs.

The preceding photos are of Chad Paronto, an outstanding pitching prospect with the Cleveland Indians who attended my pitching camps back in New Hampshire. Chad marries great size (6´5˝, 250 lbs.) with flawless pitching mechanics. While his bulk surely is impressive, his mechanics are even more impressive. The ten essential steps to a solid delivery being taught and illustrated in this book are caught in Chad's outstanding control of his body and consistent rhythmic flow and follow-through. Chad has very good control, keeps the ball low, exists in the 92-94 mph range constantly, and goes over 95 mph frequently. His fastball is basically a power sinker with movement and bite. Broken bats are consequence of the hard sinker on the hands, and this spring I was even surprised to see how readily he broke those being wielded by Major Leaguers. While he throws plenty hard enough now, Chad feels his best velocity is in front of him, and he believes this because of his mechanics.

Coached and Coaching

A good teacher will encourage the individual and let him know when he is improving. If you're afraid that by giving praise you'll create a swelled head, then you've been ignoring the mental aspects of coaching.

Good players take responsibility for their own thinking. Good coaches encourage this to happen.

The instant cure is rare and rarely holds up under extensive testing.

When you discover that you're lost, it is foolish to assume that the last turn you made was what got you lost in the first place. If you got lost three miles earlier, making a left turn at your present location instead of a right won't much matter. A solid understanding of mechanics is like a road map. If you get lost along the way — and all pitchers invariably do — it will allow you to retrace your steps back to the point where the wrong turn was made.

Whether it's because of laziness or because of the erroneous belief that pitchers are born not made, too many diamonds in the rough never receive adequate polishing. Time by itself is rarely an elixir. Consequently, there are those pitchers who are two-year projects that after two years, end up being two years away still. This is often the anatomy of a wasted career.

Good information is what makes good performance. There is a lot of bad information out there. It is not intentional but it's there!

Coaches can screw you up by what they don't do, as well as by what they do!

There are few — if any — expert coaches, but there are plenty of good ones.

Coaching pitchers is a teaching phenomenon! The most effective pitching coaches are teachers, not gurus. A good teacher adapts to the student's learning style rather than the other way around.

Train the marginal pitcher until he is no longer marginal. Mediocrity is a compromise negotiated with one's limitations. In such a negotiation, cut yourself the best possible deal, rather than accepting the first terms offered.

Baseball is really not a simple game. Good coaching however is one thing at a time.

Game Sense

Hitting an above average amount of homeruns does not guarantee a team offensive success. However, better offensive teams are usually adept at drawing walks. There's at least one lesson in this for pitchers.

Getting called strikes early on is necessary.

THIS BUSINESS OF CONTROL

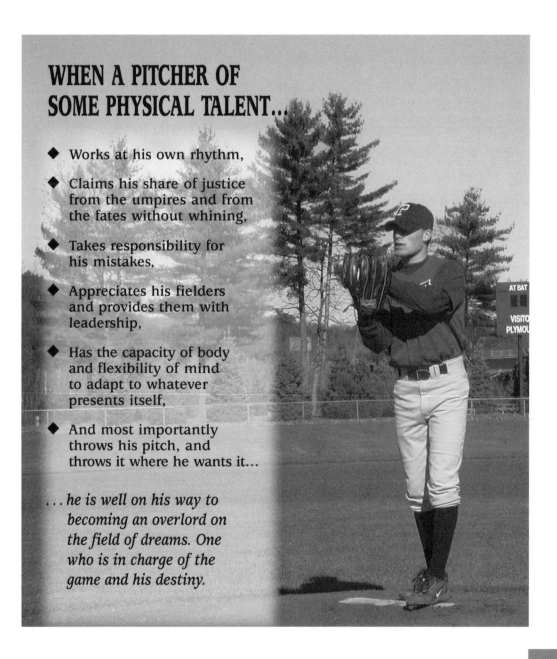

WHEN A PITCHER OF SOME PHYSICAL TALENT...

◆ Works at his own rhythm,

◆ Claims his share of justice from the umpires and from the fates without whining,

◆ Takes responsibility for his mistakes,

◆ Appreciates his fielders and provides them with leadership,

◆ Has the capacity of body and flexibility of mind to adapt to whatever presents itself,

◆ And most importantly throws his pitch, and throws it where he wants it...

...he is well on his way to becoming an overlord on the field of dreams. One who is in charge of the game and his destiny.

PART I

MECHANICAL ASPECTS OF CONTROL

When pitchers speak of control, they are talking of the precious yet elusive and ephemeral capacity to place the ball exactly where they want it. Once the ball leaves a pitcher's hand he has control of it no more. What control he can exert is determined by the thousand and one large and small things he must do before the ball spins off his fingertips. Experience teaches every pitcher, but the most hardheaded, that control attained in one moment is no guarantee that it will ever become permanent or automatic.

> There are legions of decent pitchers who never become masters of control, but there has **never been** a great pitcher who has **not developed great control.**

Masters of efficiency like a Greg Maddux or a Tom Glavine or a Pedro Martinez create the *illusion* of high work loads. They throw more innings while facing fewer batters and throwing fewer pitches, which helps lead to their longevity. When it comes to consistency, control certainly isn't the *hobgoblin of fools*. You won't find any three hundred game winners who didn't develop great control and maintain it year-in and year-out.

Many outstanding prospects have never materialized, because this critical skill has eluded them. Long-lived pitchers have always been able to harness this important facet of pitching to enhance and lengthen their pitching prowess, so that even after their prime, they continued to be among the elite.

Warren Spahn, Steve Carlton, Robin Roberts, Don Sutton, Gaylord Perry, Ferguson Jenkins, Tom Seaver, Roger Clemens and even Nolan Ryan (who finally mastered the strikezone) are all great examples of pitchers who made the strikezone their ally rather than their antagonist. Control is the added element that has metamorphosed Randy Johnson from a fearsome pitcher to an awesome one.

Especially at the earliest levels of play, he who walks the fewest batters wins the most games.

Obviously, the wear and tear of throwing a lot of pitches will shorten the career of a pitcher. Those, who through control, consistently minimize their pitch counts, simply by way of the *Law of Conservation of Energy* should prolong and enhance their careers.

The rules of the game — eight fielders patrolling the turf and only three swings per batter — creates odds which are strictly on the side of the pitcher. To confound this situation by falling behind in the count and putting runners on base via the *base on balls* avenue is to negate the pitcher's natural advantage. Nearly forty percent of baserunners score — so needless to say, walks are rarely the pitcher's friend, and to walk a lead-off batter is nothing short of a heinous sin. That is not to say that there are no situations where throwing balls and risking walks are not mandated. When you fall behind a hot slugger with runners in scoring position and first base open, discretion may be the better part of valor. However, one of the great maxims of baseball is that walks will always come back to haunt you.

THIS SHOULDN'T COME AS ANY SURPRISE . . .

A discussion of control can't have much meaning if the pitcher is not devoted to mastering his mechanics. If you are skipping around in the reading of this book, please be advised that mechanics comes before control with good reason. Once our mechanics are strong and the delivery of our pitch consistent, we can then begin to think of ways in which we can enhance our control.

KEEPING AN EYE TO THE TARGET

When a pitcher has good mechanics, but still is having difficulty in hitting his *spots,* proper alignment is often the culprit. Throughout the entire delivery it is important to keep the body pointed to the target. The chin should always be pointed at the plate or target when landing or touching down. The front foot should always be pointing to the plate, albeit from a partially closed position (toes in).

1. EYEBALL LOAD

2. EYEBALL OPENING CHEST

As the pitcher begins his motion, the front shoulder and the lead hip, each in turn, must be pointed to the target. And when the pitch is being released, not just the hand, but also the bent lead knee must draw a bead on the target. This centers the body and brings the essential focal points together at this most critical juncture. Using the concept of an imaginary eyeball on the front shoulder, and also on the lead hip and knee — the pitcher is able to concentrate these vital points as though they actually were extra eyes focused on the catcher's mitt.

3. EYEBALL FOLLOW-THROUGH

To help reinforce the pitcher who is having trouble with this concept, temporarily place an image representing an eyeball on those areas that are a challenge to align, typically the shoulder and the hip.

4. EYEBALL RELEASE POINT

LOCATION LOCATION LOCATION

If you don't pitch inside, don't expect to enjoy great success on the outside part of the plate. Throwing outside can get batters out more frequently than anywhere else, particularly when thrown downstairs. The ability to move the ball inside and outside is an art that every style of pitcher should employ. Obviously, an *East/West* style of pitching is enhanced by going inside, but *North/South* pitchers can also profit from moving in and out.

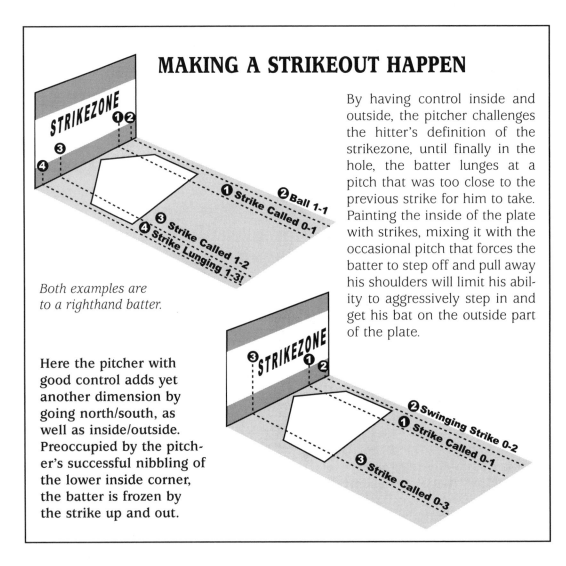

MAKING A STRIKEOUT HAPPEN

By having control inside and outside, the pitcher challenges the hitter's definition of the strikezone, until finally in the hole, the batter lunges at a pitch that was too close to the previous strike for him to take. Painting the inside of the plate with strikes, mixing it with the occasional pitch that forces the batter to step off and pull away his shoulders will limit his ability to aggressively step in and get his bat on the outside part of the plate.

Both examples are to a righthand batter.

Here the pitcher with good control adds yet another dimension by going north/south, as well as inside/outside. Preoccupied by the pitcher's successful nibbling of the lower inside corner, the batter is frozen by the strike up and out.

OUTSIDE PITCHES can be excruciatingly tempting to the hitter as the outside pitch gives the batter a great view of the ball. Most every hitter believes in his heart of hearts that if he can see it, he can hit it.

Pitching is all about command: the ability to throw the ball wherever you want— and that includes purposeful pitching outside of, as well within the strikezone.

Tom Glavine for one has made a career out of getting hitters to chase balls away from the strikezone. It's actually not easy to throw enticing balls out of the strikezone. This is a skill reserved for the pure pitcher.

> **Good control is not necessarily about putting every pitch into the strikezone.**

PITCHING INSIDE — THE CONTROL ARTIST AT WORK

The courts might look at it as reckless endangerment, but in the game of baseball, pitching inside and doing it well is a display of control at its finest. Pitchers who don't have good control of the ball can't and shouldn't do it. In such cases where the ability isn't there, attempting to pitch inside *is* morally reckless.

Besides, no pitcher (especially one with a high walk ratio) can afford to give up too many extra baserunners via the *hit by pitch* route. . . even if those baserunners are the walking wounded. And never forget that the game of baseball is no stranger to revenge. Inspiring the opposition pitcher to retaliate against your line-up is no way to win friends in your own clubhouse.

Pitchers who consistently throw strikes are more apt to get the call on the inside corner. Those pitchers can take aim for the inside, knowing that they will get a strike that's tough to hit and/or move the batter off the plate. When the pitcher sets the stage early with good inside stuff and gets it called for strikes, while keeping the hitters from setting up shop in comfort, he will be in control of the game.

It may sound hard-hearted, but pitchers cannot be overly concerned about hitting batters, any more than batters can be preoccupied with the notion of being hit. When the pitcher does hit someone, he must have the self-control to not panic, nor allow it to disrupt his concentration and rhythm, nor change his game plan.

When batters charge the mound; it's not always a bad thing, providing you can avoid harm and don't humiliate yourself with a public display of the typical baseball player's fighting skills. In contrast to the angry hitter, in most scenarios the pitcher should take the high road and not even admit that there is any kind of problem. That air of calmness wins control points as the game progresses. And when news of the incident spreads around to other teams, that hit batsman becomes your greatest advertisement. It announces to the league —

HERE'S A PITCHER WHO IS NOT AFRAID TO GO INSIDE AND TAKE CONTROL OF HIS PLATE.

ACTIVE VISUALIZATION

The system of actively visualizing oneself throwing a pitch prior to its delivery, is a habit and skill worth developing. There cannot be enough said in this area. Many top performers have a natural knack for doing this. Others need to work at developing this skill of *mind before muscle.*

With active visualization, the mind's eye should visualize as much detail as possible, seeing the entire path of the well-thrown ball, replete with rotation and location. Making a habit of vicariously experiencing the completion of a successful delivery will lead to an action that follow the image.

There's no magic about this. The unconscious mind is a marvelously complex machine that processes thousands of bits of information every instant — in contrast to the half a dozen things or so that the frontal brain, our conscious mind, can digest. When the pitcher chooses to throw a certain breaking pitch that spins a certain way, he can think of how he wants to grip the ball and a few more basics, but it is his unconscious mind that carries the brunt of the workload; it will busily send his muscles a million messages of nuance on how his body must respond from the tip of his toe to the top of his head, in order to create that particular path for the ball.

Conversely, one must be careful of planting negative images that will often get fulfilled.

Coaches are often as guilty as pitchers in this regard. "Whatever you do, don't let this guy take you downtown," is a caveat that's bound to be self-fulfilling, as the last thing the pitcher needs is to start his wind-up having just visualized the serving up of a big fat gopher ball. Coaches should always concentrate on planting the positive message of what they want to happen, rather than what they want to not happen. The last thought they should impart to the pitcher before sending him off to do his work must be a positive one!

Active visualization can be a habitual process once the individual masters the mental approach that most effectively paints the proper picture. This ability is one of the absolutes in obtaining consistent control. It's an area that needs a lot of exploration and like anything else, lots of practice so that it might be utilized to its fullest.

PITCHING IS NOT FOR THE LAZY OF MIND

THE IDEA OF THE FUNNEL

Throwing to a target (not aiming) is always more useful than *just throwing* which is what a lot of players do. A pitcher must always be focused on *throwing through the mitt*. This helps to keep the pitch focused and can contribute toward developing a fastball with a second stage, one that doesn't seem to run out of gas at the plate but rather kicks into a higher gear. Visualization is a technique that allows one to concentrate on location while emphasizing movement.

Mound

Plate

An image that works for many is that of pitching into a large funnel that narrows rapidly across the plate and through the catcher's mitt, so that no matter where the ball travels, its focus ultimately narrows into a dense laser punching a hole through the mitt.

See **through** the mitt, and you will *throw* through the mitt.

RHYTHM AND COORDINATION

Timing and rhythm are the foundations of consistent successful pitching. Good balance and body control allow the pitcher to transfer weight at the optimum time. As already discussed, the melding of striding and rotating, planting must be a harmonious balanced event if forces are to unite.

Rushing can be a problem for many pitchers. When rushing occurs striding can become shortened and one body part can get ahead of another. The rusher is apt to launch his pitch before the arm gets on top. He usually throws the ball high, as he typically ends up having to throw the ball uphill.

If the hurler releases the ball as he gets his head and shoulders over the imaginary wall and reaches forward for his release point, then finishes the pitch and gives it an ending, there should be a consistent delivery which should lead to good control.

MUSCLE MEMORY AND CONTROL

If one actively visualizes himself throwing a strike at a designated part of the strikezone and does this consistently day-in and day-out when pitching, it will undoubtedly become a part of his system. One will not always need to consciously summon the visions as they may already be on automatic pilot. The same goes for refining mechanics. With enough repetition, a dependable pattern of muscle memory is developed where a proper start invokes movement to a consistent delivery position quite naturally and fluidly, so that the ideal release point is arrived at every time.

Useful muscle memory only results when correct movements are fortified with large doses of purposeful intent. It is quite possible — in fact easier — to develop bad habits of muscle memory if that purposeful intent is absent.

CONCENTRIC RECTANGLES

A method I've utilized to teach control is to hang a heavy canvas over a wall mat in a gym. The canvas should be covered with a series of different color concentric rectangles. Using bright colors will enhance visualization. This can be done with spray paint or different colored tapes. The pitcher then standing at pitching distance will be required to call his shots or aim for specific rectangles.

This can be made into a game by assigning various numeric values to the different color rectangles with those representing the edges of the strikezone having the greatest value. Anytime you make a drill into a game even an adult will work with greater focus, especially competitive athletes.

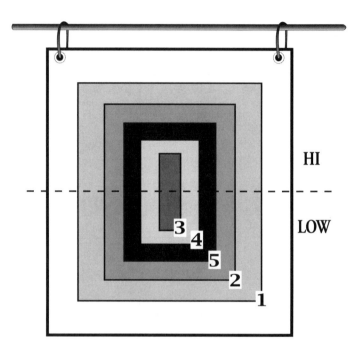

Another tool to be used by itself or in conjunction with the canvas is the multicolored plate.

With this particular plate, the darkest areas (the edges) would have the highest value. Another concept is a multi-colored plate.

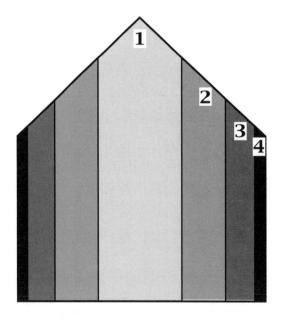

YOU HAVE TO CONTROL MORE THAN THE BALL

One of the greatest attributes an athlete could ever possess would be the ability to harness all the positive facets he possesses and unite them into an overpowering will to succeed. In his quest for achievement, he would master all the negative stimuli and eliminate the possibility of becoming waylaid by all that is in his power to control. Often times this attribute is the result of upbringing or the coaching one has had in one's early years, but it can also be very much a learned phenomenon that happens as the athlete matures.

The ability to deliver an effective pitch in a key situation, when pressure boils, disaster lurks, and Murphy's Law looms is a priceless trait, and surely the absolute precursor to success. The frame of mind that allows for such is not only a necessity for success in pitching, but for success in any walk of life. It requires the complete rebuking of our often negative and cynical world, as we take to the mound of life with a positive mindset and an expectation of success.

One is not necessarily born with this *positive presence* (although some may be). It is often acquired through battles with misfortune, both won and lost. But rarely is it acquired by accident. Firstly, it takes a conscious mind, a willingness to learn from our experience. Whether grabbing the *bull by the horns* is something that comes natural to us by way of our inherited personality or is something that is taught to us by a master of life, it requires each of us to adopt a resolve that says,

I am not a victim, because I choose not to be.

No coach should ever assume that his players come pre-packaged with this ultimate resolve; it must be continually empowered and encouraged. You may give a player a hundred compliments, but brand him a loser just once, and he may never again fully escape the shadow of doubt. Victories should always fortify us and defeats should always teach us.

Momentary positive resolve is something everyone can manifest, but it takes a constant conscious effort to make it a habit without interruption. Even the slightest interruption in the field of competition can create horrific results, as it must be assumed the opposing team is always waiting to seize upon that instant of weakness. For though our laxity may seem fleeting, we can be placed in quick disadvantage. Even a small concession is a big thing when opponents are evenly matched.

In a game of chess between two masters the tide is often turned with the loss of a pawn. One should never be into the mode of contributing to the other team; the drama of a game is too short. One bad pitch at the wrong time can destroy a season, even mark a life.

SO WHAT IF YOU'RE SCARED?

The *critter* fear must never be allowed to become so big that it becomes all of who we are. This control is a discipline. Do not give fear any additional energy; it has enough of its own.

Fear is a normal and natural occurrence. Courage is not the absence of fear, but the ability to go forward despite fear. Everyone gets afraid; even the greatest actors and the most veteran ball players feel a swelling of terror right before the spotlight shines on them. But fear itself should never stop you from doing something.

As it is with developing a positive attitude, consciousness is the tool to build courage and subdue fear. You don't ever have to deny fear exists, just tell yourself that —

> *"This fear that I am feeling is just a small part of me, and not all of who I am."*

Another good thing to remember about fear is that fear is a projection away from the present; it nourishes itself on the past and gorges itself on the future. We are either afraid of the consequence of something that has happened or we are afraid of what is going to happen. That is why deep slow breathing can be useful. As we can't breath in the past or the future, but only in the present, conscious breathing then helps pull our thinking mind into the present where if we look closely we discover we are quite okay and quite capable of dealing with the challenge on hand.

If you avoid contributing to fear by allowing it to swell to panic, the energy of fear can be converted to action; it can empower you. Don't let fear beat you. It should work the other way. It is energy that you can use positively.

Ultimately, experience will teach us that things are never as bad as they seem. If we are conscious about how we go about our business, through our successive encounters with fear we will become used to it and even welcome it as we know that we can harness its energy into a useful and positive tool, particularly in dealing with potentially disastrous situations.

I think that sometimes when players talk about losing their competitive edge, it's because *friend fear* no longer comes to visit them before a contest. Without fear's energy to beat a drum, it can be much more difficult to rally the heart.

Experience will beat fear every time — but if you don't have experience — then confidence, a positive approach and the support of others will subdue fear and help convert its energy. Having a veteran pitcher at the end of the bench who admits that he still gets scared every time out is a wonderful reassurance to the rookie pitcher that fear does not have to doom him.

TO HESITATE IS TO ERR

Taking an action that is bold and quick — no matter how risky — is always preferable to dawdling while time and distance erode the possibility of success. The Little League outfielder freezing with the ball while the winning run circles the bases is one of the most horrific sights in baseball.

In competition, hesitation is a severe detriment; the ability to quickly synthesize and execute is a priceless talent and very much related to success. It cannot be taught like a math formula but can be developed with eternal practice. Some people are blessed with the ability to see the entire game and to always be in the play. They seem to see the field with a whole extra dimension like a chess master who sees the pieces in movement on the board in constant relationship to one another. That is a gift, but even those folks who possess it, need continual practice to maintain it.

Also every player in the field should have it in his mind, that he has some role to fulfill in *every* play: covering a base, backing up a throw, serving as a cutoff, directing traffic.

NOT DOING ANYTHING SHOULD
NEVER BE AN OPTION

A certain state of the mind is necessary to pitch a ball game. What goes into the mental preparation before a game is basically a private affair. It's the inner sanctum of our personality, where the act of psyching-up, or the donning of our warrior spirit takes place.

How many games have been lost by pitchers late to cover the plate, or those who hesitate over whether to go after the runner at third or the one at first and so get neither. A player must know exactly what he will do before the ball gets to him and must have the depth of experience to weigh all the factors when a play is neither *this or that* but rests somewhere in the grayness between obvious choices.

There is no substitute here for practice. An effort should be made to simulate a game situation as often as possible, so as to develop habits of good quick decision making.

CONTROL OF ONE'S SELF

One must have control of one's self before supreme confidence can be manifested and employed. And in turn confidence will breed control. Nothing of any import can take place without self-control, whether it is revealed in an obvious, external manner, or through a quiet type of inner strength.

Confidence in one's physical and nutritional habits, strength training programs, and sleep habits creates an agreement emotionally within oneself. Confidence in one's dexterity and one's achievement in mechanical development and efficiency creates stability devoid of self-destructiveness. Confidence in one's mental approach, agenda, game plan and goals, creates a system of motivation that will prove consistent and advantageous over a period of time.

SELF-FULFILLING PROPHECIES
are often our downfall on the mound and in life.

A self-fulfilling prophecy is when we, by the way we think about something, cause it to become true. The waitress who looks at a bunch of high school kids and thinks *lousy tippers* will deliver bad service, and consequently receive a bad tip, vindicating her negative expectation.

"I knew that was going to happen," is the usual cry of one prone to the self-fulfilling prophecy.

If you think, you are going to have trouble finding the strikezone, you may tighten up in an effort to aim rather than throw the ball. That is why often times one wild pitch will beget another.

Going into a contest with the assumption you are going to lose creates a disaster in waiting.

In that moment after a great upset, the victorious underdog is rarely surprised by the end result. Later as he reflects, he might find himself surprised, but unless he stumbled into victory, he will have already assumed its occurrence.

TEMPER TEMPER!

I would be lying if I told you that great pitchers never lose their tempers. Even some of the greatest were known for Roman Candle dispositions.

It took a catcher with the diplomacy of a Tim McCarver to work with a snarling Bob Gibson. Teammates of Lefty Grove were known to skip their showers and head from the field to the parking lot when they erred behind the great Lefty. It took the feigned insensitivity of an Earl Weaver to balance the sulkiness of a Jim Palmer.

The majority of big league pitchers could probably recall a day or two on the Little League mound when their ears burned and tears of anger and frustration blinded their eyes. The truth of the matter is that highly competitive spirits often come with fiery tempers. But the only ones who continue pitching are those who have learned to cope with their own natures.

> You can never change an individual's basic personality. **The fact of the matter is** that some folks are just wired with shorter fuses than others.

The trick of course is not to let your temper take over to the point that you lose your composure, and with it, your capacity to be effective. Great coaches have a knack for helping players funnel their anger into productive energy. If you get to the point that you start thinking the whole world is against you, suddenly you find yourself in a battle not just with the other team, but with the umpire and maybe even your own teammates.

> *"If you can rattle him, he's done,"* has been the scouting report on more than one pitcher, at any level of competition.

Often times a short fuse or over-sensitivity is the result of a lack of confidence. Often times it is about ones own questions about one's adequacy. When the ego is attacked or bad luck occurs, the fear of having one's assumed inadequacies revealed, creates a knee-jerk defensive lashing out. No doubt, the temper tantrum was a coping mechanism developed in early childhood to externalize frustration and self-anger. And as a child, it did serve its purpose, only now as the pitcher moves into selfhood, such behavior has outlived its purposefulness.

AS WITH FEAR, IT'S IMPORTANT TO NOT LET THE ANGER BECOME ALL OF WHO YOU ARE

Breathing serves as a great tool in helping to calm one's anger. Slowing things down when one becomes angry or upset is crucial, as wild anger often gives us a frantic energy that does not serve well the fine motor coordination needed to pitch, and will often lead to self-fulfilling prophecies. Here of course the coach and catcher can be greatly helpful. Sometimes the pitcher must be assured that he is still a great person; sometimes humor will break the mood.

But eventually the mature pitcher should begin to recognize the early signs of his temper being lost, learn to step outside of himself as an objective observer and employ whatever tact is required to keep himself grounded. Sometimes merely recognizing it happen can be enough.

MURPHY'S LAW

The phenomenon known as *Murphy's Law* states that if anything at all can go wrong at the worst possible time, it will! The mythical Murphy has destroyed a lot of potentially great performances — sometimes because the performer was not aware of such a thing (perhaps he deluded themselves into thinking Murphy played favorites) and sometimes because the person was ill — prepared for looming disasters.

Maybe since I have always been associated with the Boston Red Sox I have a leg up on understanding the power of Mr. Murphy.

My premise is to actively attack Murphy by keeping an extra wad of positive energy in my back pocket to use at critical times. Ignorance of Murphy allows for the unexpected to take over. This is intolerable if one is to be a consistently effective winning pitcher, which after all is our prime directive. You don't have to expect disaster or court it to be prepared for it.

Operating effectively in the presence of disaster is probably the best indicator of a true competitor, because more often than not, we mortals allow disaster to win out. Steve Carlton winning 27 games for a Phillie team that couldn't collectively field a ball or score a run is one of the greatest real life examples of a pitcher who tussled with Murphy and came out on top. Jack Morris and Dave Stewart are two examples of pitchers who tangled with Murphy and still came away with World Series Rings. The ones that *get going* when the situation gets tough and then still tougher, are true heroes whose value goes far beyond the quality of their *stuff*.

Pitching in Little League is probably as great a training ground as any for learning how to deal with Murphy. No lead is ever safe, no play is routine; anything is possible, and more often than not, anything *does* occur. To watch some eleven year old kid who is pitching beautifully only to have his effort sabotaged by a desperate outfielder or a nearsighted ump, or an infield filled with potholes and launching ramps, yet keep going about his business without a loss of composure is true testament to the limitless strength of the ordinary human spirit.

The success of a hurler can be greatly dependent on his relationship with his catcher. The two youngsters pictured here have already worked together for four seasons. Though they have personalities as different as night and day, they will often make plays that surprise everyone but each other.

A catcher's affect on your performance can be even greater on any given day than the quality of your pitches. A good catcher solicits the best there is in a pitcher. There can't be any antagonism, because there is enough pressure as it is. A pitcher must trust that his catcher has no agenda besides winning, so that he can respect the catcher's observations and suggestions as objective. If the relationship is such that the catcher is afraid to tell the pitcher that his breaking pitch just isn't breaking, then a homerun will end up delivering the message. The catcher must be as sincere as the boy who saw that the emperor's *new clothes* were actually no clothes.

However a catcher should probably handle his pitcher with care, baby him to an extent — not confront him or increase the pressure already existent by the nature of the position.

BABY . . . CAJOLE . . . SCOLD . . . MOTIVATE . . . CALM . . . INFORM

At those times when tensions mount and tempers flare, in his relationship with the pitcher, the catcher must put aside his ego; he must always remain the *adult*.

A catcher should be the pitcher's greatest advocate and if need be, his protector. The catcher is the pitcher's *partner in crime* with regard to the inside pitch. He can't leave the pitcher out to hang, by saying, "Hey it wasn't my idea."

Many pitchers perform admirably when catchers persuade and induce them to turn in their very best work. The bond mentally is extremely strong. Natural disagreements on the selection of the pitch are inevitable, but ultimately pitcher and catcher must be of one mind. A catcher who digs balls out of the dirt and frames pitches well is worth his weight in gold. These catchers, through their own toughness and effort, cause pitchers to strive to be their best.

He must be somewhat of a psychologist and do what it takes to bring out the best in his pitcher. Above all else, the catcher must never try to upstage his pitcher. This creates a hostile environment, which is doomed from the outset.

And while the catcher must honor his pitcher, on the other hand, the pitcher must let the catcher know that he appreciates the pain dealt out to his man behind the plate. The pitcher must recognize that his catcher can never wear enough armor to protect himself against all the insult and pain that even the gentlest of games will inflict on him.

CONTROL IS THE GREAT EQUATOR

A pitcher can be a great winner with a mediocre fastball, providing that his control is superior. Control is the unavoidable variable in the formula for turning potential into genuine success. Control must always be considered the number one priority and be attended to on a daily basis. Most pitchers are capable of giving it this attention — it they so choose.

But while command of one's pitches helps, it does not always lead to command of one's destiny. It takes presence on the mound to make a pitcher into an overlord who truly controls that *ninety percent* of the game which is his to take, and a successful future that is his to make.

CHANGING SPEEDS TO WIN

One of the magical mathematical formulas that makes baseball so special is the one defining the relationship between speed and movement. As we already know, the more speed the ball has, the less apt it is to have movement. Imagine for a moment if it were the other way around; then the game would belong entirely to the Goliaths. Guile, genius and grit would serve no purpose and our greatest heroes would exemplify the blessing of physical genetics rather than perseverance and courage.

Changing speeds is not just a style of pitching, it is an essential element necessary to any style of pitching. Great pitching does not occur without it. No matter how good your stuff, the hitters will ultimately tee-off on you if you do not find a way to change speeds on them. When faced with a must win situation, if I don't have a Seaver or a Koufax to call upon, I would rather send to the mound a pitcher with a good fastball and a great change-up than the other way around. A good fastball, a great change-up and a brain that knows how to use them are ingredients enough to create a consistent winner.

After studying college pitchers over the years, it has become apparent to me that pure velocity is no guarantee of success. At that level, I've seen pitchers throwing in the high 80's and low 90's who get hammered by little better than average hitters. Conversely, I've seen many pitchers throwing in the high 70's who could get the ball by the hitters because they mixed it up with good change-ups and breaking pitches. What this has led me to conclude is that if there is any one factor paramount to creating success, it is the ability to change speeds. This is true at any level.

Certainly, pure velocity can buy you wins in high school where the talent is not dealt out with a fair hand, but even at the scholastic level I've seen kids grow into better pitchers when they developed something off-speed. At the professional level, achieving success without the ability to change speeds just doesn't happen. Many people have made the claim that hitting a 90 mph fastball is the most difficult challenge in sports — but that isn't true. If hitting 90 mph fastballs was all that it took to excel at hitting, Michael Jordan might have made it to the big leagues. What *is* the most difficult challenge in sport is hitting a 75 mph change-up, when the batter just saw a 90 mph fastball the pitch before and an 85 mph slider the pitch before that.

Ultimately, when athletic skill is evenly matched, when the bat speed of the hitter is well-matched to the arm speed of the pitcher, pitching then must become a game of deception. And to carry out that deception, it is essential to change speeds so that hitters aren't just swinging in the wrong place, but are also swinging at the wrong time.

THERE IS CERTAINLY MORE THAN ONE WAY TO SEND A HITTER BACK TO THE DUGOUT MUMBLING TO HIMSELF, BUT NINE TIMES OUT OF TEN THAT WAY INVOLVES A CHANGE OF SPEED.

Changing speeds can be accomplished by using a straight change, by taking a little off the fastball, or by employing other pitches in your repertoire as change of pace offerings.

The straight change is probably the most deceptive of them all when it comes to change of pace. But before we consider the straight change, let's take a look at some other pitches that can play havoc with a hitter's timing.

The fact is that you might already possess a change-of-pace pitch and just don't know it.

THE CHANGE-UP MENU
A. TAKING A LITTLE OFF

Taking a little off the fastball is a delicate and dangerous art, which few pitchers have mastered. Jim (Catfish) Hunter was one of the best at it. On first study it seems rather simple. Essentially, it does not require any special grips or changes in motion. The pitcher just throws hard sometimes and not as hard other times. The difficulty with this is that the human body is not an easy machine to calibrate.

And as we've already talked about, putting spin on the ball is a very fine art. The exact amounts of pressure required to impart the ideal spin can't help but be impacted by *putting on* or *taking off* a little mustard. So with this method there is always the danger of tossing a flat fastball that hangs over the plate like a big old piñata. If Catfish Hunter had one weakness, it was the long ball (even during one of his twenty-win seasons, he gave up thirty-nine dingers).

> Taking a little off or putting a little back on requires an **internal regulation** that can't be corrupted by fatigue or adrenaline to be effective.

The other danger with this kind of change-up is that a pitcher, especially an inexperienced one, is apt to get sucked into the rhythm of the hitter without realizing it; and even if this only happens for a pitch or two, the results can be catastrophic.

Aspiring to reach the point where one has absolute control over velocity is a noble venture as it requires that the pitcher be incredibly tuned-in to his body and ability and the reality of what he is throwing. But before trying it in a game, have someone put a radar gun on you while you try to predict the speed of your pitches. And even then, if you get good at guessing, you're probably better off using the skill for winning stuffed bears at the local fair than winning ballgames.

B. SHIFTING GEARS WITH UNCLE CHARLIE

Using a breaking pitch as a change-up is extremely effective, as the breaking pitch should be coming at the batter with a good deal less velocity than a fastball if it is going to give you more than a slider type break. When you throw breaking pitches or change-ups too close to the velocity of your fastball, you lose the effect the change of velocity should make.

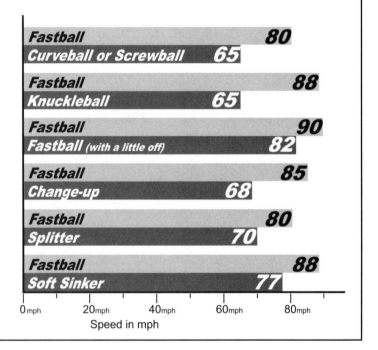

A NOTICEABLE DIFFERENCE

In order to make both pitches more effective there should be a significant difference in mph from your fastball to your change of pace pitch. For a hard thrower as much as fifteen mph or more is desirable. To the right are some more typical ratios between fastball and change of pace pitches.

Fastball	80
Curveball or Screwball	65
Fastball	88
Knuckleball	65
Fastball	90
Fastball *(with a little off)*	82
Fastball	85
Change-up	68
Fastball	80
Splitter	70
Fastball	88
Soft Sinker	77

0 mph   20 mph   40 mph   60 mph   80 mph

Speed in mph

The big curve is extremely effective as a change-up mainly because an ordinary fastball seems a whole lot faster after the batter has just seen your big curve, plus you're also forcing him to be concerned with variations north and south as well as in speed. But if you decide to throw a big Charlie as your leadoff pitch, it needs to have the habit of crossing the strikezone so that the batter knows he must pay it some mind, rather than just take it for a ball as he sits on your fastball.

The game of *down and away* and *up and in* is the essence of the North/South technique in pitching. Once you add in the element of differing speeds, you've achieved a very potent method for getting batters to respect you —and probably dislike you a bit as well.

The screwball has the same advantage as the curve. It usually cannot be thrown hard and almost always breaks down.

Changing speeds is always enhanced if the change of pace pitch moves down. This keeps the batter from seeing the whole ball and does not allow for a level swing.

C. SPLIT-FINGERED FASTBALL—AN ATYPICAL CHANGE-UP

Typically, the split-finger is thought of as a velocity pitch. However, many pitchers can't get a handle on delivering it as a fastball, so they end up discarding it, without even considering its value as a change of pace pitch. If used intentionally in this roll, it can be extremely effective, especially if it breaks downward.

One should keep in mind that any velocity-intended pitch that fails to cut the mustard with regard to speed could be used as a change-up providing that it stays down and has good movement on it.

D. KNUCKLEBALL

Since it is generally difficult to throw a knuckleball hard, the good knuckler can be used to change speed in a most dramatic fashion. But keep in mind that a well-loved knuckleballer is a rarity. Catchers don't like them as they can make the already difficult job of receiving into a nightmare. Managers don't like them because they generally don't care for any pitcher who can't guarantee strikes. And opposing hitters don't like them because it's insulting to be fooled by a pitch thrown at Little League velocity.

Even the best knuckleballers are apt to wear out their welcome with wildness, and they tend to wander about from team to team like gypsies. My advice is that you're best off experimenting with every other kind of grip and delivery, before you settle into the unloved role of a knuckleballer.

However, also keep in mind that if you just don't have the right stuff to be a good hard thrower or breaking ball pitcher, exploring the knuckler is not a bad option. When they get to this crossroad, some fellows can't make the switch simply because of their sense of pride. To them getting hitters out with *junk* just isn't a *manly* thing. They just don't realize that in the world of baseball there's room for all kinds, and it's the results rather than the method which ultimately leads to respect. To be accomplished at throwing so-called junk requires the highest level of craftsmanship and years of diligent work in the pitching lab.

Some coaches who have a knuckleballer or other type of junkballer on their rosters like to start off a series utilizing them, as when they are effective, they can mess up a hitter's timing for days afterward. This impact can also factor in the choice of a reliever to use.

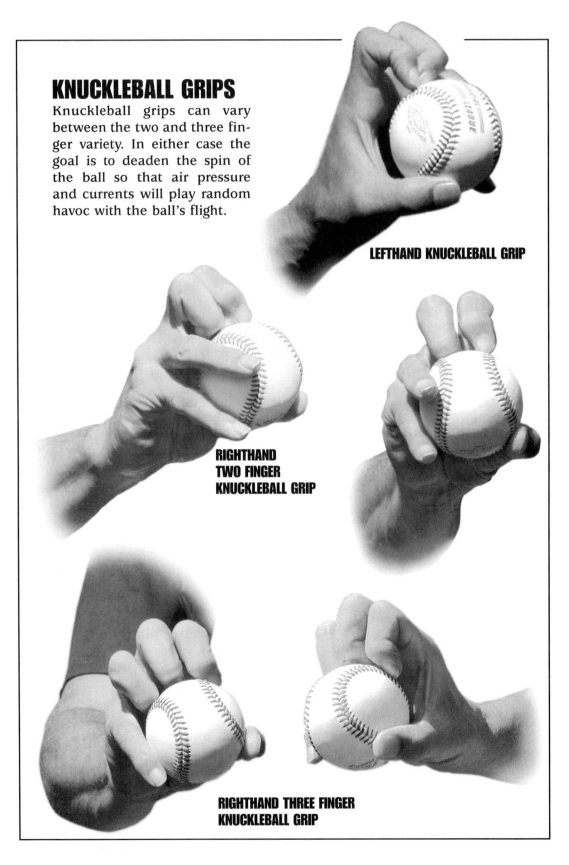

KNUCKLEBALL GRIPS

Knuckleball grips can vary between the two and three finger variety. In either case the goal is to deaden the spin of the ball so that air pressure and currents will play random havoc with the ball's flight.

LEFTHAND KNUCKLEBALL GRIP

RIGHTHAND TWO FINGER KNUCKLEBALL GRIP

RIGHTHAND THREE FINGER KNUCKLEBALL GRIP

E. THE SOFT SINKER

Coupled with the hard sinker, the soft sinker makes for an effective change of pace pitch. It does not require as significant a difference in speed variation as other pitches to be effective because the action is so different from one to the next. If you throw a hard sinker at 88 mph, a soft sinker at 80 will keep hitters off balance. Both drop down but the drop is so much more dramatic and sharp with a hard sinker. Sinkers are illustrated and talked about in depth in both Chapters One and Ten.

F. STRAIGHT CHANGE-UP

It's no coincidence that just about all the big winners of this generation possess a mastery of the straight change. Watching Greg Maddux or Tom Glavine warming up can cause a hitter to salivate. Their stuff just doesn't look that good. Yet, they win again and again because they follow the two essential tenets of effective pitching: mix up the speeds and hit the corners. And what allows them to do this is their mastery of the straight change.

Straight changes come in many varieties. Whereas a sinker, knuckleball, and curve are change of pace by happenstance, a true straight change is a pitch that is designed to look like a fastball and includes the classic, the palm, the three-finger and today's most popular choice, the circle.

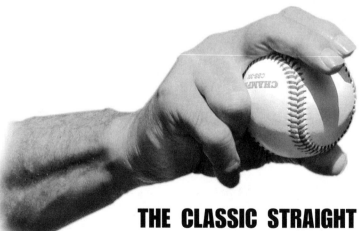

THE CLASSIC STRAIGHT CHANGE shown above has a fastball grip, only pushed back deeper into the palm, here with the fingertips off. Arm speed alters very little. What slows the ball is resistance created by the snugger grip. With a fastball, the fingertips are the prime activators of spin which determines quality and velocity. **The fingertips do not play a role in any of the straight changes**. The classic change should be throw with a stiff wrist, rather than the snapping wrist of a fastball.

The straight change can be a great equalizer of talent. An 85 mph fastball is plenty fast enough when it's paired with a 70 mph change-up. And when an extreme talent like Pedro Martinez — who throws in the 90's — adds a straight change to his repertoire, his talent lifts to greatness. An average pitcher throwing a good change-up can make even a good hitter look bad. A great pitcher can make him look downright silly. Martinez has often stated that his fastball — with all its movement and velocity — is only his second best pitch. His best pitch? The change-up.

When Pedro Martinez has just thrown a 95 mph fastball into your kitchen, it runs counter to the instincts of self-preservation to think about leaning in to get that diving change-up on the outside corner that might be coming next. It's almost impossible to sit on a pitcher's change-up. Physically, it is much more difficult to shift gears to high speed when you're expecting a change-up than the other way around. Mentally it is almost impossible. A great pitcher can literally immobilize a hitter with a 65 mph pitch if the batter is looking for an 88 mph slider or fastball.

The straightness of a straight change has
nothing to do with the path of the pitch.

Although it's not a prerequisite, the best straight changes have movement and go down. A straight change is a ball created for deception and nothing more — but that is enough! It is thrown with near fastball arm speed, with fastball arm angle and comes off the hand like a fastball. Only, despite all of that hurrying-up, the ball travels at a more leisurely pace — a pace that's not easily adjusted to in that fraction of a second allowed the batter after recognition.

Even if the batter ends up just a few inches ahead of the pitch, his bat will have lost a good deal of its pop. And when this alleged fastball not only shifts gear, but also sinks — due to the finesse of hand angle and finger pressure — you end up with a frustrated hitter who is reduced to a hacker diving for pitches that often end up outside of the strikezone.

While movement is a plus, it is not a prerequisite. Batters, especially those intent on reading the spin of the ball, will have difficulty telling the straight change from a fastball until it's too late. But again it needs to be stressed that to be effective, the pitch must remain low enough that the batter can only pick up the top of the ball.

Throwing a change-up perfectly straight doesn't negate all of its advantages. As a rule of thumb, a pitcher who throws a four-seam fastball needs to throw a four-seam change-up and anyone who is primarily dependent on a two-seam fastball should be throwing a two-seam change. This will create all kinds of recognition problems especially for those hitters wanting to *read* the spin. But whether the pitch has movement or not, it must be kept low. High change-ups will greatly compromise a pitcher's chance for survival! Adjustments to a high change-up are much easier for the batter. Not only is it more visible; it's also far easier to hold back one's swing when the plane of that swing is higher rather than lower.

Because it looks so darn much like a fastball coming off the hand, **a straight change** is going to totally frustrate the hitter who tunes his bat in at fastball or slider speed — as most do.

STRAIGHT CHANGES

Along-the-seam change (2 seam) ▶
The ball is gripped along
the seams.

◀ **Cross-seam change (4 seam)**
The ball is gripped across the
seams with the thumb kept in
tight on the bottom seam.

With both the two and four-seam change-ups the ball is gripped along the
seams with the fingertips off and the ball pushed back deep in the palm.
With the palm-ball and the classic straight change the wrist should be kept
stiff on release.

Many pitchers today will opt for the two-seam change-up regardless of their
fastball, as the two-seamer will tend to have greater movement. You want
to avoid the snapping motion that will put extra velocity on the pitch. By
pushing the ball deeper into the palm, friction will aid the cause of slowing
the ball. Keeping the fingertips up or holding them very lightly on the ball
will eliminate the urge to put a tight fastball spin on the ball.

PALM-BALL puts all the fingers on
the ball with the ball pushed back deep in
the palm. The hand can be turned slightly, in either direction, to give the ball
movement.

The palm-ball is very similar to the classic
change, with the four fingertips off the
ball. Here a stiff wrist can also help to cut
velocity. Locking the thumb is one way to
assure that the wrist remains more rigid.

THREE-FINGER CHANGE

The ball is pushed back with the fingers split wide so that the first and third fingers straddle the sides of the ball and the middle finger runs right along the center. The thumb is directly under or to the side. Placing the thumb to the side seems to make the ball sink.

The three-finger was Tom Seaver's preferred change-up. This type of grip can really encourage the pitch to sink. Placement of the thumb will vary and each pitcher should experiment to see how thumb placement adds or detracts from sinking movement. You must be especially conscious to keep your fingers straddled wide on the sides. If they start to creep together, you're liable to end up with a home-run derby fastball rather than a change-up.

CIRCLE or OK CHANGE

Here the index finger and thumb form a circle on the *inside* of the ball. Pressure comes off the closely positioned second and third fingers. This kind of grip makes it extremely difficult to throw the ball hard.

The circle change has become the change-up of choice today. Maddux, Glavine, Martinez, and many others rely on this kind of straight change to keep the hitters off balance. For many, this seems to be a way to get excellent motion on the ball. The position of the index finger can cause the ball to break right or left.

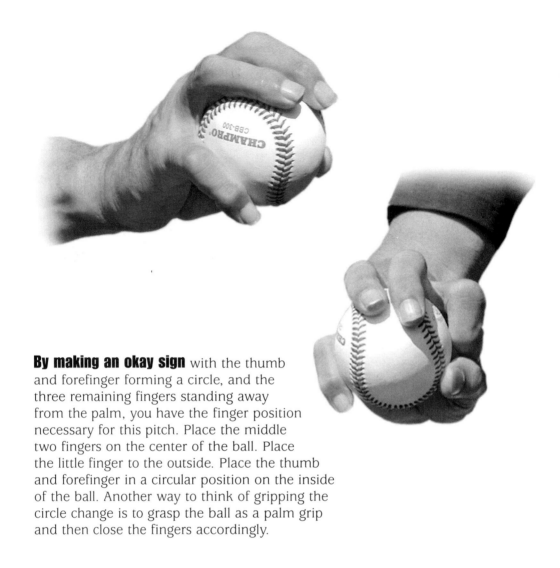

By making an okay sign with the thumb and forefinger forming a circle, and the three remaining fingers standing away from the palm, you have the finger position necessary for this pitch. Place the middle two fingers on the center of the ball. Place the little finger to the outside. Place the thumb and forefinger in a circular position on the inside of the ball. Another way to think of gripping the circle change is to grasp the ball as a palm grip and then close the fingers accordingly.

Don't attempt to throw the ball with less arm speed than your fastball. **Trust in** the friction of the grip to do the work of cutting speed.

Once the grip is established, the intent should be to throw the pitch low. Placing the middle fingers so that the ball is released off of them should guarantee downward movement on the pitch. As it is virtually impossible to throw the ball hard off the middle fingers, the pitch will come off the hand well below fastball speed. When first developing the circle change, one should try to throw the pitch hard with fastball arm action, then gradually work into a comfortable release.

Never forget that the effectiveness of the pitch is totally dependent on the batter's inability to tell it from your fastball.

GETTING CHANGE-UP TO SINK

Getting the change-up to sink by slightly turning the hand will add to its effectiveness. Some pitchers are blessed with the proper hand anatomy that will allow for a natural pronation. However, for those less blessed, a certain amount of *doctoring* can turn the trick. Experiment with the following to encourage the ball to break down and in.

POSITIONS FOR BETTER DROP

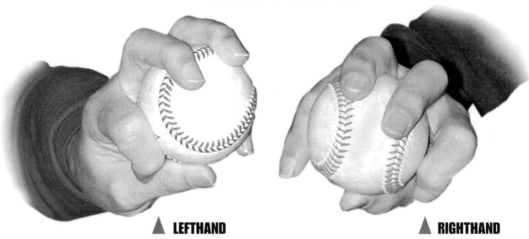

▲ **LEFTHAND**   ▲ **RIGHTHAND**

Typically, when the pitcher turns his hand slightly inside (counterclockwise for rhp, clockwise for a lhp) the ball will get better drop. Turn the thumb inward. Push forefinger down and in. This will cause the ball to sink. By subtly shifting the wrist towards the inside, the pitch can take on a screwball-like action. Some circle changes will even behave like a screwball. This is due to reduced speed and rotation. Rarely do these pitches get hit long.

One can also get a change-up to break the other way — away from a right-handed batter or in on a left-handed hitter for a right handed pitcher. Although some hurlers get away with this type of change, it's not usually effective in terms of movement and results.

To make the ball break away, the middle fingers should exert pressure inward with the thumb also turning inward. This will cause the change-up to fade like a cutter or a slider. The very real danger with this pitch is that it is not apt to break downward. Consequently, it must be thrown low.

IT TAKES HOURS AND HOURS and hundreds upon hundreds of pitches to create the right grip to compliment one's anatomy, arm speed, and ability to impart spin. However, because the success of the pitch is so dependent on the batter's read and reaction to it, ultimately a good change-up can only be refined in game-type situations,which is probably why pitchers are usually slow to develop them.

> It's almost impossible to sit on a change-up if the pitcher has a half-decent fastball. But there's absolutely no reason to throw a change-up in an important situation if the hitter is totally overmatched by your fastball.

STRETCHING THE STRIKEZONE

One thing about hitters is that they love to hit what they can see. Probably since Little League they've had to constantly re-teach themselves not to swing at that fat pitch outside of the strikezone. Compared to any fastball, the change-up is easy pickings for the eye. Perhaps that's why umpires often seem willing to call a strike on borderline change-ups. Like many hitters, they feel the ball looks just too good not to swing at. . . even if it is a tad out of the strikezone.

Glavine and Maddux have made careers of hanging out on the away side of the plate. Gradually, over the course of a game, they will inch the ball further and further outside, expanding the strikezone until the batter doesn't feel safe in letting anything go that he might reach. This is one reason why this type of pitcher often seems to get tougher and tougher as the game progresses.

The ultimate change-up is one that the pitcher can throw with confidence when behind in the count, 2-0 or 3-1. Batters almost always look for the fastball here, and the pitcher can sometimes get himself out of trouble without extending himself. It takes awhile to gain the confidence needed to throw change-ups under adverse conditions, but once the pitcher matures to the point where he recognizes that velocity isn't the only way to challenge a hitter, he will generally enhance his effectiveness and extend his career. Mentally, it can be a tough step to take and almost requires *an act of faith*.

Those five inning pitchers who have trouble going through a batting order more than once or twice will find that a good change-up can make all the difference.

Knowing that you can change speeds will keep the batter from getting comfortable at the plate, no matter how many times he's seen you. Mastering this pitch is worth the time.

There are many styles of pitching; in the next chapter we'll identify twelve. Each of these styles can be greatly enhanced by the use of the change-up. As much as I love the curveball, I know that next to the fastball, the most important pitch one should possess is a good change-up. Straight change-ups are perhaps the most difficult to master, but the guy on the mound does not become a true pitcher until he has one in his repertoire.

THE THINGS WE FORGET

If you've ever been around toddlers, you probably realize they have incredible change-ups. Sometimes they'll pick up some squeeze toy and nail you with a line drive; other times, they come at you full arm speed and as you cover up, you watch the toy pop out from their hand and fall three feet in front of them. Don't they have a good laugh?

As toddlers we begin experimenting with throwing long before we master walking. And from the get-go, most of us have pretty good palm-balls, as that is our first throwing grip. Then someone says, "Throw it to me," and we find ourselves being encouraged to learn how to throw things straight so that by the time we get to organized ball, our change-up is pretty well gone. Recapturing a change-up will help you get that good laugh back. . . this time at the expense of the hitter.

Coaching **TIP** Its amazing how many good pitchers have the change-up as an out-pitch.

LEARN A CHANGE-UP AND GET A CLUE

When you start tinkering with a change-up, you begin to realize that with a little increased pressure or by setting the ball a notch further back in the palm, ten to fifteen mph can be taken off a pitch. There's a lesson in this!

When you first started pitching in Little League, your technique probably consisted of picking up a ball and throwing it as hard as accuracy would allow, with lit-

tle concern for grip or motion. At that level, the belief — probably fostered by your coach — was that the harder you threw, the better, and throwing harder meant more arm speed and greater *oomph*. What you probably didn't realize at the time was the significance of having great mechanics — and how subtle variations could make a world of difference.

Developing a good change-up forces you to be conscious of all the little things, such as finger placement, release points and arm angles. The trick then, is to go back to the pitching lab with those things in mind and apply them to your other pitches. Maybe better finger placement will give you a little more movement on your slider, better follow-through, a couple more miles on your fastball.

Great pitchers are never done tinkering, never done with inventing new pitches. As you grow older, your body changes, and if you don't have an open mind towards making adjustments, you will fail to grow and your game will stagnate. Keep in mind that growth is a natural part of the human condition, and anything that doesn't continue to grow will fade to nothingness. This applies as well to the act of pitching.

The give-away on an effective change-up is often the great finish that a hurler will give the pitch. For example while both Martinez and Maddux give all their pitches solid finishes, the follow-through on their change-ups is even more dramatic. That kind of follow-through tends to emphasize the sinking action of the pitch. Of course reading the follow-through is of no help whatsoever for the batter.

PITCHER AS ARTIST
THE BREAKING PITCHES

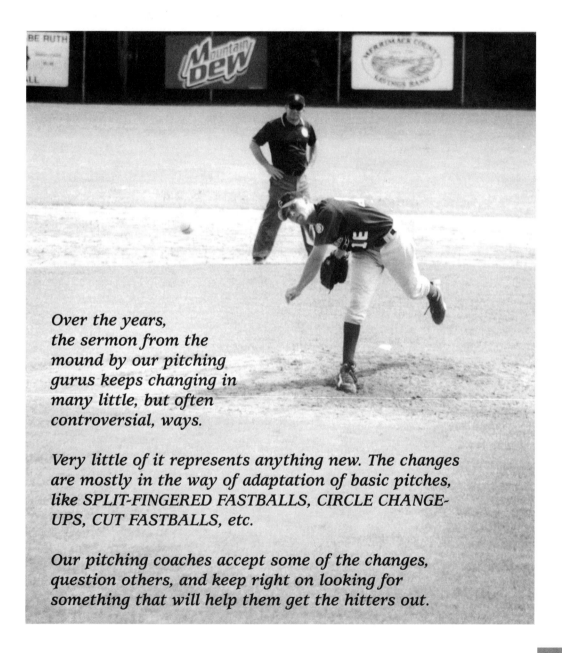

*Over the years,
the sermon from the
mound by our pitching
gurus keeps changing in
many little, but often
controversial, ways.*

*Very little of it represents anything new. The changes
are mostly in the way of adaptation of basic pitches,
like SPLIT-FINGERED FASTBALLS, CIRCLE CHANGE-
UPS, CUT FASTBALLS, etc.*

*Our pitching coaches accept some of the changes,
question others, and keep right on looking for
something that will help them get the hitters out.*

MASTERING THE BREAKING BALL

PHYSICS 101
THE CURVEBALL

A curveball can be explained by way of the Bernoulli Principle. The Bernoulli Principle states that the faster an air stream moves, the lower its pressure.

With a proper curve, the ball leaves the pitcher's hand spinning. As the ball spins, the air closest to the ball moves along with it. This means that the air on one side of the ball will be moving faster than the air on the opposite side.

This also means that on one side of the ball there is lower air pressure than on the other. The slower moving air on the high-pressure side of the ball exerts greater force on the ball than the faster moving air on the low-pressure side.

The ball is then pushed to one side by the uneven pressure as it moves forward. The greater the spin, the greater the differential in pressure and the greater the break. Getting it to drop is a question of the downward trajectory from the pitcher's hand and the plane of flight caused by hand and arm angle.

And while the technique from one pitcher to another might be similar, the results of any two hurlers are rarely the same.

Nowadays in some Major League parks they have little neon signs near the scoreboard that will tell the fans the velocity and type of pitch just thrown. *Slider, sinker, splitfinger*. Rarely does the word curve ever pop up. And when it does, fans will say, *"Well I guess it must look different down on the field, because I sure didn't see it curve."*

Many fans of today still believe there is no such thing as a curveball, and from their view, you'd have a hard time proving otherwise. But back a generation ago, you didn't need a sign to announce a curveball.

When Sandy Koufax or Steve Carlton threw a curveball, everyone in the stadium knew. A true curveball is a beautiful, majestic sight — an aesthetic event that stuns a hitter and inspires awe. But the truth of the matter is. . .

GOOD CURVES ARE COMMON, GREAT ARE FEW AND RARE.

THE STATE OF THE MODERN BREAKING BALL

It continues to bother me that two of the breaking pitches I like very much are on the endangered species list. Perhaps because I had a pretty good one, I was always partial to my Uncle Charlie, a pseudonym for the curveball, *bender, roundhouse, hook, or outcurve.* Today, it might simply be referred to as a *big curve.*

As right-handed pitcher, I knew my curve was working when the pitch would move inside or over the plate to the right-handed hitter and then curve down and out.

From everything I see these days, this kind of so-called *old-fashioned* breaking pitch is on sabbatical. You just don't see it as much as you did prior to the 60's. Its once intimidating cousin, *The Yellow Hammer,* has practically vanished. The Hammer is the epitome of a sharp-breaking curve — a pitch that breaks suddenly and *falls off the table*, its movement resembling the darting action of the Yellow Hammer bird as it sharply dives for an insect.

The newcomers on the block are the *power slider* and the *cutter.* These new boys are good, but they are quick fixes — much easier to learn than a curveball and much more likely to be called for strikes. For those reasons, they have become popular with the current generation of pitchers.

Oh, I've seen some pretty decent ones, and I even taught both sliders and cutters to college pitchers to enhance their repertoire and increase their survival kit. But given my druthers, I would preach Charlie to the high heavens. A well developed Uncle Charlie or Yellow Hammer is majestic and lifts pitching to an art form. These are pitches that can stun a hitter. Too often, however, they stun the umpire, who is unwilling to recognize their brief intersection with the strikezone. Ultimately, the hitter learns that chasing such a challenging target is foolish, especially foolish when eight times out of ten they will not result in called strikes. Consequently, such rude treatment has placed Charlie and the Hammer on the endangered species list.

Let's take a look at the pros and cons of the traditional curve and compare it to the power slider, today's weapon of choice.

THE PROS AND CONS OF POWER CURVES AND POWER SLIDERS

	CURVE	SLIDER	EDGE
STRIKE-ZONE	Hard to get over. Tough to get called strikes.	Easy to throw for strikes. More apt to be called for strikes.	Slider
BREAK	Great two-dimensional break.	Modest break. Great rotation can give it second stage life.	Curve
BATTER'S READ	Early break may tip it off.	Late break is hard to recognize.	Slider
RECEIVING	Catchers may have trouble, especially when low.	Little trouble for good catchers. Easier pitch to frame.	Slider
EFFORT	Takes time to master.	Easy to learn.	Slider
ARM WEAR	Easier on arm.	Hard on arm.	Curve
LOCATION	Can get away with a pitch right over the plate.	Can't locate up in strikezone. Hanging slider is a homerun pitch.	Curve
CONTACT	When it goes down, it is extremely difficult to hit.	Most hitters develop bat speed to hit it. It can overpower weak hitters.	Curve
VERSATILITY	Off-speed nature enables it to be used as change-up. Angle and delivery can vary.	Has to be thrown with velocity. Dependent on great rotation which won't always take.	Curve

You don't have much gray area on the rotation of Uncle Charlie. There is no compromise. The spin must be 6/12 or 7/1 (go back to Chapter One for an explanation of how spins are defined). Much less than that and the pitch becomes a *slurve,* which isn't much of a pitch at all. And if the elbow drops, you wind up with a flat curve and an escalating ERA. A slider, on the other hand, can become a cutter or a slurve without much commotion.

Over the years, the truly outstanding curveball has gradually lost favor. We cannot say it has vanished, because pitchers like David Wells and Darryl Kile are still winning twenty games with outstanding Uncle Charlies. However, the strikezone — as reinvented by Major League umpires — has given rise to a preponderance of short curves, hard curves, sliders, and cutters, which tend to spend a great deal more time over the plate.

It will be interesting to see if the Major League's current intention to raise the strikezone will encourage more curves to be thrown.

Though I favor the traditional curve, the slider is not a pitch to take lightly. One could liken it to comparing a newer beauty like Gwyneth Paltrow to an older beauty like Sophia Loren. Both women, like both pitches, are creatures of beauty and will turn heads. Both have shapes that can delight, but there are curves and there are curves. . ..

ANATOMY OF A POWER SLIDER

What constitutes a great slider or even a good one is a matter of opinion. Many pitchers claim they are throwing sliders when in reality what they are throwing isn't anything more than a poor curve. Some pitchers have the aforementioned *slurve,* which is questionable in terms of effectiveness. Some have a cut *fastball,* which can be effective, but for most is not as effective as a slider.

PATH OF THE SLIDER
(thrown by a lefty)

The slider is a pitch that was developed in the thirties and according to many experts played a large part in the extinction of the .400 hitter. Ted Williams for one, said that as his career progressed, the slider, and not the fastball, was the pitch that he began to look for. Batters of today are beginning to catch up with the wisdom of Williams and with the slider as well. Today, most tune their bats in at slider speed. Consequently, a mediocre slider will inevitably betray a pitcher. Mediocre sliders are probably one of the greatest contributors to the homerun barrage of recent years. That doesn't mean the pitch should be scuttled. Instead, if it is to be used, it must be perfected.

THE EFFECTIVENESS OF THE SLIDER LIES IN THE BATTER'S DIFFICULTY IN DIFFERENTIATING BETWEEN IT AND THE PITCHER'S FASTBALL.

The fastball habits of a good slider—

◆ The slider should move like a fastball until it drops across the plate.

◆ It should be nearly as fast as a fastball. (within 5 mph to be a power slider)

◆ Like a fastball it should have extremely tight rotation.

◆ It should be thrown with fastball arm speed.

A pitcher with an average fastball might apt to become overly reliant on the slider, but for it truly to be effective, it must be intelligently mixed in with the fastball. A good slider that gets the hitter thinking about it and timing his bat for it will make a pitcher's fastball, even an average one, more potent.

THROWING THE SLIDER

As with any pitch, the pitcher must bring his slider into the lab and discover for himself what finger pressure and grips work best and which arm angles best enhance those grips. However, there are certain requisites necessary for the manufacturing of a slider.

1. It must be thrown from the *top* of the ball.

2. It should be given a sharp karate-chop type of cut with two fingers (index and middle).

3. The elbow must be kept high (above shoulder).

4. Wrist action is responsible for imparting extreme hand speed.

5. To get good movement and save wear on the arm, a smooth follow-through to finish is required.

READING THE BALL

The rotation on the ball is produced by the manner in which the ball is gripped and then released. As covered in Chapter One, the John Sain Spinner is a great tool for teaching an understanding of rotation.

While rotation may be enhanced by arm angle, it is produced through grip and wrist action.

A pitcher should be an expert at determining and understanding the different types of rotation that can be placed on a baseball. So too a good hitter. These spins are what make a baseball *act*. When a ball is given tight rotation (fast spin) the end of the axis reveals itself as a red dot. The location of this red dot has everything to do with how a baseball will act or react to the rotation put upon it. A 6/12 rotation will result in a straight drop. A 7/1 rotation will cause a sharp curve.

As explained in our chapter on the fastball, the ball should be looked at as a clock face with the top being twelve o'clock, the bottom being six o'clock and the sides being nine o'clock and three o'clock respectively. So with a 6/12 rotation, the axis goes through the three to nine o'clock line.

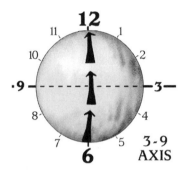

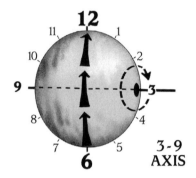

A 6 TO 12 SPINNING ACTION
STRAIGHT DROP CURVEBALL
No discernible dot

IF YOU SEE A DOT AT 3 O'CLOCK -
When the axis of 6/12 shifts so that the red dot becomes visible at about three o'clock, or for a lefty at nine o'clock, the ball might have a little more east/west movement.

PERFECT SLIDER
**Dot right in middle
LEFTHAND**

PERFECT SLIDER
**Dot right in middle
RIGHTHAND**

UNFINISHED SLIDER
Dot above center
If the dot rises above the center, with a somewhat wobbly spin, we have an unfinished slider that will probably hang.

OVER-DOCTORED SLIDER **Dot below center**
When the dot drops below the center, with enough velocity it will still have a good — although perhaps exaggerated break.

All diagrams are from the pitcher's viewpoint.

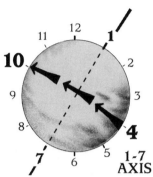

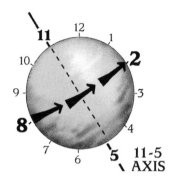

LEFTY SLURVE

Dot at around 7 o'clock

When the dot on a slider drops down and off center, you end up with a slurve.

RIGHTY SLURVE

Dot at 5 o'clock

A slurve is a compromise between a curve and slider. It breaks more than a slider, is flatter than a curve and is slower than a slider. Some pitchers have an intentional slurve which can be effective when thrown with velocity. For others though it is a pitch of accident, a curve that's thrown with too much force and not enough finesse, or an arcing slider that lacks bite.

BEST CURVE -- THE YELLOW HAMMER

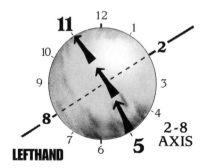

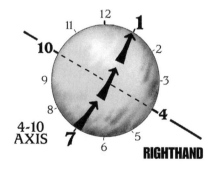

5 TO 11 ROTATION BEST CURVE

When that axis tilts a little bit, a 5/11 rotation occurs and the dot is visible at around eight.

7 TO 1 ROTATION SHARP CURVE

When that axis tilts a little bit, a 7/1 rotation occurs and the dot is visible at around four.

All diagrams are from the pitcher's viewpoint.

While the slider rotation should look like a football spiral or bullet type of spin, be careful that the hand isn't held like it is throwing a football or for that matter a dart. Such a delivery will make it extremely difficult to get velocity. Velocity is critical because it deprives the hitter of decision time and keeps him from distinguishing your slider from your fastball.

Being on top of the ball encourages the ball to go down a little. The dropping of the ball, even by a small amount, is also critical to the effectiveness of the pitch as it forces the batter to contend with north/south as well as east/west movement on the break.

It seems that a high slider typically does not *act* and is far easier to read. When it does act, it drops itself into the hitter's wheelhouse, which is why so many homeruns are hit off high or hanging sliders. Bring that same pitch down several inches to where the batter can only see the top of the ball and good contact will require a good guess.

The slider can be hard on the arm, and like any breaking pitch, if it's thrown too often it may actually start to deteriorate arm speed. A good slider doesn't have to lead to arm trouble, but often times a young pitcher will develop a decent slider without a strong mechanical foundation.

No matter how effective the slider may appear, if in its throwing the pitcher drops his elbow and puts great emphasis on the twisting snap of the wrist without properly decelerating to a full finish, he is putting his arm and baseball future at risk. If you or your charges are guilty of these mechanical deficiencies the pitch should immediately be rebuilt from scratch. If thrown properly — not overthrown — with correct and consistent mechanics, the slider can be a strong pitch without doing damage to the arm.

Sliders are much easier to master than a great curve. They don't require the same finesse. If a pitcher does not have the ability to develop an overwhelming curve, a slider could be the pitch for him, especially if he has a good fastball. For the pitcher who already has a decent curve, the slider can be his next pitch of decision. But the slider, like any other breaking pitch or change-up, should always be thought of as a companion to the fastball, not as a replacement.

A GOOD BREAKING PITCH SHOULD NOT ONLY FORCE A BATTER TO CHANGE HIS SWING PLANE, BUT SHOULD SERVE TO DISRUPT TIMING AS WELL.

Fastball to slider 5-7 mph less

Fastball to cutter 3-5 mph less

Fastball to slurve 10-12 mph less

Fastball to curve 10-15 mph less

SLIDER GRIPS

Don't grip the ball too tightly. Keep the elbow up higher than the shoulder, and accelerate the arm with fastball velocity. Typically a 3/4 to 3/4 + arm angle will give the ball the best plane. Impart a tight spin on the ball, releasing it with a karate-chop type motion, applying spin pressure with the middle and index finger. Be sure to finish strong, burying the shoulder and following through fully with the hand turned slightly upward as it completes the circle of motion by the opposite hip.

SLIDER GRIP RIGHTHAND

SLIDER GRIP, LEFTHAND

Unlike the cutter, which is virtually impossible to tell from a fastball, the slider spin will give the pitch away to batters that are sitting for one, and many a batter makes his living sitting on sliders. Therefore your slider has to be good to be useful. If it doesn't break well, or wanders up too high, it is doomed for the bleachers.

JOHNNY SAIN ALWAYS PREACHED THE SLIDER TO HIS PITCHERS AS AN EXTRA PITCH TO GIVE HITTERS THAT ONE MORE THING TO THINK ABOUT....

SLIDER RELEASE POINT

ABOUT THE CUTTER

One of the newer kids on the block is the *cut fastball* — the *cutter*. For years, pitchers have been throwing an *accidental* cutter, which is the result of throwing a poor slider or a short curve that just isn't doctored enough.

Of recent, the *manufactured* cutter has become an excellent extra pitch. You can call it a breaking pitch or refer to it as a fastball that moves away. Either way it is the same creature.

A cutter is subtle and sneaky — it breaks late and looks suspiciously like a regular fastball. The main difference with the cutter and the slider is that the slider has a more defined spin, almost bullet-like, whereas a well-thrown cutter is almost unrecognizable. The velocity is within 2 to 3 mph of the fastball. The break is flat, but quick and short.

A cut fastball works well on an alternating basis with a fastball that tails the other way. It does not break down, as a properly thrown slider should. It fades and can be thrown quite hard. Thrown from a righty it tends to jam the left-hand hitter and cause the right-hand hitter to chase it outside of the strikezone.

CUTTER GRIP, RIGHTHAND

Those with great control and great velocity, like Mariano Rivera, can also throw the cutter high and tight, forcing the batter off the plate as the pitch seems to be coming directly at him before fading over the inside corner of the plate.

With a cutter pressure comes from the middle finger and the ball is gripped more to the outside. The ball should be thrown hard with a tight 12/6 (slightly off center) rotation. Much more than this increases the break, slows the pitch and will likely decrease its effectiveness. One should work with finger pressure and experiment with slight variations on the axes. Work the spin to achieve as late a break as possible.

CUTTER GRIP, LEFTHAND

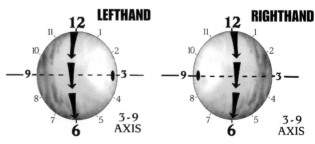

SPLIT FINGERED FASTBALL: A STYLING FORKBALL

The splitter was truly the pitch of the nineties, rejuvenating several pitchers' careers and giving many that extra pitch necessary to even have a career. And while its name implies fastball and it moves with near fastball speed, its effectiveness lies with its downward break.

With a splitter (l), the fingers are spread as with a forkball (r), though not as far. The ball should slide out with a tumbling motion, which gives the ball its downward break.

SPLITTER GRIP

FORKBALL GRIP

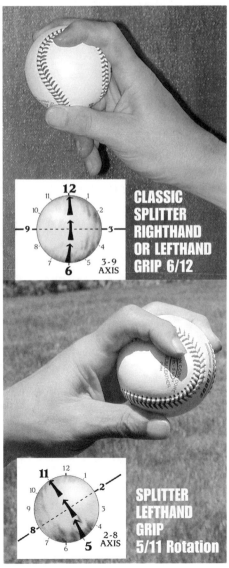

CLASSIC SPLITTER RIGHTHAND OR LEFTHAND GRIP 6/12

3-9 AXIS

SPLITTER LEFTHAND GRIP 5/11 Rotation

2-8 AXIS

Only the most discerning eye can pickup the slightly off center splitter rotation which runs between 6/12 and a 7/1 for righty, 5/11 for a lefty. ▶

Splitter arm action should be essentially the same as a fastball, but while the fingers may look to be on top, as with a fastball, pressure is instead applied with the knuckles.

Much like with the slider and the cutter, the effectiveness of the splitter is greatly enhanced by the batter's inability to tell it isn't a fastball until past the point of swing decision, when it will break down more viscously than a fastball. The splitter must be kept down in the strikezone to insure its break. Some pitchers get an additional break inward or sometimes outward, making the pitch doubly difficult to hit.

THE GREATEST PITCH IN THE WORLD

FOR ME, TEACHING THE CURVEBALL IS A MISSION

Aside from my purpose of helping pitchers become the best that they can be, I admit that I have a few more specific missions which have fueled the writing of this book. One is this business about *pushing* or *not pushing off* the rubber about which I've already let you know how I feel. A second — which I will get to in a later chapter — is how we can curb this *homerun orgy* and get the pitchers caught up again with the hitters. A third mission of mine — the one we'll cover now — is restoring the most beautiful pitch in baseball, the curveball, to its proper place of high esteem and ultimate usefulness.

> *In this section I will give you all the ingredients necessary to concoct an exquisite curveball. All you have to do is add sweat, patience, mindfulness and a supple wrist.*

My curveball defined who I was as a pitcher — it is the pitch of which I am most proud. I'm long past the point where I have anything to gain by self-delusion. I know that in my salad days, I was a blue-collar pitcher who always pitched tough but didn't always pitch smart. I know that although I had a fastball with good velocity, it lacked movement. But I also know that I had *some kind* of curveball. In fact I still do.

The goal should be to develop a curveball that doesn't have a great big loop, but rather one that seductively offers itself to the batter before breaking sharply down and away on entering the strikezone.

I tell pitchers at my clinics, if they can't learn a curveball from me, then they never will. I threw it competitively for fifteen years and it

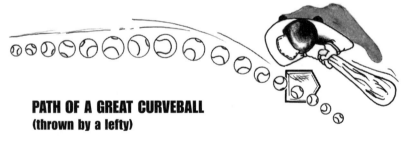

PATH OF A GREAT CURVEBALL
(thrown by a lefty)

helped me to win 117 games of baseball. Over the course of the last few decades, I've taught a lot of young men to throw the curve with authority and success. But I'll tell you up-front: there are no shortcuts, no tricks that will replace the kind of work you need to do to develop a magnificent magical curveball.

Some coaches won't teach the curve for fear that young men will destroy their arms. And they're right. Young men *will* destroy their arms throwing a curveball, or any pitch for that matter, if someone doesn't show them the right way. Because those who have seen a masterful curve delivered, and fallen in love with its majestic beauty are going to try to find their own curve, no matter what the caveats.

SHOULD KIDS THROW THE CURVEBALL?

Until you mature, you probably don't want to be fooling with a full-fledged curveball. Instead you and your coaches should think about developing a Little League curve (see next page).

Even if you have a Great Curve, you still need a fastball to go with it. No matter how good your curve, your fastball is what you should practice the most. If you practice the curveball to the point of neglecting your fastball, you will lose arm speed; you will lose velocity.

I think keeping kids away from the curveball has as much to do with mental maturation as it does physical maturation. At a young age, boys especially, are apt to be reckless with their bodies and will impulsively allow results to guide form rather than building results out of good form. And it certainly is easier to do damage to your arm before your bones have calcified, and your sinew is etched.

So what I am saying is definitely geared towards the more mature pitcher who is now past the stage where developing a curveball might jeopardize his career. Also, as good as this book may be, it's still not enough. You will need to work with a knowledgeable coach who is strong in fundamentals and can help you build technique that is not self-injurious. As we talked about earlier, if we want good results in anything we do, we must approach it with a strictly positive attitude. Instead of thinking, *If I throw curveballs, I'll hurt my arm,* think, *My curveball will take me to a whole new level of pitching mastery.* You needn't be afraid of the curveball; just approach it as you would any other pitch. First, solid fundamentals are a must. Secondly, don't over-do it.

You cannot learn a curve for a career in an afternoon. Arm pain is not a prerequisite for developing a curve. The *no pain, no gain* school of thought does not hold here. If your arm ever starts hurting, you need to stop throwing until it can be figured out what you're doing wrong. And if it keeps hurting, seek medical advice from a qualified physician. Throwing through pain is stupid, especially for a young man who has most of his career in front of him.

THE LITTLE LEAGUE CURVE

The Little League pitcher who has developed his fastball, and has solid mechanics and good control, can add a breaking pitch to his toolbox, providing he doesn't get carried away. The curve should be an occasional pitch thrown some at the end of practice. Little League pitchers must throw a lot of fastballs to develop a strong arm and nothing should take priority over that.

With this pitch the idea should be to emphasize hand and arm angle as opposed to any twisting or snapping motion. With the elbow up, the hand should turn as if throwing a football, and through release the arm should come down as if delivering a karate chop. Some spin action can be given with the thumb and middle

finger, but rather than encouraging a snapping movement, the Little Leaguer should be taught to release the pitch with the thumb finishing up. Follow-through is a must. No discomfort should occur with this delivery. If there is any discomfort the pitch should be abandoned immediately.

Another alternative for the Little Leaguer looking to get movement is to throw a slightly off-center palm-ball (see chapter on changing speeds). The palm-ball can be thrown exactly the same as the fastball and when done properly will tail downward.

I also strongly encourage younger kids to really work at getting movement on their fastballs. The Wrist Drill explained later in the book is an ideal way for kids to learn the concept of spin and experience the burn of the spin coming off their fingertips.

I'm of the school that says, "If you do something right, injury and misfortune will not plague you." I even think that if you are taught a curveball correctly at a younger age, tendonitis or tennis elbow will not automatically occur. In fact, all the pitchers that have great curves, will probably tell you that they started pretty early.

There are various ways to throw the curve, some better than others. Having possessed a rather strong form of it, I will pass on to you a certain technique that I know works because I have already passed it on to many young men who developed great curves.

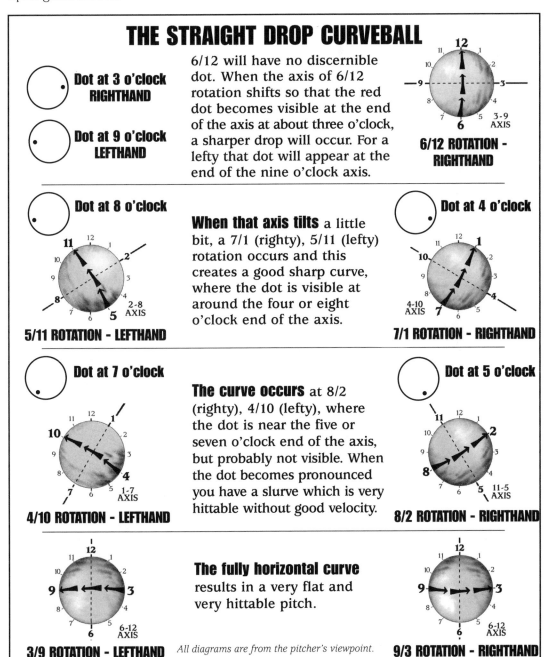

THE STRAIGHT DROP CURVEBALL

Dot at 3 o'clock
RIGHTHAND

Dot at 9 o'clock
LEFTHAND

6/12 will have no discernible dot. When the axis of 6/12 rotation shifts so that the red dot becomes visible at the end of the axis at about three o'clock, a sharper drop will occur. For a lefty that dot will appear at the end of the nine o'clock axis.

6/12 ROTATION - RIGHTHAND

Dot at 8 o'clock

When that axis tilts a little bit, a 7/1 (righty), 5/11 (lefty) rotation occurs and this creates a good sharp curve, where the dot is visible at around the four or eight o'clock end of the axis.

Dot at 4 o'clock

5/11 ROTATION - LEFTHAND

7/1 ROTATION - RIGHTHAND

Dot at 7 o'clock

The curve occurs at 8/2 (righty), 4/10 (lefty), where the dot is near the five or seven o'clock end of the axis, but probably not visible. When the dot becomes pronounced you have a slurve which is very hittable without good velocity.

Dot at 5 o'clock

4/10 ROTATION - LEFTHAND

8/2 ROTATION - RIGHTHAND

The fully horizontal curve results in a very flat and very hittable pitch.

All diagrams are from the pitcher's viewpoint.

3/9 ROTATION - LEFTHAND

9/3 ROTATION - RIGHTHAND

1. REACH BACK TO HIGH COCK

OVERVIEW OF CURVE FROM THE LEFTY

Be careful that you don't develop any little habits that can tip off your curveball as you go through the windup. Legend has it that when Babe Ruth was a pitcher, he went through a period where the hitters were teeing off on his curveball. Then someone pointed out to him that every time he threw a curve, he would stick out his tongue.

2. ESTABLISH ARM ANGLE & FINGER POSITION

3. LEAD WITH ELBOW

4. CUT THROUGH RELEASE POINT

5. GIVE IT AN ENDING

6. STRONG FOLLOW THROUGH

The main ingredient of a great curve is great rotation. When one is first developing the curve, the rotations should be one of 6/12. Later on this can be adjusted to 7/1 or 8/2. Anything flatter than this is not acceptable! The direction of the spin is paramount.

FOUR-SEAM CURVE LEFT

FOUR-SEAM CURVE RIGHT

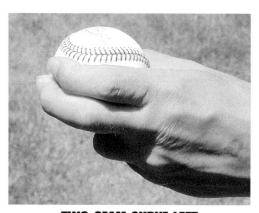

TWO-SEAM CURVE LEFT

TWO-SEAM CURVE RIGHT

Pressure should be placed on the middle finger. It is important to have a consistent but relaxed grip so that the spin is not smothered. The tip of the middle finger should be resting on the seam, which will make its job of spinning the ball easier. The classic curveball is one of the four-seam variety and that's the one I tend to prefer as I was able to get greater spin with more fingers on the seam. In recent years several pitchers have gone to the two-seam curve, preferring to trade-off some movement for better control. I also believe the four-seam curve is harder for the batter to identify, and as with the four-seam fastball the ball has the illusion of appearing smaller.

INDEX OFF

Utilize the thumb to assist the fingers with rotation. You can lift the index finger away to get a better feel for how the middle finger must apply pressure.

Candy Cummings —
the first curveball artist

Others may have experimented with the curveball before Arthur *Candy* Cummings, but like Babe Ruth, Cummings was a man who showed up at the right time in history with the right talent. It was said that Cummings came upon the idea of developing a curveball while tossing clamshells on a Massachusetts' beach. Just 5'9" and weighing a 120 pounds, the personable Cummings made his mark in 1872.

That was the year the rules changed which led to the development of the classic adversarial relationship between hitter and pitcher. Up until that point, the pitcher was required to throw the ball underhand with a stiff elbow so as to facilitate a hitter's effort to whack the ball. As of 1872, a pitcher was no longer required to deliver the ball underhand, but could jerk his arm, snap his wrist or bend his elbow when he delivered the ball, as long as his hand was no higher than his hip on release. This opened the door for sidearm stylists and a new generation of pitcher-magicians who could make the ball move. Cummings was the most accomplished of these.

Even after 1872, most pitchers threw as hard as they could, without realizing the way they gripped the ball or turned their wrist could alter its flight. Cummings was laughed at. But when he proved it could be done, he was nicknamed the *Boy Wonder.*

Cummings was durable, completing 194 of 199 career starts in the National Association, then considered one of the country's top leagues. He finished 124-72 with an ERA of 2.31, but National Association stats aren't counted in with his 21-22 National League record.

FOR THE IDEAL CURVE, RAISE THE BAR.

In order to accomplish the ideal wrist angle and rotation, have someone hold a bar just before the actual release point, below and beyond the visor of your cap. Be sure to lead with a high elbow and rotate the wrist over so that the hand is parallel to the bar, and the wrist bends to make that hand as perpendicular as possible to the forearm.

1. REACH BACK TO HIGH COCK

2. ESTABLISH ARM ANGLE & FINGER POSITION

3. LEAD WITH ELBOW

DETAILED VIEW OF CURVE FROM THE RIGHT

The elbow should be kept higher than the forearm. If it drops, your curve is likely to flatten out. You should think of the elbow as leading the forearm. Don't collapse the forearm toward your head — this will tend to make a big curve with a rounded trajectory. The desired trajectory should be straight and then abruptly down and away. Remember, the forearm should be held vertical — 90 degrees or more.

4. CUT THROUGH RELEASE POINT

As the arm starts to extend, snap the wrist with good action so that the hand moves from lying horizontal to a vertical position with the thumb up.

5. GIVE IT AN ENDING

—Continues

Turn the hand over as if to deliver a karate chop. Be careful not to turn it over too early. The wrist should turn towards the head as the forearm passes the ear. The arm should accelerate strongly, but don't put as much emphasis on arm speed as you would with a fastball. Instead your energy should be directed towards getting rotation on the ball. The hand ends up as if you are shooting a pistol. Don't let the hand and wrist get lazy. Don't cast the ball, but rather stay on top and visualize the hand going over the top.

Bring the pitching arm to the bottom of an imaginary circle, burying the shoulder in the process. Finish your follow-through with the fingers pointing up. Your hand can finish either by going to the side of the hip towards the back pocket or a little higher, as if stabbing yourself in the belly.

To impart ideal rotation, on release think of the hand as snapping into a pistol-like position with the thumb being on the hammer.

Don't shortchange your finish of the pitch after the release point is reached. When putting emphasis on the snap of the wrist, rather than decelerating as one should, it can be dangerously easy to establish a habit of coming to a dead halt. This is a habit that will injure the arm.

FINISH TO THE HIP

6. STRONG FOLLOW THROUGH

FINISH TO THE BELLY

SHORTENED STRIDE

If your curves end up in the dirt when you first start to get a handle on the spin, don't worry — you're off to a good start. Because of the downward break of a curve, your release point will probably have to be higher than a fastball. This can be achieved by a small shortening of your stride. Many pitchers will find their curves going into the dirt until they are able to adjust their stride, and with it, their release point.

Pitchers should do everything they can to strengthen their fingers and make their wrists strong and flexible. Wrist curls are valuable, as are using handgrips. Try to gradually increase the range of motion in your wrist through stretching. When doing wrist curls always go for the maximum range of motion; allow your hand to extend down and curl up as far as possible. (See Chapter Twelve on Training.)

Wrist Stretches

A CURVEBALL IS EPHEMERAL. If it isn't mastered properly — by that I mean with a conscious understanding of how one is achieving success — it may suddenly vanish and you will have no idea how to find it again. The occasional Great Curve can happen by accident. However, your goal should be consistency.

DEVELOPING A LATE STAGE CURVE

By adjusting the amount of rotation imparted on the ball, the pitcher can shorten the break of the ball which will give it later action so that it will do *its thing* as it passes into the strikezone, past the hitter's point of decision. When this happens, the curveball is rarely where the batter anticipates. Finding the right combination of arm speed and wrist and hand power is what is required to create this kind of break. Believe me, the befuddled look on a hitter's face is well worth the trouble.

IT CAN BE BENEFICIAL TO PRACTICE THE MOTION FOR YOUR BREAKING PITCHES WITHOUT A BALL SO AS TO FIND THE IDEAL WAY TO RELEASE THE BALL AND DECELERATE WITHOUT UNDUE STRESS ON THE ARM.

DROPPING THE HAMMER

The Yellow Hammer is the ultimate curveball. It is thrown hard and drops with great suddenness — breaking laterally and down. This sort of action makes it difficult to hit but also difficult to throw for strikes.

Sandy Koufax might have had the greatest Yellow Hammer of them all. Nolan Ryan, Dwight Gooden, and Steve Carlton all could throw it. You may have noticed that these are all pitchers who also had great fastballs. Having a super fastball isn't an absolute when it comes to converting your Uncle Charlie into a Yellow Hammer, but the greater strength and emphasis that the Hammer requires over an ordinary curve. does require great arm acceleration.

A good Hammer will require extra action from the middle finger, as well as additional action from the thumb pushing up. The third finger can assist in this motion. The goal is to create tremendous tightness to the spin. In addition to the extra finger action, hand and wrist speed must be exceptional. The arm must come down over the release point with a lot of power, the hand following through to the bottom of the pitching circle with authority.

HAMMER GRIP

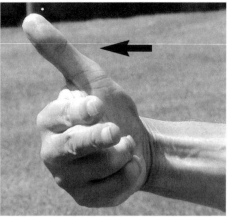

Hitters have referred to the curveball as fiendish and the truth of the matter is that a great curveball does seem to have a mischievous personality of its own — an ability to taunt a hitter only to dive around his bat.

A CURVEBALL IS A WORK OF ART, AND LIKE ANY GREAT WORK OF ART IT CAN BE ACCOMPLISHED ONLY WITH MUCH TOIL AND LONG EFFORT.

Good curves are commonplace. What moves the pitch into the realm of greatness can often times be the slightest difference in anatomy or technique. A supple wrist is a tremendous advantage. The ability to flex inward without moving or hooking the forearm helps facilitate the necessary 6/12 rotation. Finger length and strength can also affect spin, with longer and stronger being more desirable.

THE GREAT DISCRIMINATOR WHEN IT COMES TO CURVEBALL EXCELLENCE IS ONE'S CAPACITY FOR EXACTNESS.

Finding the Great Curve is a process of conscious experimentation in which one develops an aptitude for repeatedly utilizing the most advantageous combination of grip, finger pressure, angle of delivery, arm and hand speed.

Many pitchers have the ability to develop the Great Curve, but only a few actually do. The reason often is that some accept a mediocre version with the thought that it is adequate or even good.

Another reason some pitchers don't achieve a curveball early in their careers is that they become enamored of a slider, either because some coach encouraged this, or due to the simple fact that a slider is the easier breaking pitch to master. Any hesitation to use the curve is compounded when the pitcher comes to believe that umpires are reluctant to call it for a strike.

Throwing a curve is further complicated by the fact that a well-thrown curve has a relatively smaller plane of intersection with the strikezone.

It follows rather simply that if you have the skill and the discipline to gain a degree of mastery with the curve, that it will be relatively easy to develop the slider as an additional pitch. The reverse of this is rarely true. Possessing a slider does not encourage the development of a real curve. The development of a slider teaches the wrist to pronate in a habitually lazy way, which makes it almost impossible to develop the full flexion necessary for the curveball.

The truly intelligent pitcher will develop both the curve and the slider to further compromise the chances of the hitter. But if I have to choose one, I'm going to take my chances with the umpire and throw a hammer.

A great hammer isn't just a tough pitch. . .
IT'S UNHITTABLE

SLIDER, SLURVE, CUTTER COMPLEX

While the differences between a slider, slurve, and curve are often slight, they are nonetheless distinct and discernible for the astute reader of pitch spins. A cutter is between a slider and a fastball. The break is quick and lateral and late. Its velocity is generally more than a slider. It differs not so much in terms of rotation but rather in that the axis is shifted forward. When a slider is thrown well, it has a sharp break of about eight inches and will have a drop that the cutter does not. The slurve on the other hand, though faster than the curve, does not have an especially sharp break. Many a slider and cutter become a slurve by default.

Obviously there are gradations and any one of these pitches can become the other. Perhaps terminology is the differentiating factor, but to the purist there is a definite character to each pitch.

BRINGING ON THE SCROOGIE

The screwball or reverse screwball does everything the curveball does, except it typically breaks in the opposite direction. With a righthanded pitcher, a screwball will break in and down. In a few cases it will actually break away. It can be thrown both as an off-speed pitch and also with some degree of speed. Pitchers who are very flexible in the wrist area should experiment with the *scroogie*. The more rotation one gets the better the screwball.

TWO-SEAM SCREWBALL GRIP

FOUR-SEAM SCREWBALL GRIP

In throwing a screwball, the hand should pronate inward (counterclockwise for a righty) to get in-shoot, turning over on release to get the down break. One can employ a two-seam (top) or four-seam grip (bottom). Which grip you use will be best determined through experimentation. The four-seamer might give you more velocity, but for some folks, less velocity — the two-seamer — is needed for better movement.

As with the curveball, the middle finger is the trigger on a screwball. Assistance with the index finger and the thumb turning to the outside will give a good release to the pitch. To make the screwball go down, the thumb must be pointing down and the finger must be in front of the ball.

Because the downward turn of the hand is not as easily accomplished as the upward turn of the curve, the screwball is more dependent on arm angle to create the right spin. Along with finding the right arm angle, the pitcher must also find the right combination of stride and release point to perfect the downward trajectory so it does not end up below the strikezone.

> Mike Marshall threw an extreme kind of screwball which required a tremendous amount of very specific conditioning. It's a pitch that should not even be attempted without the guidance of a competent coach.

A screwball can be an extremely effective pitch, but because it is awkward for most pitchers, it can cause strain and it is difficult to control. Although it can be thrown with speed, it is more effective as an off-speed pitch. Throwing it hard will take away from the pitch's action. A good screwball artist will experiment to find the optimum speed to maximize rotation, which in turn will create the ideal break. A lot of time in the pitching lab is required to master this pitch.

This is another pitch which should only be attempted by the mature pitcher. Even then one has to be careful. The contortion on a screwball is substantial and not a convenient or comfortable pitch for everyone.

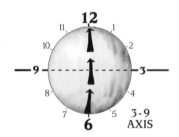

6/12 ROTATION - RIGHTHAND and LEFTHAND

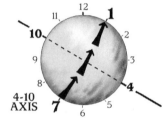

7/1 ROTATION - LEFTHAND

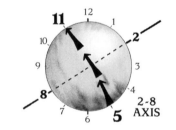

5/11 ROTATION - RIGHTHAND

DOWN SPIN can be created in a 6/12 direction, or as close as possible. If a 9 to 3 axis is accomplished (extremely difficult), the down break should be similar to the curve and will move away from the righthanded hitter. If the axis is 2 to 8, the ball should break in and down.

When first throwing the screwball, a 3/9 spin (righthand) should be the goal. A 9/3 for the lefty. Again this pitch requires very careful monitoring. I hesitate to offer any further instruction here, as the beginning pitcher is likely to do more harm than good to his body without the guidance of an experienced coach.

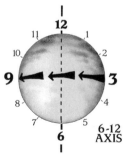

3/9 ROTATION - LEFTHAND

All diagrams are from the pitchers viewpoint.

SOME LAST THOUGHTS ABOUT THE CURVEBALL

It's always convenient to try to place blame on some *X factor* for a failed career. In the recent past it has become fashionable to indict the curveball as the culprit whenever a pitcher fails, does poorly, has a sore arm, or even is remiss in learning how to pitch. However, more likely the real culprit is improper or poor mechanics. If there is some devil's pitch that causes harm to the hurler, that would be the slider. The curve and the slider are often clumped together under the category of breaking pitches, but they are very different pitches, different not just in degree, but in method and result. Because of its strong torque and high velocity, the slider will put stress on the arm, especially when it is overused or when improper attention is given to finishing the pitch.

Orthopedic people are wise to advise against the throwing of any breaking pitches at an early age. Pitchers left alone, particularly at a young age, to fathom the mysteries of a curveball can only create a potentially disastrous scenario. However, when a young man enters high school, I'm of the mind that more good than harm will come if he receives proper instruction in the throwing of a curveball.

I have heard some pitchers, even ones with successful Major League careers, mention how they are thankful to their high school coaches for not teaching them a curveball, forcing them instead to learn how to pitch with their fastballs. And while one can find merit in such a statement, one can also find successful Major League pitchers who are equally thankful to their high school coaches for teaching them a correct curve early on in their development.

I've often times heard the line — most often mouthed by the fathers of average-at-best pitching prospects — that the boy shouldn't be throwing a curveball so as to save his arm. In most cases, the question can be asked, "Save it for what?"

The fact of the matter is that few kids are going to pitch beyond high school and even fewer beyond college. And if you take a young man throwing 74-77 mph at the age of seventeen, you are virtually guaranteeing him limited success if you deny him a curveball. Getting by with just a sub-par fastball does not bode for success in high school baseball. But when you mix that fastball with a well-developed curve, you may wind up with a very effective pitcher, one who is even capable of winning championships and having his *day in the sun*. Perhaps with a good curve and a little improvement on that fastball, and the kind of confidence that comes with winning, a Division II or III college career might even be possible.

I also see no harm in the better pitcher, the one with a lively fastball and good movement, making an effort to build his arsenal early on, as this will help him grasp the nuances of his art that he must eventually master if he is going to play Division I and/or pro ball.

On the other hand, some coaches see that a boy can deceive batters at a low level with a curveball and they will encourage him to throw it more frequently than his fastball. This is wrong — it is poor judgment. The boy's fastball will never develop with that approach. Fastballs should be thrown regularly, even daily, to develop arm speed and strength.

Show me the evidence that pitchers with good or great curveballs have any more arm troubles or diminished success or even that the curveball impedes their longevity.

Steve Carleton, David Wells, Don Sutton, Nolan Ryan, Darryl Kile, Andy Pettitte, John Sain and Sal Maglie to name only a few are pitchers who possessed outstanding curveballs that were integral to their success. Most probably learned these curves early in their careers. I hardly think that anyone capable of using good sense and good technique will ever let the act of throwing a curveball impede his career. On the contrary, used judiciously and with refinement it will embellish a career at any level.

If one can serve his apprenticeship on the mound learning to successfully pitch with just a fastball utilizing location — this is ideal. After that is accomplished, one can begin to move into the ranks of professional journeyman by adding that second dimension of changing speeds, and then move on to a master's certificate with the learning of a curve.

Learning to throw a curveball requires a young hurler to make pitching a mental act. To learn the aerodynamics of a curve, one must become familiar with variations in spin, finger position, wrist supination and pronation, elbow positioning and finally release that can impact the movement of a thrown baseball. If the same attention to information and detail required in learning a curve is transferred to every other pitch, the pitcher as artist will emerge.

> Go to any adult softball league and you will find those 74-77 mph ex-high school pitchers who saved their best fastballs and the development of a curve for a future never realized.

THE DAY OF THE RELIEVER

Even a one run deficit will produce dread and panic in a game barely two-thirds finished, when the prospects of facing a great reliever looms large. ...

6

Any discussion of pitching today would be incomplete if we were remiss in addressing the making and maintenance of the relief specialist. While we think of the relief pitcher as a modern day contrivance, from its earliest days, the pages of baseball history hold many tales of heroic firemen.

The most famous of those stories is probably that of **Grover Cleveland Alexander**, who won 367 Major League games — nearly all as a starter. Alexander remembers his greatest day in baseball as occurring in the 1926 World Series when pitching for the Cardinals, he entered the seventh inning of the seventh game with the bases loaded, his Cards holding a one run lead. Having already beaten the Yankees of Ruth and Gehrig twice in the series — both complete games with the second one having been played the day before — he faced the hot hitting Tony Lazzeri and struck him out on four knee-high pitches. He then finished off the Yanks with two more innings of stellar relief. He was nearly 40 at the time.

Despite those rare relief specialists like Hoyt Wilhelm, Dick Radatz and Lindy McDaniel from the 60's and 50's; Joe Page and Ace Adams from the 40's; Firpo Marberry and Syl Johnson from the 30's and 20's, seldom did teams of old keep an ace on the payroll used exclusively to seal a win. Often times you'd find starting pitchers who served double duty, coming out of the bullpen when necessary. Among the save leaders in baseball's early days you'll find names such as Lefty Grove, Dizzy Dean, and Christy Mathewson.

Since the 1930's the one significant exception to this has been the Yankees.

While **Satchel Paige** probably started more games than anyone in history, by the time he was allowed into the Majors, his best years were long behind. With craftiness and control he proved to be a fine reliever.

In 1930, **Lefty Grove** won the triple crown of pitching, leading the league in wins, strikeouts and earned run average. As if that wasn't enough he also made eighteen relief appearances and led the league with nine saves. Over the course of his career he saved 55 games and for a few years was the active career leader in saves for the American League.

From Johnny Murphy to Joe Page to Sparky Lyle to Goose Gossage to Dave Righetti to John Wettland to Mariano Rivera, since the time of Dimaggio, whenever the Yankees have come to the Fall Classic, they have come with a stopper who have known how to get the job done. And those relief specialists in many instances have played as big a role in the Yankees' post season dominance as the Gehrig's, Mantle's, and Jeter's

> **More than** any other team, the New York Yankees over the last half-century have led the way in creating the **role of the closer** as we know it today.

Over the decades, the rest of baseball has caught on to the point that just about every World Series of recent memory has seen the appearance of a reliever with a Hall of Fame portfolio. Aside from the aforementioned Yankees, Dennis Eckersly, Dan Quisenberry, Bruce Sutter, and Rollie Fingers, have all dramatically impacted the October stage.

THE SPECIALTY PITCH

Most relievers have had one specialty pitch that became their trademark. For Wilhelm it was the knuckleball. For Sutter it was the split fingered fastball. For Lee Smith, Gossage, Eckersly and a hundred others it was the fastball. In fact, most of the great relievers, with some notable exceptions, have been hard throwers with speed enough to challenge even the quickest bats. But regardless of what they throw, the best have always been and continue to be masters of control.

In recent years, Rivera has set himself apart from the pack primarily with his high mean cutter but can also get batters out swinging at hard stuff downstairs. Trevor Hoffman of San Diego— possibly the best reliever today — comes at the batter with three good pitches: a fastball, a slider and a change-up.

The big difference between Hoffman and relievers of years past is that, unlike most of the others, Hoffman has always been a reliever. Not long ago, just about every reliever was a recycled starter who became a reliever because he had plenty enough grit but not enough pitches to go through a line-up more than once or twice. But Hoffman from early on in his professional career has honed himself to be a relief specialist. Greg Olson is another of this new ilk, having come directly out of Stanford as a closer.

JOB DUTIES OF THE BULLPEN

Largely, in this chapter when talking about relievers, we are referring to closers, as the role and preparation of the middle and long reliever is not that much different than a starter, and that of the set-up man is little different than the closer.

LONG/MIDDLE RELIEF This role requires pretty much the same attributes as a starter. Although in middle relief, the pitcher can be successful with a lesser array of pitches as he may not be required to give each hitter in the order more than one look at him. This role is sometimes filled by a team's fifth or sixth starter. And it is often times the place where rookies are broken in.

SET-UP Usually the set-up man bridges the distance between the starter and the closer (occasionally between the starter and the middle reliever in an especially important game when the going gets sticky). He is usually the second best closer on the team and will see most of his action in the seventh and eighth innings, or the ninth inning of non-save situations.

CLOSER A closer seldom appears before the eighth and will usually enter the game only in a save situation when his team is ahead, or in a tie situation during an important game. Seldom will he come in when his team is behind. Some closers prefer to come in at the beginning of an inning rather than inheriting a situation; others — the true firemen — will answer the alarm whenever it sounds.

MOP-UP This is not a role to which any pitcher aspires. With the game out of reach one way or another, the best the pitcher can do in this situation is show he's got the stuff to perform a more important duty. For the rookie, mopping up can be an opportunity; for the veteran, a slap in the face.

RELIEF PITCHING IS NOW BUSINESS AS USUAL

Starting pitchers today are not expected to go a whole game and rarely do. To throw ten complete games in a season is a very remarkable achievement nowadays. And this attitude has filtered down to college and high school and even at times to the Little League level. I have no doubt that I lost several games in the ninth or tenth inning that could have been won if it had occurred to anyone to bring in a reliever. Like any pitcher of my era, I would never admit that I couldn't get another inning out of my tired body. I was the fellow who pitched both ends of a doubleheader in college ball, each a complete game, the second one a no-hitter. Do you think I was ever going to admit that I was ready to come out of a game? I'm not sure if baseball has gotten smarter over the years, but I do know that teams are quite a lot smarter about going to their bullpens.

A good bullpen can be a big factor for high school and college teams. Coaches at this level should give all members of their pitching staffs some education with regard to relief pitching. This should include strategies for maintaining readiness and warming up, as well as exploring the idiosyncrasies in the mental and physical training required of a reliever.

BECOMING A RELIEVER

I still don't think a youngster should start off his career planning to be a relief specialist, but he should be ready to take on that mindset when his team calls upon him to become its fireman. A young pitcher has a lot of learning to do and that learning comes with pitching a lot of innings in every situation possible. As a reliever, if one pitch is working for you, you might never develop other pitches, one of which may eventually develop into your best pitch.

Over the course of his maturation, a youngster's arm will get a lot stronger throwing seventy innings a season in high school rather than twenty-five or thirty, and in college or the early pros, a young man is much better off throwing 120 to 200 innings a season rather than the forty to sixty required of a reliever.

THE RELIEVER'S OFF-SEASON APPROACH

Off-season training for the relief pitcher should be just about the same as for the starter. The main differences being that the reliever should certainly practice more from the set (some relievers will throw only from the set) and he must develop a style that minimalizes any margin for error. The importance of control becomes magnified for the reliever who often times enters a situation where a walk could spell disaster and a wild pitch might become a headline rather than a footnote in the boxscore. Control is an absolute essential for all pitchers, but for a closer it is absolutely everything.

A relief pitcher must have one pitch he can throw for strikes nearly a hundred percent of the time. And ideally, he should have one more that is a pretty sure bet. If he has three good pitches he can go to with confidence, he will be among the invincible. Usually, the reliever wants to stay low in the strikezone, as even a fly ball can cause the battle to be lost with a runner on third. A closer must essentially be a groundball specialist if he is not a strikeout artist.

The smart reliever may not want to show his best stuff as he takes his practice throws on the mound.

GETTING THE RIGHT ATTITUDE

For the closer there is little margin for error. He must come out of the bullpen fully ready to make a perfect pitch on his first delivery. He doesn't have time to develop a rhythm or educate the umpire as to his strikezone. He must be willing to make decisions and not second-guess himself. He must let go of errors and misfortune immediately. He must tell himself that there is no room in his mind for distractions of any kind. He must not let anything or anybody rattle or intimidate him. For those few moments with the game on the line, he must be one cold-blooded creature.

Anyone with an absolute need for structure, predictability, and a set routine will probably fare better as a starter than as a reliever. When you are pitching one or two innings maybe today, and maybe again tomorrow, there must be a completely different mental outlook to your approach. It requires a personality that doesn't mind chaos or uncertainty — perhaps even one that thrives on (although preferably doesn't encourage) pressure.

STAYING READY

During the season the reliever must maintain readiness. In the chapter on training I cover just how a reliever can keep himself ready. If you are switching over to relief pitching from starting, recognize that there will be a period of adjustment before you find the right way to keep yourself physically and mentally ready. You simply have to keep yourself in prime condition for throwing all of the time. That means regular throwing with an emphasis on control.

Relief pitchers should never go two days in a row without throwing off a mound.

I've always believed and will continue to believe that there are a lot more pitchers who don't throw enough than there are pitchers who throw too much, and that more injuries come from the former rather than the latter.

Of course you have to be smart enough to take care of injuries and always throw with excellent mechanics in mind. There is a lot to suggest that pitchers are capable of pitching more often than previously thought. When Mike Marshall appeared in 106 games in 1974 while winning the Cy Young Award, it showed that there are no set rules for just how much rest one needs between appearances — particularly, shorter relief appearances. Appearance totals are on the way up, with seventeen Major League pitchers appearing during the 2000 season in seventy games or more.

Coaching **TIP** No matter how little skill you have, you're bound to get more skilled with practice. Give yourself a chance!

WARMING UP

In warming up, the reliever should begin his throwing with easy, slow-speed pitches. He should not warm up with full velocity right off, no matter what the emergency.

> **When you have to get ready in a hurry, the easiest way is to throw off-speed breaking pitches and really exaggerate the follow-through. This seems to loosen the arm quickly.**

Also, don't sit around like a lump on a log for eight innings. Move around, keep the joints fluid. Getting stuck at the end of the bench can become a cyclical self-fulfilling prophecy; if you go to the ballpark not expecting to pitch, you will not be ready when you are called upon, and subsequently, *you will not be called upon . . ..*

THE PLAN

Rookie closers are an anomaly. The closer must be a battle-tested hurler with a great understanding for all the nuances of the game. He should know the opposing hitters, not just who is stepping in against him first, but who the second and third batter are and what pinch-hitters are available on the bench. He must know where he needs to get his outs and how. If he has a base open, he can't afford to give it up to the leadoff batter when the next fellow up is much tougher. Some relievers instead of giving in to a batter, will have the tendency and tenacity to load the bases so as to get to the situation where they best like the odds.

Don Stanhouse, a flaky but very capable relief pitcher for the Orioles back in the 1970's, used to be called *two-pack*. It seems that whenever he came in to close, his manager, Earl Weaver, would be compelled to smoke two packs of cigarettes to get through the stress of watching Stanhouse go full count on every batter, typically loading the bases before getting those final outs.

> **However, there are many instances where the reliever is brought into a situation that can't get any more critical.**

In that case, the reliever's first pitch is certainly the most important. He needs to get the hitter into a defensive posture by getting ahead in the count. Usually, the first hitter you face will only swing at a fat pitch just to make sure you are ready to throw strikes.

A slight lapse of concentration can mean the difference between getting an 0-2 or a 2-0 count — the difference between a hitter being able to look for his pitch and having to protect the entire strikezone.

Of course, if you are fortunate enough to get the hitter into a hole, don't let up; make sure that he has to hit your pitch. Double plays should be an item on every reliever's menu, especially for a closer who doesn't have a high strikeout ratio. That's another reason to keep the ball low. High balls result in long balls and homeruns; low balls result in doubleplays and force-outs. Why is it so hard for some pitchers to learn this lesson?

AFTERMATH

Relief pitchers can rarely allow themselves to get too jubilant or too down, because — unless it's the deciding game of a championship — chances are, they are going to have to come out and do it again tomorrow. They never get the four-day break from the pressure cooker that starters are allowed. As erratic as the demands of their job may be, they are probably best off with terrifically consistent patterns away from the game. They can't afford to indulge one evening out of three; they can't afford to sleep four hours one night and twelve the next. They have to keep their capacity at a consistent level and know what they are capable of doing day-in and day-out.

> Relief pitchers must be experts in getting **rid of failure** almost **instantly** because their whole existence depends on tomorrow.

Nor can they afford the luxury of a conscience or the indulgence of second-guessing. Certainly, they can learn from their mistakes and avoid repeating them, but just as importantly, they can't keep rethinking them over and over again. More than one pitcher has had his ego shattered by an unfortunate moment in a big game. Coaches should be aware of this and recognize the true human makeup of that seemingly cold-blooded assassin on the mound. They should deflect blame when possible, and they should concentrate on helping their pitchers dwell on the positive rather than the negative. Even veterans need coddling now and again.

Ultimately, relief pitching is not for the timid of heart, but for the very strong of spirit. The good ones are artists of perfection and they earn their pay.

GET SET TO WIN!
PITCHING FROM THE STRETCH

It can happen. Over the course of the last century it's happened fourteen times in the Major Leagues, and chances are, over the next century it will happen at least fourteen times more. So it is possible. Indeed, the odds of your starting a game in which you record 27 outs in a row are better than winning at Powerball or better than becoming the first person to live for ever... but not much better.

> An **average pitcher** having an average day, will end up pitching with a man or men on base 75% of the time.

What this tells the pitching coach is that he had better make the skill of pitching with men on base a top priority. Learning to pitch with men on base means learning how to pitch from the set position, and learning how to keep runners from going wild. Nearly forty percent of all baserunners score, and when the leadoff batter in an inning gets on base, the odds of his scoring are about two in three. Cutting those percentages just ten or fifteen points is one difference between a winning pitcher and a pitcher who pitches just well enough to lose.

Although the catcher still tends to get most of the blame, one of the great axioms of baseball is that bases are stolen on the pitcher rather than the catcher. The catcher can't control the lead of the runner nor can he control where and how fast the ball is pitched. A pitcher with a good move and a knack for keeping the runners guessing will keep runners from taking liberties and enhance the possibility of doubleplays, force-outs, and pick-offs. He will make the journey around the basepaths an uphill battle all the way.

THE ESSENTIAL CHALLENGE WHEN PITCHING FROM THE SET IS TO KEEP THE RUNNERS CLOSE WITHOUT LOSING VELOCITY OR TAKING ANYTHING OFF ONE'S BREAKING STUFF.

Obviously, this requires a lot of practice on working from the stretch position, which most pitchers dislike. Allowing baserunners in the first place is something that goes against the true competitor's attitude of complete domination. An exception to this may be those relief specialists who inherit other people's situations. Dealing with baserunners is not any indication of a failure on their part.

Baseball, like life, hands us many raw realities and the fact of the matter is that we will be pitching with men on base as surely as we will get old. We may not like it but we better be prepared for it. Every pitcher must achieve proficiency from the stretch.

A typical program has pitchers practicing
from the set position 50% of the time. I
would stretch that to at least 60%, and not
just on the mound either. I would have the
pitcher do all his drills, even long-toss, from
the stretch position more than half of the time.

PICKING OFF THE BASERUNNER IS A BONUS

The pitcher's main objective is to keep the runner from getting a big jump and also from stealing — not just a base — but the rhythm of the inning. Certain teams thrive on the ninety-foot game and if allowed to run wild, they will take a trickle of offense and turn it into a flood.

A survival kit for pitching with runners should include a decoy move and a *got you* move to first base, a way to get off the rubber quickly, a spin step, and/or a jump pivot, as well as a variety of feints. It should include a few different ways of going to the plate — either a quick-step, a slide-step, or half-leg kick. It should also include a pick-off move to second and a strategy for dealing with runners on the corners. It should also require extras doses of confidence and patience, and a strong concept of what is and isn't allowed by the rules. And of course, it should have an ample supply of any pitcher's prerequisite for being out there in the first place, a pitch he can throw for a strike.

When a hurler gets into a jam, it's only natural to want to rush ahead and fix things as quickly as he can. That sort of thinking will more than likely play right into the hands of the other team's rising excitement. Sure, getting that instant double-play would be nice, but I would encourage the less experienced pitcher to instead slow down a bit. There are no take-backs in baseball.

Some pitchers have the attitude that having a runner get on first is irrelevant. Pitchers like Martinez and Maddux have the mindset that they will get their three outs before the runner can get past third and so will pay him little attention. But unless you can keep the hitters from batting much over .200 like those remarkable craftsmen, you might want to employ a little different strategy.

PITCHING FROM THE SET

It's always refreshing to see those consummate professionals who appear to be totally at ease pitching from the stretch. Their capacity for such is not achieved by accident nor is it a natural endowment. Those pitchers are proficient at pitching from the stretch because they have worked at it. Mentally, they have gotten to the place where the reality of pitching with men on base does not interfere with their spirit of domination — for them pitching with men on base is just another factor to be dealt with like bad weather or an unkempt mound.

HIGH-LOOP   **MEDIUM-LOOP**   **LOW-LOOP**

The pitcher may set his hands in one of three positions or loops: high, medium, or low.

He may set his feet in either a closed or open stance.

In the CLOSED STANCE, as shown to the right, the feet are placed parallel to each other, about a foot apart, with the back foot touching the rubber. A somewhat wider stance is okay if it facilitates the pitcher's move to first.

Also in this photo is another variation on the low-loop. Notice the different hand position from the low loop above.

With an OPEN STANCE, the front foot sits at about a 45-degree angle, which will afford the righthanded pitcher a better view of the runner and the bag.

However you start, pitching from the stretch will cause some loss in velocity — if that wasn't the case one would always pitch from the stretch — but you can minimize this impact with adequate practice. Control and ball movement should not be impacted by using the set position. All the mechanics talked about in previous chapters apply to the set position. Aside from the loss of some inertia, the pitcher's delivery from the set should be no different once the front hip is loaded — although there may be some variation in how high the leg rises. One mechanical area the righthanded pitcher must be careful about is the use of the lead shoulder.

In trying to keep tabs on the runner at first, the righthanded pitcher may neglect to properly close his shoulder on windup, weakening his pitch or possibly tipping off the runner that he is going to first. To be able to make that look to first, the pitcher's neck must be limber. If the shoulder follows his head, the risk of a balk is high. It takes a true craftsman to remember to put in time practicing this simple move.

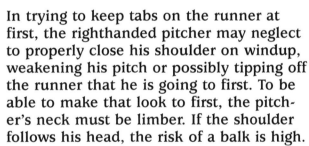

With a runner on base, the pitcher has to be strong enough to stay within himself; he can't become fearful of overthrowing and overreacting, nor can he start trying to aim the ball. He has to take the time to find his own rhythm.

Pitchers with good pick-off moves are respected by the runners. Once it's been established that a runner will be challenged with a strong move that could very well nab him, he will hesitate to take liberties with his lead.

Most pitchers do not throw to first enough. The best time to throw is when the pitcher comes down to a set position. Usually at this juncture the runner will be starting to take his lead and will have to shift his inertia to get back.

THE BALK — A QUESTION OF INTENT

A lot of pitchers go through their entire careers without knowing what actually constitutes a balk. They may have learned that if they scratch their nose at the wrong time, the game comes to a screeching halt while the opposition is allowed an advancement of base. And they might know that if they break their foot back from the rubber before making a motion to any base, they will be okay, and they probably know that once they start to the plate, they'd better finish the pitch.

And if that's all *you* know about avoiding balks, you could probably get by, but just getting by isn't what this book is about. To excel at pitching means grabbing up every little advantage that you can. Knowing exactly what you can and can't do with men on base is one of those advantages. Because while a balk is greatly up to an umpire's discretion, there are some very clear *do's* and *don'ts* that are very specifically expressed in the official rules of the game. And there are also ways to be clever and still stay within bounds of the rules that will put a little hesitation into the hearts and legs of baserunners. Included at the end of this book is a copy of *Section 8 Rules Governing a Pitcher* in its entirety. If you're serious about your craft, you will read them. As it is in a court of law, on the baseball field, ignorance of a law doesn't preclude guilt.

IN THE OFFICIAL RULEBOOK, THE PITCHER IS GRANTED PERMISSION TO TAKE EITHER OF TWO POSITIONS BEFORE DELIVERING A PITCH.
These are referred to as the *windup* and *set* positions. The rules governing these positions are very strict. In both the windup and set position, as the pitcher stands facing the batter, his pivot foot must be on the rubber or in contact with it along its front edge.

WHILE IN THE WINDUP, THE LEAD FOOT CAN BE PLACED ANYWHERE
(providing it doesn't roam beyond the plane defined by the edges of the rubber). Also before beginning his delivery, the pitcher must place both hands on the ball.

IN THE SET POSITION, THE LEAD FOOT MUST BE IN FRONT OF THE RUBBER,
and the pitcher — with or without a preliminary stretch move — must come to a distinct pause with the ball held in both hands in front of his body.

IN BOTH STANCES, THE PITCHER SHOULD BE ON THE RUBBER AS HE TAKES HIS SIGNAL FROM THE CATCHER; failure to do this can result in a warning and repeated failure may result in the pitcher's ejection from the game (a quite unlikely occurrence). At any time between receiving the signal and beginning his natural pitching motion, the pitcher may step backwards off the rubber providing that it does not become a practiced habit before every pitch.

ONCE HE RECEIVES HIS SIGNAL, THE PITCHER — EXCLUDING A FEW NOTABLE EXCEPTIONS — HAS THREE OPTIONS WITH A RUNNER ON BASE:
1. He may begin and complete his delivery to the plate.
2. He may throw to an occupied base.
3. He may disengage his pivot foot from the rubber by stepping backwards.

He may not change from one position to the other without stepping off the rubber.

ONCE HE BEGINS HIS NORMAL MOTION TO THE PLATE, HE MUST CONTINUE IT. Stepping away from the rubber is no longer allowable. In lifting his lead leg, once that lead foot passes back over the rubber, throwing to first or third are no longer options. However, he can pivot around in a continuous motion and throw to second, providing that the base is occupied. At no time with the pivot foot on the rubber can he throw to an unoccupied base. However, if the runner has clearly broken from first to second, he can throw to second without it being considered an unoccupied base.

THE PITCHER IS NOT ALLOWED TO MAKE ANY MOVE THAT MIGHT BE CONSTRUED AS A FEINT TO FIRST BASE WHILE ON THE RUBBER. He can turn his head to first, but he cannot turn his shoulders in that direction or even bend his knee or drop his weight in any way that is not typical of his usual delivery to the plate.

IF HE ELECTS TO THROW TO AN OCCUPIED BASE WHILE ON THE RUBBER, HE MUST FIRST STEP IN THE DIRECTION OF THAT BASE. The pitcher is allowed to feign a throw to second or third; however, if he steps to first while on the rubber, he must complete the throw. Recent interpretation of the rule says that a feint to any base must be preceded by a step in that direction. A pitcher *can* feign a throw to third and then throw to first, providing that a step towards first precedes the throw.

With all the limitations placed on throwing to a base while on the rubber, the reality is that the pitcher, especially a righthander, must become very proficient at making an expedient break from the rubber.

Remember that it is only permissible to break with the rubber by stepping behind it.

Between the time that he receives the signal, until he begins his natural pitching motion, the pitcher can step backwards off the rubber and throw or feint to any base in any way shape or form that he so desires. However if he does break contact with the rubber, his hands must drop to the sides (this is a rule that is seldom broken as the pitcher must break his hand from his glove before throwing; it's also one that I've never seen enforced).

Make sure that breaking with the rubber becomes a distraction to the hitter and the runner and not to you.

ONCE HE BREAKS WITH THE RUBBER, THE PITCHER IS JUST ANOTHER FIELDER with no specific limitations placed on him. He can throw or feign a throw to any base. He can even run at the baserunner and chase him back to the bag, a strategy that is not often employed anymore, but not a bad one — especially when you have runners on the corners and a delayed double steal appears imminent.

> The **rhythm** of the game is the pitcher's to control.
> Nothing happens until he decides to throw the ball.

THROWING TO FIRST

DECOY OR SET UP THROW

This is designed to drive the runner back and deceive him about the quality of the pitcher's real pick-off move. This throw can be made while still engaged with the rubber or after stepping back off the rubber. Remember that if the pitcher elects to throw from the rubber, he must first step in the direction of the throw.

Using a high-loop will make the setup to throw quicker; however, it might be advisable to use shorter arm action than shown in the picture.

◀ THE FAKE MOVE

When throwing to first, this involves stepping off behind the rubber and faking a throw. A fake to second or third is permissible while in contact with the rubber. Faking from the high-loop as shown in the picture can be accomplished quicker than with lower loops.

GOT YOU MOVE

This should be the pitcher's best pick-off move and should be reserved for when the runner strays too far or when he starts to daydream or lean in the wrong direction. At the very least, this move should force the runner to get his uniform dirty, diving back for the bag, and get him to think twice about making too quick a jump. The *Spin Move,* the *Jump Pivot* and other tailor-designed moves can be employed here. But they must be well-practiced.

The **Spin Move** is probably the most basic and easiest to master. It involves lifting up the heel and pivoting on the ball of the pivot foot as one steps in the direction of the throw. Remember though that this is not considered disengaging the rubber, so if the pitcher spins towards first, he is going to have to complete the throw.

The **Jump Pivot**, although used infrequently, can be a good way to quickly disengage from the rubber. The pitcher must leave the ground with both feet simultaneously, turning his body in the air. The hands should break while turning, so that on landing - with the pivot foot behind the rubber — the pitcher is set to fire or fake the throw. The suddenness of this movement will occasionally freeze the runner, especially if used infrequently. Very few pitchers are proficient at the jump pivot. If not perfected, a good throw is unlikely.

Another move one might try is that created by Jim Barr, formerly of the Angels. He would step not just behind, but off to the third base side of the rubber and then pivot on the *heel* of the lead foot and the ball of the pivot foot, placing him quickly in throwing position.

Coaching TIP
You can have hobbies and avocations that are very diverse and interesting but none of them can occupy the intensity of the focus necessary to be a successful professional baseball pitcher.

THE SIMPLE STEP BACK AND THROW

Stepping back from the rubber quickly is an essential move that every pitcher must have. The timing must be worked so that the back foot disengages the rubber a fraction of a second before the shoulder turns towards the base. The back

foot isn't required to land before the shoulder turns, so, as long as the shoulder action doesn't get ahead of the lifting of the pivot foot, the likelihood of a balk call is rare.

In all of these pick-off moves, it's important not to create any noticeable coiling action which will tip off the runner and also be subject to a balk call.

POLICING SECOND

The pick-off move at second is one of the more complicated plays in baseball. It requires that a pitcher be in synch with his infielders. Essentially, the second baseman or shortstop sneaks in behind the runner and to the bag. The keystone combo can work a series of decoys to conceal who is actually going to take the throw, but the pitcher best know for sure.

One can either employ a *time play* or the *daylight play.* The time play utilizes a 1-2-3 count, starting as soon as the pitcher looks away from the fielder and back to the hitter. On the count of two, the pitcher should begin his motion, and on three, wheel around and throw to the bag, not much higher than the knees. Ideally, the infielder will arrive at the bag at the same time as the ball, and employ a sweep tag on the runner.

The daylight play is a little more spontaneous. The pitcher will wheel around and throw to the shortstop, who is moving to the bag, when he sees daylight between the fielder and the baserunner.

TEMPO

Runners can be prevented from getting a good jump if the pitcher varies his approaches to delivery, his timing or both. A pitcher should always be in control of the tempo of the game and the play. Remember, nothing happens until the pitcher decides it will.

One should use the pause required of the set position to advantage in messing with the baserunner's timing. For example, on the first pitch, the pause can be held for two seconds; on the second pitch for one; on the third for three. Or two long pauses followed by a short pause can be utilized. Being random in breaking with the rubber is another good policy. The pitcher just has to be sure, he doesn't tip off the batter by developing various pauses for various kinds of pitches.

- ◆ **ALWAYS VARY YOUR LOOKS OVER TO THE BASERUNNER.**
- ◆ **PRESENT THE BACK OF YOUR GLOVE TO THE HITTER.**
- ◆ **WHEN UNCOMFORTABLE, STEP OFF THE RUBBER**

Create as many variables as possible in the timing and motion of your delivery. Practice stepping off so that it becomes a distraction to the runner rather than a distraction to you.

BE QUICK TO THE PLATE

In order to give the catcher a chance to throw out the baserunner, besides keeping the runner close to the bag, after his set position pause, the pitcher must get the ball from his hand to the catcher's glove in no more than 1.3 seconds. This is not an impossible task, but it does mean that the pitcher must be wise in his pitch selection and extremely efficient with his delivery.

You don't have to necessarily be that fast on every delivery, but if you are consistently slow to the plate, the baserunners will run you out of the game. Also note that shortchanging the first few steps of your delivery does not suggest permission to take shortcuts on the last steps of your delivery. You still must fully execute the pitching circle and not short-arm the pitch. You still must reach fully for the release point and have excellent follow-through. Failing to properly execute will most likely result in a pitch that stays up. So then throwing from the stretch, you will have a pitch that is not only traveling with less velocity, but is also high in the strikezone. . . .

THE SLIDE STEP

This has become a chosen tactic of many big league pitchers today. Many give credit to the slide step (also called the glide and skip step) to the drop-off in stolen bases the last decade. Conversely, it might also be one of the principal contributors to the rise in homeruns. My advice here is that those pitchers who are dependent on borderline fastballs, be discreet with their use of the slide step.

The ninth inning of a tied ball game is not the time to perfect your slide step. Like every other aspect of your mechanics, it must be stored away in muscle memory. When warming up, just as you would with your grips, you must test your slide step to make sure that it's there for you once you take the mound.

There are many variations on the slide step. One can lift the lead foot slightly or just slide it forward as shown below. Ultimately, you need to find the one that allows you to be the most effective and deceptive while avoiding the balk. Be sure not to rush. Take a distinct pause when you come to your set position!

With the slide step, the knee doesn't lift up at all. The hands break as the lead leg slides forward. Needless to say the challenge here is to gain power without a hip cock. Loading has to essentially happen with the hand break. This is not a well you want to go to very often unless you have a very lively arm.

Rushing your delivery in an effort to beat the baserunner can only make a bad situation worse.

Be efficient; if you want tobe quick but need to load the hip, shorten your leg lift, If you rush, the shoulder will fly open and your pitch to the plate will suddenly lose appreciable velocity. Most of us live on that razor's edge with our velocity, squandering another three or four mph will lead to runners advancing via the batted ball, including the fellow at the plate.

Base stealers are a nuisance; they *can* beat you ninety feet at a time once in a while. More often the running game becomes lethal when we allow baserunners to destroy our mechanics. Do your job of keeping the baserunner close to the bag. Be smart in your pitch selection. Once you start your motion to the plate and the runner takes off there is absolutely nothing more you can do; there is absolutely nothing to be gained by rushing.

The quick step allows the pitcher to load the hips a little more than the glide step. This can be especially effective when mixed in with a variety of leg lifts. But as with the glide step, you will get yourself in trouble if you use it too often. Again be sure to give the pitch a good ending.

If the pitcher feels that the slide or quick step dangerously reduces his velocity, he should change to the half-leg lift.

Varying the height of your leg lift will make it difficult for the baserunner to time your movement. Here the knee comes up to just below the belt.

More than anything, learn to be effective in going to the plate. No matter how well you hold a runner, your life isn't going to get any easier unless you can get the man at the plate to create an out.

When a batter reaches first base, the catcher and pitcher must work together to keep him close. The third baseman may also enter the picture by keeping the pitcher informed (via signals) on the runner's leads.

> No pitcher has ever had his career altered by a stolen base — the same cannot be said of the three or even two-run homer caused by distraction.

The pitcher shouldn't allow himself to be intimidated by the base runner's antics. If a pitcher finds it bothersome, I tell him to think about how much more distracting it is to the hitter. If a pitcher's mechanics are excellent enough, he could actually pitch to the plate with his eyes closed (Please don't try it!) The batter on the other hand must always be concentrating, searching with his eyes.

THE WORLD OF THE LEFTY

Southpaw pitchers obviously have a big advantage in holding the runner close. A deceptive move can make a lefthander even tougher. No southpaw should ever allow a runner at first to get a big lead. With any attention at all by the lefty, the runner invariably has to give in and shrink his lead.

In throwing to first base, the lefty should duplicate what he does to the plate. If he creates the appearance that he is going home — then the runner cannot possibly get a jump.

In throwing to first, the lefthander must step to the left and possibly shorten his arm span to get a quicker throw off. A variation for lefties would be to throw sidearm. Lefties need to work on this a lot. All pitchers — but lefties in particular — can lull a runner into a false sense of security by taking just a little something off their usual throws to the bag, saving their best throw for when they catch the runner leaning the wrong way or venturing out a step too far.

BEING GOOD IS BEING SMART

Many Major League pitchers are getting good results with their quick and deceptive pick-off moves, but there are still plenty who don't pay attention to this facet of the game and fail even to use common sense. In a steal situation you've got to put something on the pitch to give your catcher a chance to throw out the runner. You have to be aware of the game situation and the tendencies of the opposition. And you have to have the confidence to go after baserunners like the thieves that they are. They will steal wins from you if you allow them.

We should end here with a repeated note of caution about the biggest danger caused by baserunners. As a pitcher your main job is to get hitters out before they get on base. Once they are on, the next batter must be your center of focus. Stolen base percentages are down and that's all well and good, but one can't help but wonder if the homerun barrage of recent years can at least be partially blamed on the inability of pitchers to get something on the ball as they pitch from the stretch. Ignore the development of this facet of your game, fail to find a balance between dealing with the runner on the bases and the batter at the plate, and you will soon find yourself playing rec league softball.

PITCHING OUT OF THE SET FOR LITTLE LEAGUERS

Despite the fact that baserunners aren't allowed to leave the bag before the ball passes over the plate in Little League or Cal Ripken League baseball, some coach-

es at that level will encourage their pitchers to throw exclusively from the set position. These coaches believe that throwing from the set is far easier for the young pitcher to master than throwing with a full windup and delivery. As most pitchers at that age tend to throw strictly with their arms and don't utilize their bodies, loss of velocity is not an issue. Consistency is indeed easier accomplished from the set, especially when the leg lift is replaced by a simple step, so control is apt to be sharper from the start.

Although the arguments put forth in favor of Little Leaguers throwing exclusively from the set seem to make sense in terms of immediate results, one must ask whether this approach is holding back the young hurler's development. I believe the answer to that is an emphatic *yes*.

While many youngsters who have gone down this avenue have progressed from the set position early-on to full mechanics later, many others have retained their disposition toward the set position and have not developed the rhythmical coordination so absolutely necessary for improved velocity and power. One must also wonder when a pitcher is more comfortable throwing from the set whether he will unconsciously create scenarios that will allow him to return to that favored position. Feeling even the slightest sense of relief at putting runners on can't be a good thing.

The notion that the full motion is too challenging for a ten-year old doesn't impress me at all. I've worked with hundreds of kids every year for the past few decades and quite frankly find that with thorough instruction, most all of them can learn full mechanics if it is expected of them. In fact most don't think of it as especially challenging if that idea hasn't been put into their heads.

I would go as far as to say that by passing up on full mechanics, a golden opportunity is being lost. The younger the age at which physical patterns are taught, the more internalized they will become. The ability for people to learn through imitation is at its highest during the early formative years. After watching a big leaguer pitch, a five-year old can mimic him right down to the minutest detail. It makes us laugh to watch that five-year old nod his head at an imaginary catcher, tug his sleeve, dig in his feet and then commence a wind-up that includes every little idiosyncrasy employed by a particular pitcher. We see details we weren't even conscious of until the youngster replays them for us.

A child's capacity for this kind of imitation does not last forever, but begins to fade as he or she moves into adolescence. At the age of four, a child can learn up to five languages simultaneously and speak them like a native. That same child at the age of fifteen will struggle to master a simple dialog in French or Spanish101. Teach a young boy proper mechanics at the age of eight and it will become completely internalized in his muscle memory for the rest of his life.

If a Little League coach feels uncomfortable teaching full mechanics, he or she needs to find someone who can. After all we should always have a player's development uppermost in our minds. Subjecting them to our limitations of knowledge and/or patience just isn't fair.

When the youth pitcher does make the transition into Babe Ruth and scholastic baseball, he of course will have to learn how to pitch from the set. It's probably a good idea to begin practicing from the set during one's last year of Little League. Incorporating it with long toss may be the best way to start so that the pitcher can also begin working with the extra pitching distance as well.

No matter how stealthful you are with your deliveries and pick-offs, the very best baserunners will always outguess you!

The best you can do with one of those fellows is not dawdle to the plate, and throw often enough to keep him from getting greedy with his lead. Hall of Famer Joe Morgan always knew exactly what the pitcher was going to do; he claimed there was always a dozen or so clues to read. Without stealing the sign he even knew whenever a pitchout was called for. It was said that despite the hopelessness of catching him, some managers would call for the pitchout anyway just because they got a kick out of seeing him calmly standing on first with his arms crossed every single time it was tried.

THE NINTH FIELDER

Once in a while a pitcher with good range will cause problems for himself — getting a glove on a ball that could have been more easily played by an infielder. That's a problem I'm willing to live with! I would much rather have a player who aggressively goes after the ball — one who recognizes that no action is never an option when the ball is put into play.

A PITCHER NEEDS TO BE AN EXCELLENT FIELDER FOR OBVIOUS REASONS.

◆ **Plays to pitchers are often of an essential nature.** Bunts — against which the pitcher is a key player — are primarily designed to bring a runner in or put him in scoring position.

◆ **Self-defense** Smashing line-drives through the box is what many hitters focus on.

◆ **Weak hitters more typically ground the ball to the pitcher.** Giving weak hitters a free pass is a baseball sin.

◆ **It adds to the mystique of invincibility.** Making the perfect fielding play is one more way to tell the batters, *they'll be getting no breaks from this hurler.*

For a prideful batter, hitting a grounder to the pitcher can be more demoralizing than a strikeout, I don't especially like it when the pitcher takes his time, before easily gunning him down. In the constant battle between pitchers and hitters, that may be one way to answer a hitter who likes to watch his homeruns leave the park, but don't get caught up in playing this petty game. Be above it. Have some class.

It's no coincidence that since its inception 43 years ago, the Gold Glove for pitchers has been awarded to some of the game's biggest winners. Hall of Famers Bob Gibson, Phil Neikro and Jim Palmer, have each won at least four. In addition to his five Cy Young Awards, Greg Maddux has picked up ten Gold Gloves (and counting). Every year his glove makes the difference in at least two or three close games; rarely does it ever open the barn door.

When the pitcher is the ninth fielder, rather than a defensive liability, the team feels more confident about handling the tricky plays.

A PITCHER WHO –

- ■ **knows what to do with the fielded ball when runners are on board,**

- ■ **makes bunting seem futile,**

- ■ **takes charge on pop-ups,**

- ■ **never fails to back up a base or cover first**

Often times the pitcher is referred to as the Fifth Infielder. I prefer thinking of him as the Ninth Fielder, a defensive player who happens to be on the mound. Like his eight teammates, he has a job to do whenever the ball is put into play, whether it is bunted in front of the plate or slammed off the wall in right field.

has added another dimension to his game that can be as valuable as adding another pitch. Being a great fielder adds to a pitcher's mystique and is well worth the investment of time and energy.

A pitcher who saves an overthrow from going into the third base dugout is not there by accident; he is there because he has practiced getting there many times, because he has his head in the game, because he knows that is where he is supposed to be.

As the reader should have figured out by this point, I believe in being prepared. To my mind taking the field unprepared is embarrassing. And in baseball, being prepared is always about being fundamentally sound. When it comes to being fundamentally sound, there is no shortcut and no replacement for consistent, conscious practice. Fielding is no exception. The best pitchers practice their fielding skills daily.

> For some reason that might have made sense years ago, a lot of pitchers do their glovework shagging balls in the outfield. The true pitcher-craftsman will take his fielding practice as part of the infield.

BALLS HIT BACK TO THE MOUND

Unless there are runners on base, there is no reason to rush when the ball is grounded back to the mound. You should get your body low and square-up to the ball as would any infielder. Keep your weight forward, towards your toes, rather than back on your heels. Please make sure you field the ball cleanly before you begin executing your throw. Thinking about step two — throwing the ball — before you complete step one — fielding the ball — is probably the biggest cause of errors in baseball.

Get into the habit of following the ball to your glove with the throwing hand so as to trap the ball if it pops out. Also, your throwing hand in motion will make the snatch and throw a smooth continuation of your pick-up.

When throwing, if there's time, square-up your body, with the off-elbow and/or glove pointing to your target.

On balls hit to one side of the mound or the other, lefties and righties obviously can't play it the same way. The righthander's job is a little easier as his body will always be better aligned for the throw to first. The only way that a pitcher will know which way he must turn to get off the throw is by practicing situational fielding for many, many hours. The proper turn can only happen by way of practice-enhanced instinct.

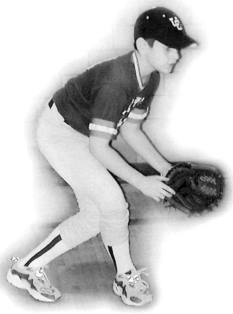

The toughest grounders to field are those hit or bunted into the no-man's land between the pitcher's mound and either first or third.

GLOVE SIDE

BACKHAND SIDE

Going to his glove or backhand side, the pitcher must get down low and lead with his glove. The first step to the ball should be a crossover.

In Little League, with a shortened distance between bases, the race for the bag between the pitcher and hitter is always much tighter. When the ball is fielded by the first baseman, it's usually preferable for the second baseman to take the throw or for the first baseman to run across the bag himself. However, when all the fielders go after a grounder to his left, his best option after fielding it might be to run across the bag, rather than risk a quick toss.

Going after the ball on the third base side is fraught with peril. With body momentum going the other way, the throw to first can be very dangerous. When there's little time to make the throw, brace with the back leg to get power.

BRACE WITH BACK LEG

1.

2.

WALKING STEP ▶

To maintain balance
while throwing to a
base, the pitcher can
either use a walking
step or employ the
crow hop. Sometimes
a second step might
be required while
waiting for the fielder
to get to the bag.

CROW HOP ▶ **1.**

3.

By the end of spring training, an infield should have all of its situational routines well in hand; and have explored every possible *what if*. Each of the infielders, including the pitcher, should have an understanding of his teammates' capabilities. During the game, it's an absolute must for the pitcher to know where his infielders are stationed for every pitch and what they can realistically reach.

It's important to maintain communication during the game, as sometimes the infielders must change things up to play a bunt or trap a baserunner. Take a look at Chapter Seven, on pitching from the set, for a discussion of pick-off's, including the pick-off play at second which can be a true test of an infield's cohesiveness.

2. **3.**

GET YOUR DAILY DOSE OF PEPPER

Pepper is an exercise that is becoming as passé as the wooden bat and pick-up games. Most kids and many uninitiated coaches think it's some kind of mischievous game fraught with danger, due primarily to the *NO PEPPER* signs on display in just about every ballpark.

While improving fielding reflexes, younger players can also develop the bat control necessary to protect the strikezone.

Pepper is an exercise designed to improve fielding while developing bat control. Ideally, no more than three fielders with gloves form a semi-circle around a batter, some fifteen to twenty feet away. For a more heightened game, you can use just one fielder. One of the fielders throws the ball crisply (enough to challenge the hitter without blowing it by him) in the direction of the batter's strikezone. The batter's job is to make very light contact using a slowed-down regular swing or by bunting the ball, with the goal of putting the ball exactly where the batter

wants it — whether it be in the air, on the ground, right or left. The fielders upon stopping the ball will immediately toss it back to the batter. The close distance forces those fielding to be on their toes and will greatly improve reaction time.

FIELDING BUNTS

Rare are those bunting attempts that come as a complete surprise, especially in this day of big-inning baseball. Better pitchers however are going to see more bunts, as the opposition will feel the necessity to attempt to score any runner who gets on base.

Know the area that's your responsibility. For example with runners on first and second and no one out, if a bunt occurs, the area on the third base side belongs to the pitcher, as the third baseman must cover the bag.

The pitcher is largely responsible for shallow bunts. How far he must go towards the plate will depend on the agility of his catcher. The catcher should field the ball whenever possible, as he will be better positioned to see the runners and make the throw. But never take anything for granted. You should charge every bunt in front of you, just in case the catcher has trouble getting out. Remember that on the squeeze bunt, the catcher is going to have to stay at home.

BAREHANDED PICK UP

Whenever the ball is rolling slow enough or is stopped, you should grab it with your throwing hand. This will require you to get even lower on the play. One common error is running past the ball when making a barehanded play as the body is in the habit of getting just low enough to field the ball with a glove. When getting low, take your center of gravity with you by dropping your bottom rather than by leaning over at the waist.

> **Know the situation.** With a big lead always go for the **easiest out.** If you're going after the lead runner, make sure that you can get him!

With bunts up the third base line, if the third baseman can get to it just as quickly, or a half a step slower, then let him take it, as his body will be in far better position for the throw. Besides, since the days of Brooks Robinson, that play is the measure of a third baseman's ability.

On any ball hit to the left side of the infield, whether on the ground or in the air, the pitcher should always react by heading towards first.

To avoid a collision and be in better position to take the throw, don't cut a diagonal from the mound to the bag. Instead, run directly to the baseline at the cut of the grass or about fifteen feet in front of the bag.

PATH TO FIRST BASE

NO MAN'S LAND
Probably the toughest bunt to cover is the one in no-man's land between the mound and first. Again, always go after the ball, and if the first baseman gets it, keep running to the bag. Practice getting low quickly.

On taking a throw from the first baseman, quickly cut left and move to the bag with a shortened stride. You will have to take the ball in motion. Don't try to stop yourself. Step onto the inside third of the bag. If he doesn't hesitate, even a slower pitcher has plenty of time to make this play.

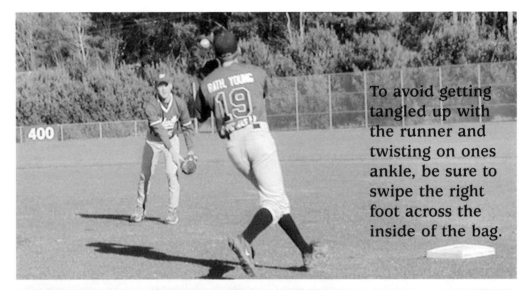

To avoid getting tangled up with the runner and twisting on ones ankle, be sure to swipe the right foot across the inside of the bag.

RIGHT

WRONG

Go hard after any ball hit to your left. If you get it, just continue on to the bag if there is time. When you need to make the throw, don't stop too abruptly; take an extra step if necessary, then plant. If you miss the grounder, go on to first to take the throw. As you approach the bag, shorten your stride so that you can more easily adjust to an errant throw.

STEPPING ON THE BAG

Don't attempt to tag the runner going to first unless the opportunity is within easy reach.

When taking the throw at first on the backside of a doubleplay, press your foot against the edge of the bag (right foot for righthander, and left foot for lefty), stretch to the ball and stay out of the way of the runner. When a body in motion collides with a body at rest, the body at rest will get the worst of it.

BACKING-UP THROWS; TAKING THE CUTOFF

Make sure you know your responsibility with regard to backing up third and home. Most pitchers remember to back up the plate; however, more than one game has been lost by a pitcher's failure to back up third. If the runner getting home is a foregone conclusion and there are other men on base, it's your job to back up third.

On occasion you will be called on to serve as a cutoff on the throw to the plate. Here you have to keep your head in the game and know when to cut the ball off and when to let it go through. Often times if the cutoff is made, the batter can get caught trying to take an extra base. Don't make things worse for yourself by letting the ball go through when it's too late to get the runner at the plate. A runner at second is more than twice as likely to score as a runner at first.

> **If you want to impress a coach with your hustle and baseball smarts, run like the dickens to back-up third. It will be noticed.**

COVERING THE PLATE — YOU'RE THE ONLY ONE IN THE NEIGHBORHOOD

Covering the plate on a passed ball or a wild pitch has got to be the pitcher's responsibility. If a pitcher doesn't learn this imperative in Little League, he probably never will. At that level, a half a dozen runs or more can pour across the plate when the game of catch between pitcher and catcher goes awry. Invariably, the more concerned about messing up the battery becomes, the more likely they will continue to mess up. In the big leagues this self-fulfilling prophecy doesn't happen often, but often enough.

Reminding yourself to cover the plate in case of a wild pitch violates one of the principles of positive visualization. As previously talked about, whatever image we place in our heads — positive or negative — we tend to live up to it. With that eager runner stretching his lead at third, and the control of the pitcher eroding, the best a coach might do is to remind the pitcher what to do if the ball *gets by the catcher,* rather than what to do if he throws it to the backstop.

When it does *get by the catcher,* the pitcher must immediately forget about the mistake; he must in fact forget about being a pitcher and instantly become that ninth fielder. Otherwise he will end up standing on the mound watching the runs cross the plate.

YOUR SUCCESS AS A FIELDER IS ABSOLUTELY DEPENDENT ON YOUR PITCHING MECHANICS

If you are a raw fielder who is constantly out of position, the opposition will exploit this. The mound is no place for weak fielders to hide. Invariably, you will be victimized by your weaknesses at the most critical of times.

Without a good clean follow-through, without proper balance, without proper positioning of the off-arm, your ability to field the batted ball or race to cover a base will be greatly compromised, as will your ability to protect yourself from a line-drive.

Life-threatening line-drives are not a regular occurrence, but all it takes is one to cause irreparable damage, both physical and psychological. Just as the batter can't allow himself to be intimidated by the fear of being hit, neither can the pitcher allow himself to be preoccupied with the possibility of being laid out by a five ounce missile traveling 125 miles per hour or better. Being as prepared as possible to deal with that danger goes a long way in building confidence and easing worry.

Taking the time to become an excellent fielder will bring you one step closer to becoming the complete pitcher.

When the complete pitcher is on the mound, there is no doubt about who is in charge. Being a skilled fielder who is always in the game allows the pitcher to become a field general. Pitchers who are respected for their competence by their teammates will often times direct fielders as to where they should play. They will back up outfielders with a wave of the hand, confer with infielders to let them know who should take the pick-off throw. They will bark out who should retrieve the high pop in no man's land and direct catchers in pursuit of a lost foul ball.

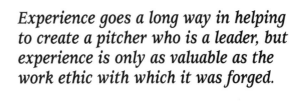

Experience goes a long way in helping to create a pitcher who is a leader, but experience is only as valuable as the work ethic with which it was forged.

Start young in developing good fielding habits and as you mature they will become instinct.

APPROACHES TO EFFECTIVE PITCHING
FINDING A STRATEGY THAT WORKS FOR YOU

Job posting in every clubhouse in the world —

WANTED, PITCHER: dependable and durable individual who enjoys both repetition and creativity. Willing to work outdoors, both days and evenings, weekends a must. Must be in love with success and able to thrive in high-pressure situations. All sizes and shapes welcome. Strong throwing arm a plus. Non-thinkers need not apply.

As this book is being written, I think it can be safely said that in pitching circles all around the world Pedro Martinez is *the man,* the hurler who stands on the mound as the best of the best. Having just won his second unanimous Cy Young Award in a row (overall his third Cy Young in four years), he's a fixture in every young baseball player's imagination. He's the imaginary titan that every *wannabe* hitter digs in against at the plate. And he's the role model for every little David standing all alone on the hill facing down some hard-swinging Goliath.

And you can bet that every teenager toeing the rubber is thinking, Fastball Change-up, that's the ticket; if it's good enough for Pedro, it's good enough for me.

Having been an active participant in the world of pitching for quite some time, I have witnessed one style of pitching after another become *the thing,* and then fade away. Usually it depends on who is *the man* at any given time, as we all want to emulate the current measure of success. This can be a good thing but only up to a point. Experimenting with various styles is part of the learning curve for any aspiring pitcher, but eventually, to be truly successful, every hurler is going to have to find his own style, a style that fits his body and gets the most out of his pitching arsenal.

I believe that by high school, a pitcher should begin to settle on a style and strive to perfect it. Certainly, one should try-on many different styles, but when you find one that fits right, stick with it and develop it. After a bad outing, there's always that temptation to abandon a chosen style. However instead of discarding it, take the time to consider what went wrong; determine what needs to be changed, what needs to be learned to make that style as close to infallible as possible. That is not to say that a pitcher should stick to a particular style when it has outlived its purposefulness. In fact as a pitcher gets older, as his strength peaks and then wanes, success becomes dependent on his ability to adapt his style to maintain a level of excellence.

Many physically talented pitchers never reach their optimum potential because they never engage their brains in the act of pitching.

THE TWELVE STYLES OF PITCHING

As a somewhat academic, but nevertheless valuable exercise, I've broken the approaches to pitching into twelve styles. Like any model that seeks to categorize, my effort is intended to help us understand the differences in approaches and the reasoning that goes behind them, rather than provide ironclad descriptions of one pitcher or another. Some styles quite obviously flow into others, and some pitchers, though primarily advocates of one specific style, will borrow from other styles as the situation dictates.

The size of a lead and whether there are men on base are two of the factors that might determine the style a pitcher utilizes in any given moment. Jim Palmer certainly gave up his share of homeruns on his road to the Hall of Fame, but he never gave up a grand slam. Was that a nineteen-year coincidence, or do you think he altered his style with the bases loaded?

Every style of pitching can boast of its share of Hall of Fame examples. But as long as getting the batter out remains the object of pitching , it doesn't much matter if the pitcher induces the hitter to fly out to deep center, ground out to first, strike out swinging or strike out looking. Any way he does it, any time he gets three hitters out before a man crosses the plate, it can be said that his style is effective.

IN LITTLE LEAGUE, THE PREFERRED STYLE SHOULD BE THROWING STRIKES. UNTIL THE YOUNG PITCHER HAS COMMAND OF THIS CONCEPT, THERE IS NO POINT — AND IN FACT MUCH RISK INHERENT — IN ATTEMPTING TO DEVELOP A MORE ADVANCED STRATEGY.

The following approaches are listed hereafter without any mind to popularity or effectiveness. As I've mentioned, good pitchers may combine three or four of these. Great pitchers may actually have several, but there are also many successful pitchers that will basically adhere to just one or two approaches.

1 EAST TO WEST

The East/West hurler throws coast-to-coast, primarily working the horizontal plane of the plate, rarely if ever throwing over the middle. One might work the inside part of the plate to push the hitter back and then go to the outside, either causing the hitter to freeze up or enticing him to lunge and flail. This style can involve a fastball and a breaking pitch or just the fastball. Tom Glavine will sometimes work this way, pushing the fastball inside and then going away with his change-up. Pitchers throwing east to west will do best to also mix up speeds as their pitches are largely traveling the same plane as the swinging bat.

Al Leiter and Rick Reed, both well-traveled journeymen, have found late-career success with the Mets as East/West style pitchers. It's not unusual for pitchers on the same team to find success with similar styles — due probably to the strengths and limitations of the defense, stadium factors, or a pitching coach's particular persuasion.

2 NORTH TO SOUTH

This was my favorite method of pitching and the one I tend to preach most often to those whom I coach. The North/South pitcher mixes his pitches upstairs and downstairs. If one has a good 6/12 down-curve or a bottom-dropping-out splitter and contrasts it with a fastball or a cutter that can be thrown high and hard enough, à la the Mariana Rivera cutter, the hitter has to buy into playing the guessing game as he knows he can't get himself ready to swing both high and low.

One advantage of this style over the East/West is that the batter's swing travels largely on the horizontal, which means there's a greater area of intersection between bat and ball with the East/West than there is with the North/South style of pitcher.

On a good day, the North/South approach puts the batter's senses on *Red Alert,* as poor guesswork on his part will lead to easy outs. Sterling Hitchcock of the Padres and David Wells of the Blue Jays offer good examples of this approach. However, on a bad day, when their curve ball isn't dropping, even weak hitters will be teeing off like Ty Cobb. And as we talked about in Chapter Five, when the umpire won't call the curveball for a strike, these pitchers are left before the mob, naked and defenseless.

Changing eye level with a four-seam fastball that seems to rise and a two-seam-er that sinks is another way to play the North/South strategy.

3 OVERPOWER THE BATTER

This is the *showdown at high noon* approach. "I'll throw my best stuff and you take your best rip." This sort of style provides for those high drama *make my day* moments when a heavy hitter steps up to the plate. Pure heat versus pure power. Randy Johnson versus Sammy Sosa. All things being equal, most of the time you get the bear, but sometimes the bear gets you.

This may be the simplest approach. "Fire it down the middle, let the ball do its thing and put another notch in your glove!" Occasionally, this type of hurler will throw the ball faster than any mortal can react, even if everyone in the stadium knows it's coming. But to date, the divine laws of baseball have not allowed for the pitcher to exist who can throw his fastball by every batter on every pitch . . .. although many a pitcher has existed who believed he could. The Boot Hill of flame-throwers long forgotten is filled with them.

To be a winner, this style pitcher better be ready to mix it up some with location and change of speed. For this type pitcher, control is often a problem. Early on in their careers, they're apt to be plagued by walks, but if they can master the strikezone, they are apt to be late bloomers who end up with long and successful careers as has been the case with Johnson and before him, Nolan Ryan.

Relief pitchers who can *bring it on* at 95 + will always find work, even if that's all they have. Currently, Armando Benitez of the Mets would be the best example of a reliever who makes his living with hard stuff. Benitez has also exemplified the danger of this style. In spite of putting up some great numbers over the last few years, he will always be haunted by that handful of times in the playoffs when one veteran or another caught up to him and converted the power of his pitch into outcome-altering homers.

On those rare occasions — about once every other generation —when a pitcher develops a masterful curveball or electrifying slider to go with that kind of heat, getting wood on the ball becomes a moral victory for the hitter. Those who faced Sandy Koufax can attest to that.

4 EVERYTHING LOW

Keep it low: that's the usual advice the Little League coach gives to his scrawny ten year-old pitcher when some six-foot twelve year-old steps to the plate. And it's advice that follows every pitcher as he matures from level to level. Keep it down and keep down the carnage. The value of pitching low is something every pitcher needs to learn as early as possible and never forget. You want a ground ball, you throw it low; you want more speed on the ball, throw it low; you want that ball to be harder to see . . . throw it low.

Unlike throwing the ball high, throwing the ball low is part of every pitcher's style. Even renowned high ball artists will work the bottom of the strikezone, but the reverse isn't true. There are some pitchers who never come upstairs on purpose. Primarily, they earn their pay by inducing hitters to hit the ball on the ground. Singles might be more common for the low-ball pitcher but homeruns are rarer. Tommy John, formerly of the Yankees, threw this way for a very long time, winning more twelve hitters than anyone would seem to have the right to.

The sinking fastball is usually the bread and butter of this type pitcher. They often complement it with a breaking pitch or a change-up that goes even lower. Those cut in the Tommy John mold can get a hitter to swing at a ball bouncing on the plate, but they don't give up a lot of walks — not if they want to be successful. With a good infield, they'll turn a lot of doubleplays.

Kevin Brown is a low-ball pitcher of a different color, and as talked about in Chapter Ten, may well represent a prototype of the new lowball pitcher. Not only does he keep it low, but he compounds the hitters' woes by throwing two kinds of sinkers — much like a fastballer who mixes up a four and two-seam fastball —

one that's hard enough to break bats and a slower one that has some serious movement.

Some pitchers will mix a power sinker with a sinking circle change-up. When you are very good at doing just that, the opposition will rarely score runs in bunches. Nobody ever exemplified this style better than Orel Hershiser, when in 1988 he set a Major League record by pitching 59 consecutive innings of shutout ball.

5 CHANGING SPEEDS

This is a style to which all great pitchers at least pay homage and was discussed rather extensively in Chapter Four. Changing speeds has not just made many a good pitcher great, but has taken a few average pitchers and lifted them to greatness as well. Changing speeds is the thinking man's game and requires a craftsman's precision and the confidence of experience. Pedro Martinez and Greg Maddux, two pitchers with very different stuff, present very strong arguments in favor of this style. A fastball with good movement and a straight change that taunts batters from the bottom of the strikezone and beyond are the most common tools of this type pitcher.

6 PAINT THE BLACK

Shaving the corners is the name of the game here. Somewhat similar to the East/West stylist, this is the realm of the sharp-shooting pitcher who will stretch the strikezone millimeter by millimeter until no one is quite sure what's a strike anymore. The ultimate result: batters who begin chasing balls they haven't a prayer of reaching. Typically, you'll hear the sportscasters claim that the batters will eventually catch up with pitchers of this ilk. Yet somehow, a Tom Glavine and an Orlando Hernandez keep winning big game after big game throwing this way.

7 JUNK 'EM TO DEATH

A pitcher throwing junk forces the batter to provide all the power. The batter must be disciplined enough to wait and wait and wait some more on the pitch's arrival to the plate. Pitchers of this ilk live in that dangerous zone beneath bat speed. Often times when the batter makes contact, his hands and his body weight will get way ahead of his bat, leading to weakly hit balls. The pitcher utilizing this style has got to stay low with a lot of movement and changes of speed (slow, slower and really slow). These guys, when they're good, manage to stick around for a long time, even coming back to pitch again long after you thought they were gone. Tim Wakefield with his knuckleball had his fantasy value plummet to $0 five years ago, but as of this writing is starting games for the first place Red Sox. Fernando Valenzuela would have hitters stumbling all over themselves to hit that seemingly fat juicy screwball of his. Stu Miller, a top reliever from another generation, was known for *slowing a hitter to death*.

8 LATE BREAK ON THE BALL

This style is usually not a pitcher's defining method, but rather one that adds effectiveness to his usual style. Late breaking pitches include the tailing fastball, the slider and the cutter. If a batter's guessing fastball, he'll end up a little ahead or find himself too stunned to react. Many a third strike is called when a pitcher has this style mastered. Maddux again is an example; he has great late action on his otherwise average fastball. Hard throwing Bartolo Colon as well as Livian Hernandez and Rick Reed are all members of the late break club.

9 POWER WITH GREAT CONTROL

From what we've seen and what history has told us, this style is the hallowed grounds where legends worked. It is the style of the take-charge ruler of his realm. Lefty Grove, Walter Johnson, and Bob Feller all had howitzer arms with sniper-like accuracy. They could whip a fastball in on the hands or up under someone's chin. Roger Clemens of the NY Yankees, beautifully and dramatically personifies this approach. He consistently registers 94 + on the radar gun, but rarely if ever hurts himself with walks. Throwing a four-seam fastball (riser) and a two-seamer (tailer) to all parts of the strikezone — including that very inside and up corner —makes this an extremely intimidating and effective way to pitch.

10 GOOD OR GREAT CURVEBALL WITH AVERAGE FASTBALL

This is a North/South type style for those with good but not great stuff. Down and away with the curve, up and in with the fastball. Here the batter must continually make vertical and horizontal adjustments to his swing. After the pitcher drops a good curve down and in, that high heat looks all the hotter. A splitter is also often employed by this sort of pitcher to keep folks from sitting on either of the other two pitches. David Wells of the Blue Jays, Andy Pettitte of the Yankees, Aaron Sele of the Mariners, and Darryl Kile of the Cardinals have made themselves into solid pitchers with this style.

11 MIX 'EM UP

This method not only involves the use of different pitches and speeds, but also different arm angles and different mechanical releases. The hitter can't ever anticipate a release point and consequently can't establish a comfortable rhythm for his swing. Some examples here are Orlando *El Duque* Hernandez of the Yankees, and to some extent, the well-traveled David Cone. One of the greatest masters of this technique was Luis Tiant, formerly of the Indians and Red Sox. This is not something that you want a younger pitcher fooling with as it can quite obviously play havoc with one's mechanics.

12 KNOW THE HITTERS AND PITCH TO THEIR WEAKNESSES

This involves doing your homework and then going out and battling the daylights out of the hitter, never giving in to him and never letting him have the pitch he wants. These pitchers have a warrior mentality and often come up big in big games. Think of Dave Stewart who dominated in World Series play for Oakland, and Jack Morris who did the same for Minnesota. This type of big hearted battler exists at all levels and must be witnessed at work to be fully appreciated, as the stat sheet rarely does him justice.

When all is said and done, no matter what style a pitcher chooses to emulate, consistent success comes down to two things — balance and control. Neither can be over-looked and neither can be over-emphasized.

All Styles Require Balance. By balance I mean the physical kind that comes from great mechanics and staying centered over the balls of one's feet. I also mean the kind of psychological balance that is the result of remaining level-headed and working in seamless harmony within the fabric of the game.

Without having total control of one's physical abilities — especially control of the ball — it is virtually impossible to subscribe to any of the twelve styles previously listed. Any plan is meaningless if a pitcher surrenders his control to circumstances, to the batter, to the umpire, or to any of the opposing forces that might preclude him from success. Balance comes from control and control is born out of balance. Neither comes about by accident or divine decree; you have to work at them. Even the seasoned veteran has got to put in his time working to stay sharp. No matter how long you have been pitching, you must always be willing to learn and never grow complacent.

Coaching **TIP** You will only have your best stuff 25% of the time. The other 75% is when you need to be mentally tough..

WAYS TO HONE YOUR PERSONAL STYLE

PITCH BATTING PRACTICE. This will allow you to get used to various batters and stances and provide you with an opportunity for a hitter's feedback. A word of caution here: don't allow yourself to get overly competitive while pitching batting practice. The last thing you want to do is to destroy the confidence of your own run support. When you're in one of those untouchable grooves, make sure you give in and allow them something to hit.

PITCH TO A CATCHER REGULARLY. Work with your catcher and help him develop a way to frame those borderline pitches.

VISUALIZE THOSE PERFECT PITCHES. Both while practicing and in games, see the ball travel your desired path to its exact location. Whether they are conscious of it or not, all great pitchers visualize positive results.

SHADOW PITCH. This is something that every pitcher can't help but do, so you might as well do it consciously. Rehearse your mechanics in front of a full-length mirror or in front of a camera with a monitor set up for immediate feedback. Be picky; attend to the details of your mechanics with an emphasis on balance, always visualizing the strikezone and that perfect pitch. Anytime you make an alteration, replay it several times until it becomes part of your muscle memory.

THINK POSITIVELY. Don't allow negative or even *what if* scenarios to creep into your thoughts. Baseball games last only a couple of hours. As a pitcher your time under the spotlight will be just a tiny part of your day. Stay on target and stay aggressive, not allowing yourself mental lapses. Anything less than a striving for perfection during the entirety of your brief opportunity is not an unreasonable thing to demand of yourself. Stay tough and when the going gets tough — make a choice and get still tougher.

Finding the right style is about finding what works for you in terms of keeping hitters off balance and guessing. Whether we're talking East/West, North/South, late break or change of speeds, it's all about cutting reaction time and destroying the hitter's timing. There are few, *very few* pitchers who have one unhittable pitch that they can throw every time. In fact, if you could do this, you'd be the first. Hitters only have to be successful three out of every ten at bats (they need to hit the ball well no more than half a dozen times out of every thirty pitches) to ruin your day and your career. Hitters can be choosy; they can make mistakes. Pitchers can't. They have to be as close to perfect as they can with every ball thrown.

If at all possible I would recommend that you try to adapt some sort of North/ South style. Changing the horizontal plane of a swing creates the most problems for the hitter. But if you don't have the kind of fastball that allows you to go upstairs, keep the ball down and find a way to go east to west. Also make sure that you have something in your repertoire that will serve as a change of pace pitch. Above all else, you don't want to give a hitter the opportunity to dial into your pitching speed.

YOUR STYLE WILL PRESENT ITSELF IF YOU BUILD YOURSELF A TOOLBOX THAT ACCOMPLISHES THESE FOUR THINGS:

❑ DO MOST OF YOUR WORK ON THE LOWER PART OF THE PLATE.

❑ THROW SOMETHING THAT WILL KEEP THE HITTER FROM BEING ABLE TO LEAN OVER THE PLATE.

❑ DEVELOP THE CAPACITY TO HIT THE OUTSIDE CORNER.

❑ CHANGE SPEEDS.

Being good at what you do requires that you choose to do what it takes. Nobody can force you to become a great pitcher. Ultimately, motivation has to come from within; and as with anything else, learning how to motivate one's self from within takes practice.

PITCH SEQUENCE & PITCH SELECTION

Pitch selection is a creative endeavor and the more advanced the competition, the more creative and clever the pitcher must become. With the exception of a few precocious youngsters, the only choice of pitches the Little Leaguer has is the four and the two-seam fastball. As he progresses with his control he can experiment with moving the ball in and out, but by and large, he should always be encouraged to stay around the knees.

As a youngster progresses into Babe Ruth, the next step would be to develop a change-up, probably a straight change or a circle change, experimenting with grip and rotation that will give the ball some downward movement. Unless he can throw a four-seamer with significant power, he is best off staying downstairs, perhaps with some east to west movement, but mostly following a theme of low and lower. As the young hurler begins to progress into the high school game, unless he has a topnotch fastball, it should be time for him to develop a good breaking pitch (one that performs as it should at least seventy to eighty percent of the time). Of course the development of any off-speed or breaking pitch should never preempt a continuing effort to improve the fastball, getting more late movement out of it and more velocity.

At the high school level, if the young man has put in his time, he would be able to begin utilizing a North/South style of pitching with an emphasis on the southern end of things. With regard to choice of breaking pitches, I would prefer to see the young man put more effort into the development of a curve rather than a slider for reasons fully discussed in the chapter on breaking pitches.

Once the young man has achieved a fastball with enough velocity and movement. a change-up, and a breaking pitch, it's time for him to start developing what he feels is his most effective utilization of them. This needs to be an individualized process. Ultimately, he will find himself falling into one or more of the twelve aforementioned styles, but getting there should come about through the recognition and development of his own unique set of strengths, and not through any attempt to fulfill the requirements of a particular style.

Making the right pitch choices and putting them together in the most effective sequence requires confidence, courage, intelligence, intuition, and a bit of luck. Some outside considerations must be factored in, especially the habits of the batter. You obviously want to dictate the game from the mound, but no matter what your strength, if a particular batter always looks for a fastball on the first pitch, why throw him one? And of course you have to pay attention to what is and isn't working for you on any given day.

By and large, the good pitcher will follow a sequence that fortifies his particular style of pitching. But what does that mean exactly?

THE MATHEMATICS OF SUCCESSFUL PITCHING

Let's employ a little algebra so that we may recognize all the factors involved in throwing a sequence of pitches.

QUALITY x EXECUTION = EFFECTIVENESS

1. **Quality of Pitches and Quality of Plan**
   Any of the twelve styles or combinations are obviously dependent on having quality pitches and having a quality short and long term plan. A shortage of either plan or pitch can be compensated with a surplus of the other; however, a shortage in the planning department requires an unequal amount of physical pitching talent to compensate.

2. **Execution**
   Potential for execution rarely equals product in any human endeavor. We are not robots when it comes to execution; we are subject to a far greater array of variables than any machine. Execution thus is the sum of many parts positive and/or negative including skill, preparation, effort, desire, and luck. Our capacity for execution is subject to environmental and internal factors at so many more levels than that of any robot — including the emotional and interpersonal.

> Every style is dependent upon at least one of three approaches in keeping batters from making contact.
> ## POWER
> ## MOVEMENT AND LOCATION
> ## CHANGE OF SPEED

Possessing mastery of all three is not necessary. If you've mastered just one, the Hall of Fame is still a possibility if that mastery is of the highest level. Here Nolan Ryan comes to mind. Mastery of two can place you in the class of elite winners. Consider Roger Clemens and Bob Feller(not known for their change-ups) and Greg Maddux (not known for his power). Of course one could argue that throwing a fastball 107 mph like Feller makes that *garden variety* 94 mph pitch something of a change-up.

You can probably name on one hand those pitchers who were true masters of all three. Sandy Koufax probably qualifies as well as anyone. From all accounts Lefty Grove probably made the grade; like Koufax he relied on a great fastballs counterbalanced by a great curve. Pedro Martinez has possibly slipped into that select category thanks to developing a *go to* change-up with movement that complements a tremendous fastball with strikezone action and the kind of control that makes hitters believe his mistakes inside aren't mistakes at all.

CONSIDERATION OF SEQUENCES

A pitcher with conventional pitches such as a fastball, curveball, and change-up could conceivably employ any of the pitch sequences listed below in getting hitters out. Obviously, to effectively employ these sequences requires good control both on the horizontal and the vertical, with the ability to get the first pitch over for a strike We are working with the concept of four-pitch sequences as going any deeper into the count is not to the pitcher's advantage.

THE MOST IMPORTANT PITCH IS ALWAYS STRIKE ONE

SEQUENCE ONE
1. Fastball low
2. Fastball high
3. Fastball out of strikezone
4. Curveball down

SEQUENCE TWO
1. Fastball in
2. Fastball in
3. Fastball up and in
4. Curveball outer part

SEQUENCE THREE
1. Fastball up and in
2. Change-up down
3. Fastball up and in
4. Curveball down

SEQUENCE FOUR
1. Fastball lower outer half
2. Fastball lower outer half
3. Curveball away
4. Fastball up and in

SEQUENCE FIVE
1. Fastball outer half
2. Curveball low and away
3. Fastball in
4. Change-up low and away

SEQUENCE SIX
1. Curveball low
2. Fastball outside
3. Fastball in
4. Change-up low outside

LET'S CONSIDER A FOUR-PITCH SEQUENCE THAT MIGHT BE EMPLOYED ESPECIALLY BY A NORTH/SOUTH STYLIST.

1. Fastball inside on the fists
2. Fastball or drop curve low and outside
3. Out curve away
4. Fastball up and in across the corner

A curveballer with strong control like David Wells, Darryl Kile, Aaron Sele, or Andy Pettitte could utilize the curve on the first pitch to put the batter on *red alert*. If the batter knows right off that he can't afford to lay off the curve, he won't be able to sit on the fastball.

ALTERNATING & REVERSING ROTATIONS

In arriving at a viable and useful style of pitching, particularly one that fits individual specialties, I would encourage utilizing the idea of changing rotations to further confound the hitter's ability to anticipate a pitch. The two-seamer down and four-seamer up could be employed in this scenario. Not only does the batter have to adjust to the up and down element, but also to the variation in rotations and what they will mean in terms of second-stage movement.

A four-pitch scenario might look like this:

1. Four-seam fastball 12/6 rotation (riser)
2. Curveball 6/12 rotation (drop)
3. Two-seam fastball 1/7 rotation (tailer)
4. Curveball 7/1 rotation (outcurve)

Here the batter is forced to consider north and south, and fully alternating rotations. One could also end with: 3. Fastball 2/8 (sinker-tailer) 4. Curveball 8/2 (slurve-slider)

Maintaining a 3/4 or 3/4 plus angle, the North/South style is still in effect with some lateral movement as well.

If the fastball takes on a 9/3 rotation and the curve 3/9 (Frisbee), an east/west approach is more obviously applicable which can be effective but does not create as many variables for the hitter in terms of swing plane.

To force the batter to consider reverses in rotation while coping with changing eye levels (up or down) and late movement in a multitude of directions is ultra-challenging, even to the best of hitters. Add in the factor of changing speeds — the curveball is always 12-15 mph slower than the fastball — and we have a devastating way of attacking hitters.

A FEW SEQUENCES FOR OTHER STYLES

With an East/West Style of pitching, the first time through the order, start with a fastball low inside, and on the second pitch, a slider away. If you can get them called for strikes, you can throw successive sliders or fastballs without the batter being able to sit on either one.

Change of pace pitchers need to take away the rhythm of good hitters by establishing a change-up early on in the sequence of pitches. Once you utilize it as an *out*-pitch, the impact is even greater.

Low-ball pitchers can establish a sequence where successive pitches are thrown lower. Doing this early on can help establish the bottom of the strike-zone which can be subtly expanded downward in the eyes of either the umpire or the hitter. Get one strike called below the knees and the batter will have a tough time laying off anything above the ankles, especially if the pitch has late action downward.

While some of the material in this chapter has a certain level of complexity to it, many of pitching's simplest concepts are its most important.

THROW FEWER PITCHES.   Fewer pitches means more innings thrown. It also probably means less walks and a more aggressive attitude. Strategically, it's best not to give a hitter a look at all your pitches the first or even second time through.

GET THAT FIRST PITCH STRIKE.   This does not mean throwing it down the middle of the plate.

STAY AHEAD IN THE COUNT.   Always be conscious of the count. Recognize that hitters have the highest batting average on a 2-1 count. The hitter is more likely to swing on 2-1, than on 3-1 and we're apt to be less careful than on 3-1 so fearful are we of the 3-1 count.

LOCATION IS THE MOST IMPORTANT QUALITY.   A poor pitch thrown in the correct location can still get a batter out.

THROW STRIKES.   Nobody wins baseball games without throwing strikes. Even when the ball is hit, the average batter will record an out more often than not.

WHO CALLS THE GAME?

A pitcher knows his stuff better than anyone else, and those who are quite cerebral about the process should be allowed to call their own games; however, there has to be strong two-way communication with the catcher. The best pitch is always the one with which the pitcher is comfortable. There are times when a pitcher's lack of faith in one of his pitches is unwarranted. In such a case the veteran catcher may be wise to take control.

It's best if the catcher can actually keep the pitcher from worrying or even thinking about what to throw. Some catchers are quite good at this. A team's ERA can often be lower with one catcher than with another.

The catcher shouldn't call a game that's foreign to his pitcher's style. A North/South style pitcher who uses a breaking pitch to set up his four-seam fastball shouldn't be coerced into a location type approach, or be encouraged to throw everything low.

THERE IS NO ULTIMATE IDEAL STYLE

A good coach will recognize this and not attempt to make clones of his staff. Part of baseball's beauty is the opportunity it provides for individuality to be expressed through athletic endeavor. Being known as a Maddux or Martinez type pitcher is not a bad thing, but ultimately you have to remember that you are not Martinez, Maddux, Johnson or Clemens. You are your own person with your own unique blend of skills, talents and personality. If you do enough right things, your style will find you and allow you to express the best part of who you are though the act of pitching.

Practice

Practice getting good.

Do enough right things and something good happens — one can't help but achieve. You can do everything right and still fail, but it is less likely.

Once you have control of yourself, get a plan.

The beauty of this game is you can get very good at it.

Baseball presents adversity every day.

Success is consistency.

A tremendous work ethic without interference results in success.

There is a time when a thrower becomes a pitcher — I was a thrower for a good part of my pitching existence. Crossing that line when a thrower goes into the hallowed area of pitching probably is at no set time. The magic moment may or may not be noticed.

How good you get is an open-ended issue; however, there may be some limitations as to how far you can go. These limitations should never be self-imposed.

Technique

Most outstanding pitchers have a slow and easy tempo or rhythm, but are explosive into the release area, which is when great arm and wrist speed has to be exerted. The ball will only go as fast as your arm does. This is due to laws of physics. There are no exceptions to the laws of physics.

I believe you can teach a fastball if you put the same attention to it as you would a curveball. Velocity is only half of the equation. Character is the other half. Character is all about imparting rotation. Each pitch you learn will teach you a little more about the pitches you've already learned. A change-up will teach you of the relationship between finger pressure and velocity for your fastball. A curve will teach you the relationship between rotation and movement that is applicable to your fastball and your change-up.

Attitude

Recognize limitations, but don't give into them

The difference between our best game and worst game may not be stuff but mental condition.

Success comes by seeing yourself succeed. It's not an accident.

I'm a positive person now. Wasn't always that way — certainly not when I played pro. So I believe you can certainly develop this.

STOPPING THE HOMERUN BARRAGE!

10

A BRIEF HISTORY

In 1920, popular Cleveland Indian shortstop Ray Chapman was killed with a ball pitched by submariner Carl Mays, and the baseball gods angered by such hubris (what gives these hurlers the right to have a say in matters of life and death?) placed a curse on all pitchers and their descendants from that time forth. They banned dirty balls, introduced the lively ball and the homerun went from being an occasional occurrence to a mainstay of the game. Up until then, a pitcher could coast by on mediocre stuff until men got on base, and then he'd have to bear down. With the advent of the homerun, all pitchers were required to toil without rest, because to get sloppy or lazy, even for a single pitch, could spell doom. Slugging percentages jumped a hundred points. ERA's rose like modern gas prices. The balance between pitchers and hitters shifted dramatically as behemoths like Ruth and Foxx ruled the game as dinosaurs had once ruled the earth.

It took about twenty years to stop the carnage. And the elixir that brought an end to the vengeance of Chapman's ghost was a new variety of pitch. According to Ted Williams, it was the advent of the slider that shifted the balance of power back to the men on the mound. In the decades that followed the age of Ruth, pitchers developed all sorts of nickel curves that came at batters like fastballs, only to break in or out or down, too late for the hitters to make adjustment.

Consequently, for half a century, averages tumbled, run production dropped, and for a while in the late sixties and early seventies, .300 hitters became rarer than honest politicians and anyone who could jack eighteen balls out of the park was a candidate to bat clean-up. To counterbalance the over-dominant pitching, Major League Baseball dropped the height of the mound and continually shrunk the strikezone until it was no bigger than the Cheshire Cat's grin.

Then about ten years ago, whether it be due to smaller parks and livelier balls, to hitters' improved strength training or increased intelligence (if you can call taking thirty years to learn to sit on a slider, intelligent) , the pendulum began to swing back. And now it has swung so far in favor of the hitter, even the mythical records of Ruth have become subject to assault.

Pitchers have tried to stem the tide by employing further descendants of the slider. The last in this long line of souped-up breaking pitches was the splitter, first made popular by reliever Bruce Sutter. The splitter pretty much became the big league pitch of the 90's and it has had its moments. Mastery of that pitch is what allowed Roger Clemens to move back to the head of the class and claim another pair of Cy Young awards. But as good a pitch as the splitter has become, it has still not proven to be a match for the slider-tuned bats of the modern hitter.

I think several factors have contributed to the power surge in Major League hitting. Some strictly reside with the hitter, such as improved strength training and the abandonment of a few Pied Piper theories that had erroneously taken hold. Some are logistical: the advent of smaller parks, a ball that may be wound a little tighter, corked bats. Those factors are beyond our control. But that doesn't mean the modern pitcher has no chance to re-establish dominance from the mound.

I love the beauty and artistry and drama of the 1-0 ballgame. And those rare occurrences when they still happen make me think that it is still quite possible for pitchers to regain control of this game. As a pitching technician who spends his hours trying to make young men into better pitchers, I can't accept the idea of patting some kid on the back and saying ,good enough, when I know that good enough isn't as good as he can be.

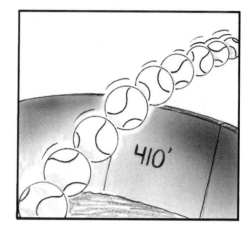

We needn't stand idly by. In fact I feel it is the duty of my coaching brethren and me to develop new ways to befuddle the sluggers and bring a halt to the homerun barrage.

What follows here are four practices that I believe can be utilized to help keep the ball in the park. The first three are fairly obvious and need little explanation. However, the fourth is a different story. we will spend the better of this chapter in consideration of it. There is a fifth. But I'm not even going to give it mention, as I've already beaten that drum a dozen times. Keep the ball ___. . . . I'll let you finish the statement because if you haven't mastered this simple concept yet, than your future as a pitcher is suspect.

FOUR PRACTICES TO CUT HOMERS

1. IMPROVE UPON PITCHING FROM THE STRETCH

Notice here I don't say working from the stretch, but rather pitching from the stretch. Overall pitchers have done a good job of getting the running game back under control and I think that statistics would back me up on this. But in doing a better job of holding runners there has been a tendency to sacrifice the quality of pitches being made to the plate. Too many pitchers are not throwing enough to first — which is still the best way to hold the runner — and are instead often rushing to the plate.

Any pitch that is rushed will end up short on strength and character. Working on one's pick-off moves is important, but pitchers today need to put greater emphasis on learning how to throw from the stretch without an appreciable loss in power or movement.

2. ENCOURAGE STRATEGIES THAT DON'T TAKE ONE SO DEEP IN THE COUNT

Strikeout totals are way up; there's no question about that. But is a strikeout all that superior? Statistically, it has little if any added value over other kinds of outs. It's become the slam dunk of baseball. I think that strikeout to walk ratios tell us an awful lot when it comes to evaluating talent, but give me a pitcher who gets three outs on three pitches any day.

Going deep in the count means that a pitcher will tire quicker; it means that his fielders are more likely to end up sitting on their heels. It also gives the batter too many opportunities. If I can get a fellow to ground-out on a first pitch sinker, it means he still has no clue as to the quality of my four-seamer or my curve the next time through the line-up. If we looked closely at the flow of the game, I would suspect that games now taking three hours have to do mostly with high pitch counts. High pitch counts are not a pitcher's friend. Pitcher's arms do not get stronger as the year goes on. Over the course of a long season, come September it makes a difference whether you've averaged ten or sixteen pitches each inning.

3. AVOID OVERUSE OF THE RADAR GUN

MPH is not an accurate description of a fastball's effectiveness (see the live ball factor at the end of Chapter One). Velocity is just one quality. Greg Maddux's fastball is one of the best in the business, yet in winning four Cy Young awards, he's probably thrown very few that ever broke 90. Getting movement, preferably late movement, is the key to a good fastball, and you haven't been paying attention if you haven't realized by now that the key to getting great movement is great rotation.

4. DEVELOP PITCHES THAT CHALLENGE THE HITTER NORTH AND SOUTH WITH LATE BREAKING ACTION.

As I've already noted, I believe the curveball should have a place in the repertoire of the modern pitcher. I also believe that having some kind of change-up is almost as essential to good pitching as having a fastball.

But ultimately if we are going to turn the tide and tame the modern hitter, we need to think in terms of late-breaking fastballs — particularly the power sinker.

Also included in this category of late-breakers would be the riser and the tailer. The cutter is not of that variety. Although the well thrown cutter does have second stage life — unlike the riser, tailer, and sinker which drop — all of the cutter's action occurs on the horizontal plane. So even if the pitch breaks after the batter makes his swing decision, he still stands a good chance of getting wood on the ball if his timing is right. In fact, when talking about the homerun barrage, we can look at the average garden-variety cutter as one of the primary culprits.

NOT TOO FAST, NOT TOO SLOW

The tailer, the riser, and the sinker when they are working are balls that have a second stage that kicks in as they approach and travel through the strikezone. They essentially do their thing after the hitter's swing decision has been made. When thrown perfectly, these pitches will drop significantly during those last few feet when the ball is too close to track anymore. Contrary to myth and imagination, no hitter sees the bat and the ball meet.

As I explained in a previous chapter, pitches break due to the Magnus Effect where the spinning of the ball creates imbalanced wedges of pressure that cause the ball to veer in one direction or another. However with the Magnus Effect, *more* doesn't necessarily mean better. In fact if a ball is thrown with too great a spin at too high a velocity, the effect will be negated, which is why 98 mph fastballs are usually pretty straight.

Roughly speaking, a pitched ball slows down one mph over every seven feet after it leaves the pitcher's hand. Consequently, what creates the late break is the pitched fastball slowing down just enough to allow itself to be impacted by the Magnus Effect as it comes across the plate. Figuring with what strength and rotation to throw the ball so that it decelerates at that critical instant can only be accomplished through relentless trial and error.

Truth be known, flukes of anatomy may have more to do with it than anything else. Some people are just blessed with the ideal finger length, strength, and curvature to impart the proper force and rotation on the ball. But no matter how fortunate one may be in terms of anatomy, many hours must be spent in the pitching lab to create a late break that is available on demand rather than by accident. On any given day the air temperature, the humidity, the wind, as well as one's flexibility and energy level will have their share of impact on the pitched ball. Therefore, the pitch has to be reset in warming up every single time out. And until such time that we are capable of reproducing this effect with scientific certainty, discovering that ideal convergence of speed and rotation will be an art form that will be utilized by many and mastered by the rare few.

THE RISER

Baseball players are stubborn folk, and even in this age of high-speed photography a ball player is more apt to believe his eyes than the hard results garnered by scientific study. As far as we pitchers are concerned, *that's not such a bad thing.* Many a baseball pitcher has made a living off the batters' willingness to trust their mistaken eyes, and if hitters want to think there is such a thing as a rising fastball, I say, *let 'em believe it . . . .*

Throwing a pitched baseball fast enough to create enough backspin that will allow it to escape from its downward trajectory is possible; it's just not humanly possible; that has been proven beyond any shadow of doubt. Certainly a few pitchers — mostly the legendary one's — have been credited with possessing a rising fastball. Bob Feller is maybe the prime example. Others were Goose Gossage, Sandy Koufax and Jim Palmer. And you'll find no shortage of victimized hitters who come dragging back to the dugout mumbling in colorful terms about some pitcher's capacity to deny gravity its due.

What high speed photography might show is that, although Bob Feller couldn't

I myself would swear I've batted against pitchers whose fast balls hopped right over my bat.

make the ball rise, he could throw it hard enough that it dropped significantly less than the average mortal's fastball. When imparted with extra spin, the ball resists the efforts of gravity, and what the hitter gets is a pitch that doesn't drop as much as anticipated; hence he is apt to swing under it. The so called hop the ball takes is really the difference between programmed expectation and reality — the food-stuff of all optical illusions.

From a vantage point of some sixty feet away, the trajectory of the ball is easy to follow, but when the same thing is happening three feet away, the head and eyes just can't move quick enough to keep up with it.

Think about how slow a car appears to be moving when it's several hundred feet away to how fast it appears when it whizzes by you. In both instances the car may be traveling the same speed, but once it's on top of you it is moving across your field of vision faster than you can track it. Because of this visual limitation, there is always that blind spot as the ball approaches the plate where a hitter's eyes cannot possibly follow the ball. What gives the riser its advantage is that the ball arrives at that blind spot and then travels through it, dropping somewhat less than the hitter has learned to expect through previous experience. Consequently, the hitter swings at an imagined point of impact that may be a good five or six inches too low. It's the mind's eye catching up to reality — not the ball — that does the hopping.

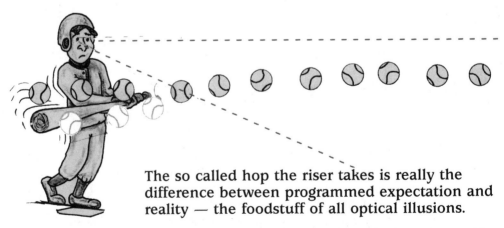

The so called hop the riser takes is really the difference between programmed expectation and reality — the foodstuff of all optical illusions.

Being a North/South pitcher myself — even though I don't think it exists — I love the concept of the riser, and believe that for a select few it is a great pitch. The trouble is that when pitchers buy into the same myth that preoccupies the hitter, they start wasting their time finding a way to doctor a ball to give it that hop. And they might even convince themselves that their four-seam fastball has enough velocity to hop if it is thrown correctly. On the four-seamer your efforts should just be spent on working to increase velocity. Certainly one should attempt to angle the wrist slightly to see what kind of impact it has on the pitch. But by and large, if you want to spend time experimenting with various grips and spins, doing so with the two-seam fastball will probably prove more fruitful.

Dropping down sidearm will not allow you to create an upward trajectory. For starters, due to the height of the mound you'd have to be throwing the ball from just above your shoelaces and you would need to have been born on Krypton to possess the kind of strength such a throw would require. Quite simply too much speed is sacrificed any time that you drop down to create the riser effect. Virtually all risers are thrown from right around the 3/4 + arm angle.

To master the various grips for the four-seam riser, as well as the two-seam tailer, refer to Chapter One.

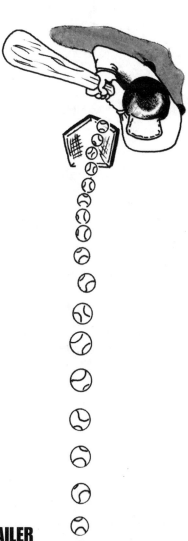

THE TAILER

This is a great pitch when mixed in with a slider or cutter or another high-velocity pitch. The tailer is a late breaking fastball that must be thrown with great velocity. The fingers need to impart a 1/7 to 2/8 rotation to make the ball tail away. And of course, the later the tail, the better.

The ideal fastball would be a tailer thrown with such velocity and late break action that it would seem to hop up like a riser in addition to moving away. If it could be taught with any kind of consistency, and was not dependent on incredible arm speed, every fastballer would be relying on it as his bread and butter. Some rare few can get a little tailing action with their four-seamer; however for the rest of us, gripping the ball across two seams is the best place to start. Pronating the wrist slightly may also help, as will putting a little extra pressure on the inside of the ball.

TRAJECTORY OF THE TAILER
(righthand pitcher to righthand batter)

THE POWER SINKER

The power sinker is a pitch that can blur the distinction between a fastball and a curve. Aerodynamically, it travels like a breaking pitch, with a 2/8 to 3/9 rotation. However, it is thrown hard with fastball arm action. Because of the sharp downward action of the ball, hitters will typically hit on the top of the ball and drive it into the ground. When it's working, a sinker is extremely difficult to hit out of the park, although one should never forget that some hitters can hit anything long. Groundballs are usually the result of a great power sinker, or in the case of a Kevin Brown, who has such good velocity and movement, groundballs and strikeouts.

Darren Driefort is another pitcher with a good power sinker. But at present they are a rare breed. The kind of good power sinker that breaks bats and results in groundballs must be thrown in the nineties, but if one throws it too hard then it will start to flatten out. Chad Paronto of the Orioles, pictured throughout this book, has a bat-breaking type of fastball which indicates sinking action.

It is quite possible to have two types of sinkers: 1) Slow sinker — which breaks perhaps more in amount and more consistently in frequency. 2) Hard sinker — which bites hard and down when thrown properly, but doesn't always break as much as its slower cousin.

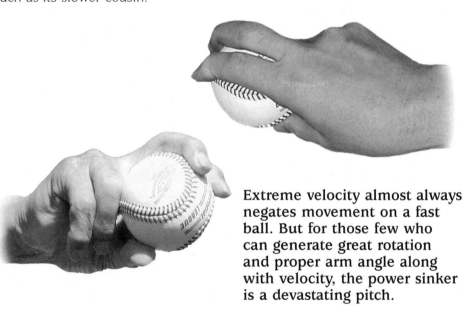

Extreme velocity almost always negates movement on a fast ball. But for those few who can generate great rotation and proper arm angle along with velocity, the power sinker is a devastating pitch.

The index finger should come down on the inside of the ball on a sinker. The wrist pronates with the thumb turning to right (rhp). Good hand-speed creates fast rotation and this gives character and sharpness to the pitch. However, slower velocity will usually allow for a greater downward break. Therefore, a sinker comes in many different shades. Some pitchers will employ a slow sinker as their change-up. Many pitchers can create a sinker type action by using the circle change grip and throwing the ball low.

In the near future we'll probably begin to see more relief specialists employing the power sinker. There is no better pitch to throw when a groundball is needed and a homerun would prove the ultimate disaster, providing of course that the pitcher has enough mastery to keep it out of the dirt. If I had a big hard throwing pitcher in the pen who needed another pitch to compliment his four-seam fastball and hard breaking pitch — be it a cutter or a slider — I would encourage him to develop the power sinker.

No one pitch is going to tame the homerun barrage; however, the good power sinker is the hardest pitch to take deep, so we can probably expect to see more and more pitchers coming to rely upon it.

One other point to keep in mind is that the sinkerball pitcher must be an adept fielder as when the pitch is working to perfection, ground balls are the most typical product and often that means a hard chopper back to the mound.

IT'S US OR THEM

We should be heartened by the fact that some of the most dominating pitchers in the history of the game are at work today. Martinez and Maddux stack up well against anyone who has ever taken the mound. And a pitcher like Brown seems to flirt with perfection at least every other time out. Those three mentioned all have very different approaches. Martinez has his pinpoint fastball with a change-up that utterly destroys a hitter's timing. Maddux does it with late break action in the strikezone. And Brown throws as effective a power sinker as the game has ever seen. The one thing they have in common is that they all keep the ball low.

The newly increased strikezone is something of a tease in that not many pitchers have the kind of mustard that allows them to go after those high strikes. The enlarged zone may help bring back the curveball as those umpires who gauge a strike by how the ball enters might give the curveballer a few more strikes. But if the Major Leagues really wanted to crimp the power hitters, they would have stretched the strikezone at the bottom rather than the top.

The implied message here is that if pitchers want to get control of the game then they have to take it upon themselves to do so. Baseball, like life, is all about adjusting to change. Those who adjust survive; the rest go extinct.

Challenging bat speed is no longer a meaningful exercise. Bat speed has improved so dramatically, that the best way to get an edge on today's hitter is to make him aware that he may be called upon to change his bat angle in the very last instant. Mixing in good off-speed stuff — in particular, a good change-up — will make him even more susceptible to late breaking fastballs. Then add in a good breaking pitch which forces him to swing early. Accomplish this and you will hear hitters pining for the good old days when the slider ruled.

Coaching **TIP** The best way to develop a positive outlook is to work hard at your craft. Success will never be a permanent thing unless you believe in your own mind that you deserve it.

MENTAL TOUGHNESS

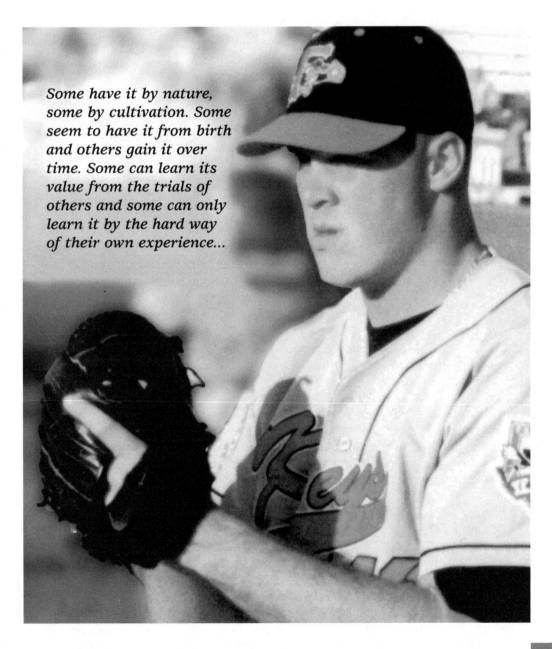

Some have it by nature, some by cultivation. Some seem to have it from birth and others gain it over time. Some can learn its value from the trials of others and some can only learn it by the hard way of their own experience...

Certainly a lot of the game of baseball is about physical talent and much of what occurs on the diamond is accomplished by reflex. But physical talent by itself is a very poor predictor of success in the game of baseball. We all know what Yogi Berra meant when he said *fifty percent of the game of baseball is ninety percent mental.* I would amend it to say that ninety percent of the time, a hundred percent of the brain is required to lift ones game from potential into purpose. This I feel is especially true of pitchers.

You can never place too much value on the mental aspects of pitching, the most important of which is mental toughness. All great and good pitchers possess merit badges in mental toughness. Mental toughness is a many-colored, multi-faceted phenomenon that defies precise description. But, we can invariably recognize it when we see it in action. We can invoke a hundred different terms: *operating under pressure, finishing off, overcoming adversity.* We can call it *discipline, concentration, poise, self-confidence, or dedication* — and still we are left short of a complete understanding.

Setting goals and adhering to a regimen of accomplishing those goals surely exhibits a long-range utilitarian version of mental toughness. And battling a tough hitter, pitch by pitch, represents the kind of gritty *in your face* toughness that lives in the *here and now.* Both types of mental toughness are of value and they need to be adequately addressed, as today more than ever it seems that many good prospects fall to the wayside because that toughness necessary to maneuver the difficult turns is missing from their portfolio.

> Though mental toughness is something that can't be taught, **it can still be learned.**

I've seen too many kids *grow into toughness* to say that lack of it is reason for disqualification when evaluating young pitchers. Many pitchers without the obvious characteristic of mental toughness can be encouraged to develop this important yet elusive quality. And in ones growth as a pitcher, it should be given as much daily attention as one gives to control and velocity.

Lapses in mental toughness have certainly cost this author games in the ninth and tenth inning. These games were often pitched extremely well, but were not ended well. One could certainly come to the defense of a pitcher like me who might pitch a great eight-inning game, only to come up a little short in the ninth.

Certainly, it is very true that the hitter's bat speed does not diminish in late innings the way that a pitcher's arm speed and velocity will. But though it may seem like toughness to keep coming right at the hitters the same as you did in the first and the fourth and even the seventh — that's not toughness at all, but rather resignation by stubbornness.

SELF-DELUSION IS NOT TOUGHNESS

A pitcher must recognize when his pitch is no longer lively enough to dance unscathed across the heart of the plate, and then he must adjust. Toughness in such an instance is seeing that *drop in velocity* as a hindrance to get over, rather than something to ignore.

Failure is a great teacher as long as you don't become absorbed in it or identify with it. The idea of learning from ones mistakes is not just a consolation prize; it's essential to a pitcher's growth. One must evaluate performance regardless of the results, not giving luck — good or bad — too much credit.

> No matter how tough you are, you will **still experience failure.**

THE NEGATIVE MONKEY ISN'T PICKY —
He'll climb up on anyone's back!

A favorite pet of people who are afraid of accomplishment, the negative monkey is an opportunist, a malingerer, a sneak, and a crook. You can't always tell he is there. Sometimes the monkey will even convince you that his is the voice of objective reason. He has a habit of deceiving people about his intentions, but be assured that he never means well. Other times he's not so subtle, but heavy-handed, maudlin, and dominating with his bleakness. But always he is useless.

WHENEVER YOU ARE ABLE TO DUMP
THIS GUY, GOOD THINGS HAPPEN.

Despite his assertions to the contrary, this monkey is just extra baggage. He serves no purpose. The earlier this guy is shown the highway, the quicker you can get on with taking charge of your destiny and directing it toward the positive. Only by eschewing this intrusive freeloader will you be prepared to be serious in your efforts to succeed. But watch out! — just give him a little room and he'll dirty everything with doubt, even the value of your accomplishments.

He is encouraged to come forth if we hesitate when faced with the prospect of commitment, success, or responsibility. But even without encouragement, he'll find his way. No one is immune to his visits; in fact his visits are quite inevitable and if you're foolish enough to let down your guard, he'll jump right on you at the peak of your hubris.

Just wish him away and he'll go! The trick is to keep him from coming back, because you can never insult him enough to keep him away for good. Undeterred, he waits, always ready to second any negative thoughts that pop into your head.

It's amazing how easy it is to get rid of the monkey.

The secret then to disarming him is to never allow negative thoughts to go unchecked. That's a tall order, but recognize this: It's a choice.

If one is fully committed to a purpose the choice then is simple. You do what you have to do. You starve him out and he'll give you some space, but continue to give him tidbits and he'll squat right down on the rubber with you, licking his fingers while filling your head with hearsay.

Not allowing the monkey to have his way is the essence of mental toughness. And so if we wish to acquire this toughness, we must make this banishing of the monkey a continuous relentless practice. This can be done with mental composure, the expression of confidence, attendance to details, and unwavering concentration, all of which we'll now address.

KEEPING YOUR COMPOSURE

Whenever we lose our composure, we are most susceptible to negative thoughts. Pressure that builds to too great a level is what causes us to lose composure. When, and if, you eventually figure out human nature, you will realize that pressure can only come from within.

Some people never give themselves a break. They internalize any hint of pressure and live in a constant state of tension. When we look at such a person, it is easy to say, "Hey, why are you putting so much pressure on yourself?" The funny thing is that in observing other people, we know full well that their taking on all that pressure is a choice. Yet, we have so much difficulty in recognizing that any pressure we put on ourselves is also a choice. We can be much more in control than we think; we just have to exercise that control, which of course isn't an easy task if it's not part of our conditioned habit. Like anything else, defusing pressure starts with recognition and gets easier with practice.

In baseball to eliminate pressure one has the very easy solution of saying, "It's just a game; win or lose no one dies." And that is absolutely correct. But even if the game is not a mortal struggle, it will have powerful impact on our psyche; it *will* mean a difference about who we are in this world. The game can give us a healthy sense of identity when we are successful. But when we get shellacked seven or eight outings in a row, it's pretty hard to make the assertion *I am a baseball pitcher.*

And when that doubt occurs, the negative monkey — always ready to assure us that the worst part of who we are is all of who we are — jumps in and says *you're not just a pitcher; you're a losing pitcher.* Such thoughts can ease the pressure but entertaining the negative when things go awry is the sort of pure self-indulgence that will compound your problems beyond repair.

You must believe things will improve before they will. Keep telling yourself things will improve and though you may not believe it at first, with enough repetition your resolve *will* become stronger.

CONFIDENCE IS EVERYTHING

When a pitcher knows that no one in the world is more qualified than he to take care of the job at hand, when he knows it and believes it, the feeling that is experienced is one of the strongest that can run through a human body. This is confidence at its peak, the kind of confidence that one can see, feel, even smell; it is unassailable, beyond the reach of negativism, doubt and even misfortune.

You can be a four foot Little Leaguer and still be standing tall. And a pitcher who stands tall is a glorious sight. When any big leaguer reaches this state, if you could eavesdrop on his self-talk, you will hear the phrase, "I trust myself." You will hear him say, "This batter can be mine, this inning can be mine, this game will be mine." And when misfortune occurs, you will hear him say things like, "It's really no matter. See the target, hit the target, one pitch at a time."

Such a pitcher is usually one who has paid his dues one pitch at a time, one who knows what he has, and knows what it takes, and sees no discrepancy between the two. For him dealing with adversity is *old hat*.

RELENTLESS CONCENTRATION

Being mentally tough in baseball terms means being consistently present. The tide can change rather quickly on a pitcher; it can grow suddenly wild when there's not a storm cloud in sight. The masterpiece that disintegrates into a heartbreaking loss has been experienced by many; it surely has left me with some unpleasant mementos. Just the shortest lapse in concentration can result in that one bad inning that ruins an otherwise great game.

Some pitchers seem to have a habit of pitching just good enough to lose. They will be cruising through a game, all is under control, then suddenly an error occurs. And the error is followed by a walk . . . and then that one bad pitch to the wrong hitter and it's all over. Chances are that the pitcher walked the batter because his mind was still on the error, and then with the greater part of his concentration preoccupied with the potential of disaster, the lazy fastball, or the curve without a break leaves his fingertips, and then the proverbial horse is out of the barn.

Staying in charge is definitely an art, but it is quite manageable, providing one is ready to focus fully on the task at hand, which is always the next pitch. It's the only thing that can matter.

Listed below are some ways in which a pitcher can develop a strong capacity for staying present — but remember it's all for naught if you don't want it bad enough.

CONCENTRATE ON EXECUTION Once the pitcher becomes set on the rubber and takes the signal, his concern should be with the execution of the pitch, rather than the result. For this, one must have practiced enough to know that good technique will bring about a good result.

VISUALIZE Lay out a blueprint for your body to follow before you begin your windup, by actively visualizing not just the result, but your most perfect delivery.

FIND YOUR RHYTHM Staying with it makes concentration far easier.

GET INTO THE RIGHT MIND-SET Doubt can be a horrible burden on concentration. Even if you've done the work to get yourself ready, confidence isn't going to happen until you assert it. Exclaiming your confidence to yourself is the first step to projecting it.

MAKE PRACTICE TIME QUALITY TIME It's awfully tough to maintain two sets of habits. If you don't concentrate when you practice, it won't be possible to do so in a game. Take attendance now and again during practice and make sure that you're really present. Attentiveness needs to be part of your routine.

SIMULATE GAME SITUATIONS Practice in dealing with adversity should be a prime directive. Whether you're shadow-pitching or going through *dry* mechanics, or whenever throwing to a catcher, create hypothetical game experiences. By the time you get into a game, you should have already attended to a thousand and one full count situations and know just what you can do.

BE A STICKLER FOR DETAIL Great players are detail oriented and they realize success is dependent on repetition with concentration. They leave as little to chance as possible. Your instincts will sound an alarm to tip you off when your delivery is going awry. Listen to that alarm and scrutinize. Never forget the seven for one rule. When you change your stride by an inch, or somehow else alter your release by an inch, the difference at the plate will be magnified by seven inches. In other words, release the pitch one inch too high and that pitch over the knees will suddenly become a waist high watermelon.

IT'S A CHOICE

As you must have surmised by now, being mentally tough is all about making good choices. Whatever percentage you want to apply, the fact is as Mr. Berra more or less said, in the game of baseball, it's the use of the brain that separates winners from losers. Throwing is a physical act, but pitching is mental and the game will always belong at any level to those who not only understand this, but also practice and project it on a daily basis.

TRAINING & CONDITIONING

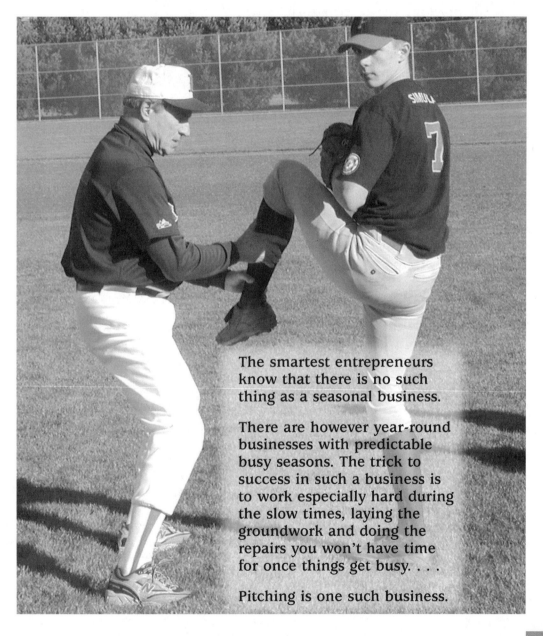

The smartest entrepreneurs know that there is no such thing as a seasonal business.

There are however year-round businesses with predictable busy seasons. The trick to success in such a business is to work especially hard during the slow times, laying the groundwork and doing the repairs you won't have time for once things get busy. . . .

Pitching is one such business.

12

Over the course of a year, dozens of people will pull me off to the side and ask me in a hushed voice, "What's the best way to become good at pitching?" — as if there is some secret that I am holding back from them as I coach or conduct seminars. High school kids ask me how they can become flame-throwers; parents of Little Leaguers ask me how they can turn their kids into aces; and college players asked me how they can develop the *right stuff* to make themselves ready for the pros. To me the answer is obvious and hardly a secret:

"YOU GET GOOD AT PITCHING BY THROWING BASEBALLS!" It's that simple.

"Yes but," the questioner will go on to say, "How do you *really* get good at pitching?" And again to their dismay, I repeat myself, "You get good by throwing baseballs, lots of baseballs."

No matter how many times they ask, that's the only answer they are going to hear from me. There are lots of good ways to develop one's body, but ultimately if you want to be a good pitcher, then you better plan on throwing a lot of baseballs. . . and not just three months a year, but all year! Because no matter how much rope jumping, running, or weightlifting you do, no matter how many protein shakes, and colloidal minerals you take, you are only going to get good if you throw a lot of baseballs.

Certainly, being fit improves one's performance in any sport. I don't disagree with that, but what I do disagree with is the notion that athletic shortcuts exist and that there are ways to get good at pitching that don't involve throwing baseballs twelve months a year, every year. If you can't commit to doing just that, you will never realize your full potential as a pitcher.

Many well-intentioned people will argue that throwing year-round will cause injury or wear out one's arm. To my mind there is a lot more proof that arm injuries more often come from throwing too little, rather than from throwing too much. People support the notion that *less is better* by pointing to the fact that big league pitchers are more effective on four days rest rather than three, and by pointing out that the typical Major Leaguer loses velocity off his fastball as the season wears into September. And they will also point to a phenom like the Cub's Kerry Wood whose career was said to have been jeopardized by high pitch counts.

I agree that pitchers can wear down. Major League pitchers today have to throw harder and more carefully to keep apace with ever-improving hitters and consequently, they do need more rest. Managers — with their jobs always on the line — tend to think in terms of short term results rather than long term consequences, and so will go with that strong young pitcher until he runs out of gas. In one organization I played for, they would have you throw batting practice the day after a start and *that* I agree that is detrimental. But to my mind, the arguments in favor of regular throwing shouldn't be negated by individual acts of foolishness.

The most successful pitching staff in baseball — the Atlanta Braves — believes their success is based on their between-game throwing program. And consider the incredible influx of terrific Latin American pitchers who come from areas where competitive baseball is played year-round. I think any study would prove that the Latinos have stronger arms; that despite being typically smaller than their US counterparts, they throw harder and with less incidence of injury.

Olympic skaters don't take summers off because skating is a winter sport. Swimmers don't take off the winter because they're involved in a summer sport. Not the ones that are the world's best.

> *Again, let me repeat:*
> **Injured arms** don't usually come from throwing too much; in fact more often they come from **throwing too little.**

With questionable inning limitations, and rules against off-season training, in our effort to help protect young throwers, we may well be setting them up for injury and impeding their effort to achieve excellence. When a Little Leaguer or high-schooler develops a sore arm early in the season, usually the culprits are under-developed mechanics and unconditioned arms. More than likely most of those kids hurting themselves are the ones who pick up the ball a few weeks — if that — before the season begins.

Certainly, one can overthrow and overtrain if one chooses to be thick-headed about it. I agree that kids should have the chance to be exposed to many different sports and that great care needs to be taken so as not to stress their still-forming bones and tendons. But in order to pitch well, it's important to have a strong arm and, there is no exercise that simulates throwing a baseball better than throwing a baseball.

Up where I come from in New Hampshire, God's country, you have to possess an awful lot of baseball spirit to excel at this sport. The season often opens with ice and snow encroaching on the field. If you don't have the stamina to play in the cold rains of late spring, if you can't stand mosquitoes and can't stomach a game in 95 degree sunshine followed by a night game played in finger numbing coolness, you won't be able to play North Country ball. New Hampshire produces tough ballplayers, but it doesn't produce many. You have to want it bad enough to shovel out out the driveway in spring or find a warm enough barn, as well as a friend or brother or father who knows how to catch.

Kids should start out playing a wide variety of sports, but when they decide they want to pursue baseball with seriousness, especially pitching, they need to begin training those arms year-round. But please make sure that you understand we're not talking about overtraining. Throwing until it hurts, throwing through pain, throwing with mindless tedium is overtraining.

PART I

FIT TO PLAY

When you step onto that mound for the opening of the season, you should feel like you're in great shape. I know that the best games I ever pitched were when I happened to be in the best shape of my life. Confidence and poise increase with conditioning and proper training. Success and excellence follow right behind.

If you are going to pursue the business of pitching, if you are going to give yourself a fair chance, you owe it to yourself to pursue a fitness regimen that involves a year-round commitment.

Being in great condition seems to strengthen every aspect of one's game, including confidence, stamina and the kick needed for a late inning finish. It's hard to be in great condition all the time, but it should be the basic goal of all serious pitchers.

There are many legitimate conditioning methods available and most of them are acceptable, providing they recognize aerobic fitness, muscular strength, flexibility and specific skill training as the primary building blocks necessary to the development and continuation of high level pitching efficiency and performance.

There is a significant, very self-evident difference between good and great condition. You'll know it if you get there.

My personal preference has always been to build stamina and endurance through regular running. Besides good shoes, no special equipment is required and progress is easily measured. One can set time and distance goals and gradually work up to them.

Don't aggressively stretch the muscles prior to running. Loosen and lubricate the joints first with rotational stretches (arm circles, knee circles, hip circles, etc.) and as you start out, gradually increase your pace from a brisk walk into a trot. Throw in some occasional sprints once you've achieved a good pace. Always stay light on your feet, and when possible run on softer surfaces to avoid pounding the knees.

One good way to build a running program is to allow yourself a half hour, alternating walking and running, gradually building yourself up over the course of a few weeks until you can run for the whole half hour and then gradually work it up to forty-five minutes or so. During off-season, the goal should be to run at least every other day. Everyday running won't hurt you providing your joints are strong and you don't run a marathon every time out. During the season get in at least one running session between starts. Two would be better.

What a gift it is to have a training partner who shares your love for the game. Someone whom you can experiment with, someone to push you a little harder and a little further, someone who will also be there to pick you up when you're feeling down on yourself.

Running isn't the only way to build endurance. Stationary bike work is another equally good way, especially when weather prevents outdoor work or when one is recovering from an injury where the jarring motion of running would prove counterproductive.

Swimming when done in a consistent measured fashion will also build endurance, but one should give consideration to not overbuilding muscles that may impede arm velocity. I would caution against swimming during the season and especially before a start. The muscles of the arm go through enough tearing down and rebuilding cycles over the course of a season.

Pools aren't just for swimming. Pools provide an opportunity for gravity-free exercise, which can be ideal for injury recovery and for those with bad backs or joints that need exercise. Working in a pool can be just the thing for post-operative physical therapy. Aerobic routines can provide variety to a workout, but you should approach any group program with caution as peer pressure might encourage you to push your joints beyond personal limits.

Tai-chi, karate, and yoga programs when taught by qualified instructors can help develop muscle tone, flexibility, and breath control as well as mind control, but you should

probably avoid postures that put too much stress on the joints. Also avoid martial arts programs where contact and groundwork is emphasized.

Martial Arts programs can provide the answer. Youngsters who start in the martial arts early will develop their coordination and reflexes more quickly, as well as the poise and confidence necessary for competition. Countless Japanese ballplayers practice the martial arts, and it is now becoming more popular with American ballplayers. Having the confidence to defend yourself will also make you less apt to be intimidated by batters, especially those who take exception to inside pitching.

Aerobic routines can provide variety to a workout, but you should approach any group program with caution as peer pressure might encourage you to push your joints beyond personal limits.

WIND SPRINTS

If you can motivate yourself to do wind sprints (affectionately known as suicides) on your own, give yourself a pat on the back for having great self-discipline. In training camps, nothing elicits bigger groans than ending a training session with wind sprints. Wind sprints should be something the pitcher is religious about, and when executing them, he should constantly push himself to the max. They will teach the mind and body to bring forth those explosive emissions of energy critical to any athletic endeavor. By doing them at the end of a training session, you will teach yourself to call on those reserves of energy so essential for success at the end of a long game when the body feels like it has nothing left to give.

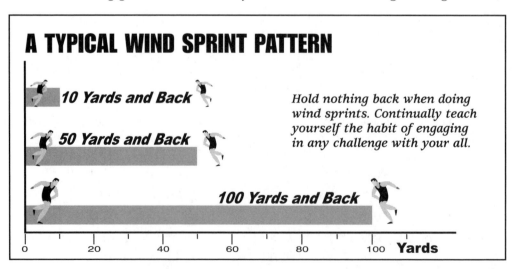

A TYPICAL WIND SPRINT PATTERN

10 Yards and Back

50 Yards and Back

100 Yards and Back

Hold nothing back when doing wind sprints. Continually teach yourself the habit of engaging in any challenge with your all.

0   20   40   60   80   100   **Yards**

STRETCHING

Stretching is best done after the body is warmed-up and should become a habitual part of any cool-down period after intensive exercise. Flexibility will improve one's range of motion and will make the joints more fluid and the muscles longer and suppler. The limits of flexibility are genetically determined, but anyone can improve his stretch. The more flexible you are, the less resistance your own body will provide to the act of pitching. It's wasteful to have to use your strength to overcome the limits of your flexibility.

Ballistic, bouncing, forced stretching should be avoided as a rule. Stretching should be individualized, and when stretching, the goal should be to gradually increase one's limitations by pushing the body just slightly beyond its comfort zone. Don't shortchange this important component of training. One can work on stretching while watching television or in-between activities, but always be sure to listen to your muscles so as to avoid injury. Breathe into your stretch and focus on relaxing the muscles.

During sleep, our bodies are incredibly flexible, so think in terms of relaxing. Stretching when you are all wound up about some problem will probably be counterproductive. A good stretching routine after a hard workout should leave you feeling loose and just about ready for bed.

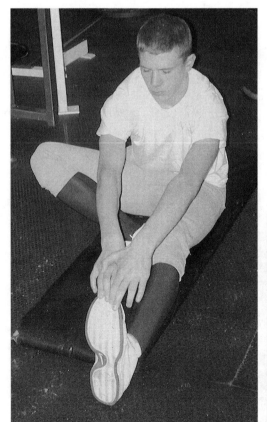

In just about every stretching routine, be conscious of keeping your lower back straight, especially when doing leg stretches. Whenever possible, always attempt to keep the crown of the head aligned with the butt. When performing the leg stretch, pull forward as well as down so that ideally you end up with your forearms on the ground.

IDEAL LEG STRETCH

You can gain a little extra stretch in your thighs (improving your leg kick) by trying to squeeze the knees back together for about three seconds while you keep them propped open and offer resistance with the elbows, or by having another person pressing the thighs open with his or her hands. When relaxing you should find that you gained a little extra stretch. Limit this exercise to a few reps; don't overdo.

Stretching involves tearing the microfibers of the muscle tissue so they can grow back more elastic and longer. This does not mean that you should feel your body tearing apart as you stretch. Work gradually, without hurry.

Some folks get right into stretching the first thing. I would rather see pitchers do some shoulder, wrist, and hip rotations and then warm up by throwing very lightly. Just ten feet or so for the first few tosses and then stepping back a pace with every other throw.

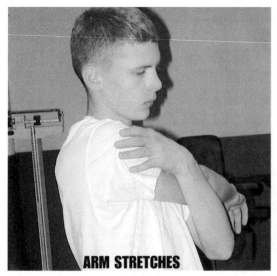

ARM STRETCHES

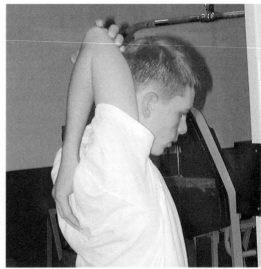

After the muscles are warmed, I would then engage in the stretches shown above and right before doing any purposeful pitching. With all stretching, go slow and be thorough. Hold each position for at least three breaths, extending the stretch on the out-breath.

WRIST STRETCH

It's also a pretty good idea to start with some Wrist Drills before throwing, especially early in the season to get the wrist fully involved and to remind the hand to emphasize rotation.

WRIST DRILL

CROSS-TRAINING

Playing other sports is a good way to stay in shape during the off-season. However, if baseball is your main thing, you want to be careful not to do anything that will interfere with your ability to pitch, such as building up bulky muscles.

Multi-sport athletes are often surprised to discover how sore they get after the first day of training camp, thinking that they are in great shape. While the aerobic conditioning does carryover, most sports are very muscle specific. Playing basketball will not keep you from getting sore when you pick up the ball to pitch again. If baseball is important to you, no matter how many sports you play, you must have a year-round regimen that targets baseball skills.

> It's important to not delude yourself into thinking that just because you're in basketball or soccer shape, that you're in baseball shape.

STRENGTH TRAINING

If you intend to get heavily involved with weight training, then you need to actively study this intricate art and seek out the guidance of a competent strength coach. It would take another entire book to cover all the do's and don'ts of lifting. These next few pages are intended only as an overview. For some recommended reading material on strength training, see the end of this book for some suggested titles. But be advised: no amount of reading can replace the value of a personalized and skillful strength coach.

THE DANGERS OF WEIGHTLIFTING FOR A PITCHER ARE SO SERIOUS THAT YOU SHOULDN'T EVEN THINK ABOUT ENTERING THE WEIGHT ROOM IF YOU DON'T HAVE YOUR PRIORITIES STRAIGHT.

Weightlifting can present two career-ending problems for potential pitchers: injury and improper muscle balance. Both of these are almost always caused by mental laziness and/or by losing sight of your goals. It is too easy for a young man to look at every weightlifting session as a contest rather than as a training. One must always be conscious of this trap. When large muscles and the capacity to push large numbers of plates become the goals, the would-be pitcher is headed for a world of trouble. As a rule, good baseball pitchers do not have massively muscular upper bodies. They will not win bench press contests, nor will they ever compete for Mr. Olympia.

While the science of weightlifting has improved, it is still a very tricky business to develop pitching strength through lifting. The specific synchronicity of firing muscles that is needed for pitching can be enhanced but not fully replicated by pushing iron. By over-lifting, you could end up slowing your arm through the development of muscle firing patterns that are counterproductive to pitching. And just because your muscles are strong enough to push huge weights doesn't necessarily mean that your joints are strong or stable enough to handle the workload. Also, watch that you don't hyperextend — the elbows are especially susceptible to such. Once developed, joint problems rarely go away. Whenever a joint is injured, arthritis moves in. Immediately stop lifting at the first sign of joint pain. If you're presently having joint pain talk to your doctor about utilizing glucosamine-chondroiton which can help lubricate and rebuild aggravated joints.

Hopefully the above paragraphs have encourage mindfulness while lifting, as my intention is not to discourage you from entering the weight room. Weight training can be an incredibly valuable adjunct to training.

Toning and working specific muscles is the key to lifting. Through lifting one can develop arm and upper body strength that will help stabilize the joints and thus reduce injuries. Weightlifting can be especially useful in the development of muscles necessary for deceleration of the arm, thus improving mechanics and also helping to avoid injuries. Lifting is also a good way to keep tone and to rehab when an injury curtails your ability to pitch.

We've all heard stories of the petite mom who lifted a car off of her trapped child. Such an action is possible and what it points out to us is that each of us already possesses enough muscle mass to perform just about any Herculean task. The real trick is sending the message to those muscles to do the work. That's all about developing the neural system to fire the right muscles in the right order. This is partially a function of adrenaline, but mostly a function of mind. That's why all lifting must be done with extreme mental focus, willing the muscles to fire.

When lifting, one should remember that in the development of strength, muscles are only a part of the story.

When we see a pitcher who is especially strong and has good mechanics but lacks good arm speed, a stodgy neural system is most likely the weak link. Lifting more and lifting heavier won't accomplish anything in this case. Instead one should focus on improving mind to muscle communication. This can be accomplished in a diverse amount of ways, all geared towards reducing reaction time and improving the muscles' burst capacity. Long toss and use of the weighted baseball both talked about in this chapter can be utilized to enhance arm speed. With long toss make every effort to throw line-drives with a little bit of juice on the ball. With the weighted ball, make the snap of your wrist as quick and crisp as possible. Starting on the following page are few other less traditional methods for improving arm speed.

WORK A SPEED BAG

As a group, no athletes possess faster arm and hand speed than do boxers. For developing lightening quickness, the speed bag continues to be the tried and true tool of preference. Work the bag at three to five minute intervals, making your punches come in flurries. Keep the arms loose and the shoulders down. The object isn't to knock the bag off its swivel, but to work a steady rhythm gradually picking up speed. Wear light gloves to protect against bruising and cuts. A variation on the speed bag is the double-ended ball. This inflated leather encased ball has an elastic cord attached to top and bottom, so that it can be suspended between ceiling and floor. The idea with the double-ended ball is to keep moving closer and closer so that you end up striking the ball before it can fully rebound back. A word of caution: while the double-ended ball can be a lot of fun, if you get lackadaisical it will reward you with a smack in the nose.

READY, FIRE DRILL

This drill can be done with the elastic tubing talked about later in this section. Bring your arm up into the pre-launch position and hold. Have a partner say, "Ready, fire!". On the command of *ready*, pull the ball forward, so that the cord has no slack in it. On the word *fire* explode the arm forward. Keeping the cord tense at the start will encourage you to explode forward without any movement backwards (double-clutching) which would be indicated by the cord's going slack. Even a slight double-clutch in the launch position will rob you of tremendous energy. When batters double-clutch, they refer to it as having a hitch in their swing. But whereas a batter can compensate with timing, for pitchers there is no compensation. Once a pitcher double-clutches and breaks his flow, he's forfeited all the stored energy that his motion has collected to that point.

DEVELOP YOUR OWN REFLEX DRILLS

You can come up with hundreds of them. If you happen to have a biofeedback machine kicking around that's the best tool for teaching the brain to trigger muscles. Ultimately you will find more and more of them being used in sports training. But until they start making those units available at WalMart, you'll need to utilize some more old-fashioned training that will encourage reflexes both specific to throwing and non-specific as well. In hammering a nail or shooting a basketball, explode through the movement, going from stillness to full throttle. When employing the Stride Drill talked about in the next chapter, practice going from the high-cock through the release with explosive movement.

UNDERLOAD TRAINING

This is one of the newer concepts being bandied about. The idea is that when throwing a ball or swinging a bat, one would use a lighter ball or bat than typically employed which will allow one's movement to be quicker. By practicing a quicker movement, the athlete will train the neural and muscular system to accomplish the task with greater acceleration. The quicker movement will consequently become embedded as muscle memory, so that when the regular ball or bat is used, the motion will end up being just as quick as when using the lighter equipment. And while the theory makes some sense, school is still out on whether underload works with as complicated an action as pitching. Shadow pitching could be considered a form of underload training. When shadow pitching, if one is as true as possible to one's mechanics, I see no harm in practicing full acceleration now and again.

Lifting more weights is not necessarily going to improve mind-muscle communication. Improvement can only happen if you are willing to work your mind along with your muscles.

Approach the weight room with the same focus and purpose with which you should be approaching the mound. So many people just drop their bodies off in the weight room. Then their minds go off elsewhere until the body's all done. When you hit the weight room, put all your focus into learning how to best communicate with your muscles. Focus on contracting and controlling the muscles with every rep. Be conscious of you breath. Be so attuned that you know when the muscle has hit its limit. Learn to use your mind to supply the muscle with extra energy. Such a skill will stand you well in the later innings of a close game.

WORKING THE ARMS & SHOULDERS

When working the arms and shoulders, stay away from heavy weights. Work to increase your number of reps, rather than poundage. You're best off using dumbbells as opposed to a straight bar so that one side isn't allowed to cheat and you can mentally focus on one set of muscles at a time. Do exercises that are muscle specific. Maximize the range of motion with full extension and contraction.

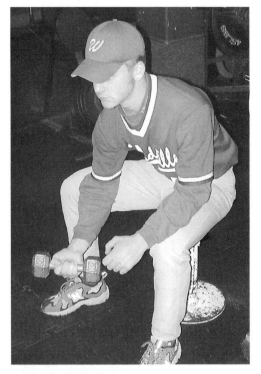

Weight training shouldn't really start until the pitcher is at least thirteen years of age. The old adage of *start lifting when you're old enough to shave* is still a pretty good one. And then start off slow and get some good guidance.

BICEPS CURLS Focus on one arm at a time. Don't swing the weights. Utilize a full range of motion, from full extension to complete contraction.

WRIST CURLS Keep the movement slow and smooth.

TRICEPS (FRENCH) CURLS Keep the upper arms parallel to the head, slowly straighten the arms, lifting up. Good arm speed does not happen without strong triceps.

Remember with the upper body to emphasize repetitions rather than weights. Think in terms of doing two or three sets of 10-13 reps.

TRICEPS PULLDOWNS

This is a preferable exercise to French curls when a pull-down device is available. Freeze the upper arms against the sides of the body, pulling the bar down from chest to thigh by straightening the arms.

LAT PULL DOWNS

Pull the bar straight down to the top of the chest. Focus on the lat muscles (the wing muscles just under and to the rear of the armpits. If you're not focused on the lats, the biceps will end up doing more of the work.

ARM EXTENSIONS FRONT & SIDE
Work with very light weights. Keep the shoulders relaxed as the straight arm rises up. This series is designed to strengthen the shoulder structure.

Start off light and chart your weights and reps to measure progress.

SHOULDER SHRUGS
Hold the weights with loose arms at your side and shrug the shoulders to the ears, hold for a second and relax. Concentrate on one side at a time.

BENT OVER ROW Lead with the elbow pulling it to the center of your back. As with any exercise, resist gravity on the way back down, rather than just dropping the arm.

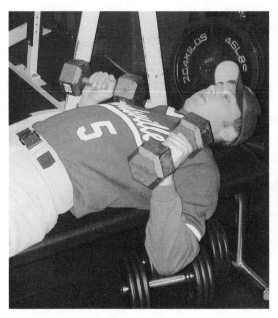

BENCH PRESS Using dumbbells will allow you a greater range of motion. As you push up bring the weights up even with the center of your chest so that the weights click together at the peak of the lift.

ELASTIC TUBING

If it's available, you can use a pulley system to imitate the throwing motion, but if you employ this method, practice just a piece of the motion at a time, working as smoothly as possible. You probably want to work the off-arm as well to maintain symmetry.

As opposed to using a pulley to simulate the pitching motion, you might want to consider utilizing elastic tubing or a sports cord. There are some commercial products available that are designed specifically for baseball pitchers such as the Armstrong device, and they typically include training programs that are designed to muscles use both for accelerating and decelerating the arm. The nice thing about them is that they are easily portable and can be utilized by attaching an end to a doorjamb (inside), or a fence post (outside). By doubling up cords or starting at a point with the cord already stretched, you can increase resistance.

More and more big league pitchers are currently using cord devices for in-season training between assignments. One can use it to tune delivery muscles. This should be done with limited resistance with focus on form rather than speed. In the off-season it can be used more aggressively to pick up arm speed by exploding the arm forward from the pre-launch position as shown on page 254.

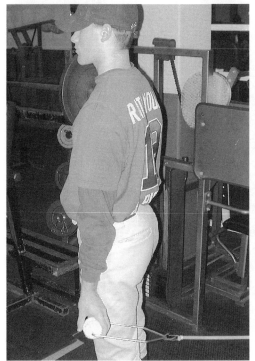

Coaching TIP

Conditioning cannot overcome freak injuries, but it will prevent fatigue-related injuries.

WORKING THE LEGS FOR EXPLOSIVENESS

Contrary to the upper body, the pitcher's lower body can greatly benefit by heavy lifting. Just look at the legs of Tom Seaver or Roger Clemens; those huge thighs are where their fastballs originate. Leg strength will also promote endurance, as the first thing to tire are the legs, and when the legs get tired, the stride will start to shorten and the ball will start to come up.

Squats, lunges, and leg presses are simple exercises that can develop the butt, quads, and hamstrings with great effectiveness. It's not crucial to do a lot of targeting exercises. Each of the aforementioned exercises will get all those upper leg muscles firing.

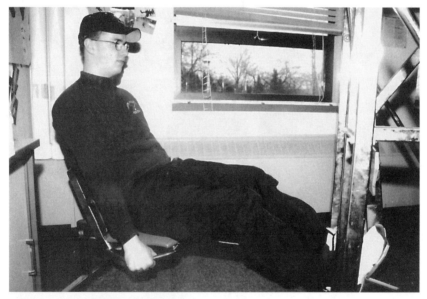

Be careful of your knees when working the leg press. Never lock out. When doing lunges keep the weights light enough not to stress the arms. Keep the back straight.

A pitcher might want to consider the leg press as opposed to squats and lunges. Squats can put a lot of pressure on the shoulder and require two spotters. With lunges, you can avoid neck and shoulder problems by holding the weights at your side, but if you go heavy, you might be putting undue strain on the arms. With the leg press, make sure you go deep enough to feel the work in your butt. Allow yourself plenty of recovery time. One day of rest is not usually enough after a heavy leg work out.

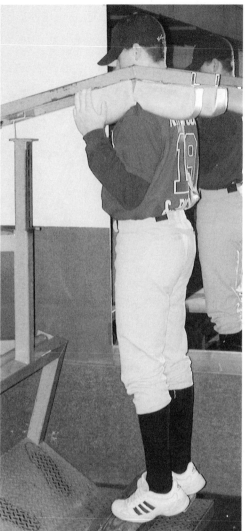

CALF RAISES can be done on the leg press or with a specialized machine as shown here, or by holding a dumbbell in your hand and standing on the edge of a board.

Calf raises are valuable and can be done every second or third day. Contrary to some opinions, alternating the way the toes point will not dramatically alter this exercise. You will not shape muscles by varying foot position. Muscles either fire or they don't fire.

Baseball players seem to be especially susceptible to hamstring injuries as this is an area that is often under-trained. An excellent exercise to help develop the hamstrings is the leg curl.

LEG CURLS UP With leg curls make sure that you concentrate on a full range of motion — sacrificing weight if necessary. Really work to squeeze the ankles to the butt (it's okay for the pelvis to lift slightly from the table).

Don't forget to warm up before you start, and to stretch between sets and after the workout.

LEG EXTENSIONS work the quads to exclusion. Make sure you do an equal amount of leg curls to keep leg strength balanced.

During the off-season work the legs to their max once a week with heavy lifting and then, once or twice a week, do maintenance work with leg curls, leg extensions, lunges and calf raises. The maintenance routine can be continued with moderation during the season.

ABDOMEN

Strong stomach muscles are an absolute must. A strong abdomen will take a huge load off the lower back forestalling problems in the structurally weakest part of the human body (at some point during active years, as many as 80% of people will develop lower back problems).

YOUR MIDSECTION PLAYS A VITAL ROLE IN THE MECHANICS OF PITCHING.

Essentially the midsection is your control tower. It coordinates the upper and lower halves of your body. When movement is initiated in the waist, the arms and legs will act in concert with each other. Strong abdominal muscles will also encourage deeper breathing, getting the focus of your breath out of your chest and into the lower part of the lungs, which are much richer in capillaries and hence provide more oxygen to the blood.

My advice when exercising the abdomen is to stay away from the one size fits all mechanical contraptions found in the gym. Crunches, knee up and leg lifts will give your stomach all the work it needs. Once in shape you can do stomach work six out of seven days.

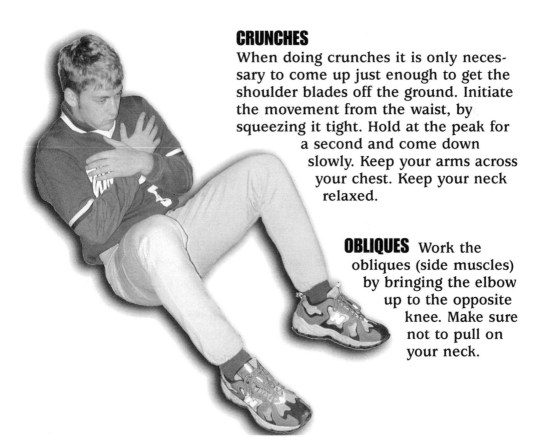

CRUNCHES
When doing crunches it is only necessary to come up just enough to get the shoulder blades off the ground. Initiate the movement from the waist, by squeezing it tight. Hold at the peak for a second and come down slowly. Keep your arms across your chest. Keep your neck relaxed.

OBLIQUES Work the obliques (side muscles) by bringing the elbow up to the opposite knee. Make sure not to pull on your neck.

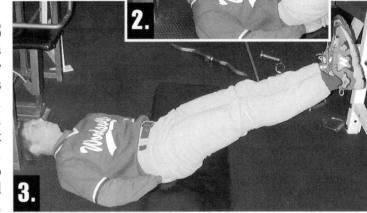

LEG RISES

With the leg lifts avoid strain by pulling bent legs up to your chest, then straighten the legs and let them down slowly. Use your hands to support the small of your back.

KNEE UPS

With knee-ups, rather than throwing the legs up, squeeze the belly so that the contraction of the stomach pulls the legs up to the point that the butt rolls off the ground. Go back down slowly, never letting the toes touch the ground between reps.

HANDS AND FINGERS

A pitcher can make up for a lot of deficiencies with strong fingers. The movement on Steve Carlton's fastball was often attributed to his superhuman fingers. Ones finger strength will improve with weightlifting without any special exercises as the act of picking up and gripping the weights requires the constant participation of the fingers.

I always carried handgrips with me, working them in free moments. Squeezing a rubber ball or wax will also turn the trick. For awhile the medical community believed that finger exercises contributed to carpal tunnel syndrome, but now the exact opposite has been found to be true. Typists and other people involved in repetitive movement can actually forestall carpal tunnel with squeeze balls and handgrips.

It's important to be kind to your hands and fingers; they are the tools of your craft.

Wear gloves in the winter. Apply lotion to keep the skin from cracking. Don't ignore blisters. One of the most frustrating things for a pitcher is to have his season curtailed by a blister problem that won't go away. Pitchers have been sidelined by paper cuts, by hitting their fingertips with a hammer, by ingrown nails caused by nervous chewing. Treat your hands and fingers with as much care and kindness as would a violinist.

SOME WEIGHTLIFTING RULES OF THUMB:

◆ Work from larger muscles to smaller muscles both on the upper and lower body. Do bench presses before you do curls. Do squats before you do calf raises.

◆ Never lift through pain.

◆ Continually stretch during and after lifting. If done properly, lifting will increase your flexibility rather than impede it.

◆ POUND THE WATER TO YOU! Don't wait until you're thirsty to drink. Thirst is not a warning of oncoming dehydration, but rather an indicator of its presence. Drink plenty of water before, during, and after a workout. Allowing yourself to work while water deprived is a foolish way to gain mental toughness.

◆ As you get older, the onset of delayed muscle soreness will occur later but will last longer. Make sure that your muscles have had plenty of recovery time before lifting again.

◆ Denser muscles can be worked more often. This means that calf and abdominal muscles require less recovery time between workouts than the chest or quads. In fact sit-ups can probably be done every day in moderation.

◆ During off-season use light to medium weights once or twice a week and heavy weights (legs only) once a week, with at least two days off from lifting following a heavy workout. In-season keep it light!

◆ Don't forget to work the waist.

You can target specific areas by hitting the weight room every day or do an overall workout every other or every third day, depending on recovery time. When considering recovery time make sure to listen to your body and not your calendar.

As a rule of thumb, 48 hours should be adequate recovery time; however, this can vary. When you get into your thirties, chances are you may need more than a two-day recovery period. Other factors affecting recovery are the intensity of the previous workout, general physical condition, as well as the amount of water, rest, and nutrition utilized to replenish your system.

We don't have the space to get into a lengthy discussion on nutrition, but that doesn't mean you needn't study the topic. Michael Colgan's *Optimum Sports Nutrition* might be the best book covering nutrition and supplements and is well worth the read.

There are literally hundreds of lifting exercises, and it is easy to keep adding more and more until lifting becomes the centerpiece of your training program.

REMEMBER YOU ARE A PITCHER — NOT A BODY BUILDER — AND THROWING A BALL IS THE MOST IMPORTANT THING YOU DO. EVERYTHING ELSE SHOULD BE SUBORDINATE TO THIS.

If you are spending more than four to six hours a week in the weight room, you are either not working very efficiently or you may be overdoing it.

WEIGHTED BASEBALLS

Overload training with weighted baseballs is as close as you will come to a magic tonic for increasing velocity.

I use weighted balls in my training camps. And unless my radar gun is lying, their proper use yields immediate gains. The weighted ball is not a toy. It has been

carefully researched by many knowledgeable baseball people over the years (I for one did my doctoral thesis on the weighted ball's relationship to increased velocity). Their consistent controlled use results in improved arm strength, improved arm speed, improved velocity and, interestingly, improved control.

The weighted baseball should be thrown crisply — not real hard — with as little arc as possible. It's easy for kids of all ages to get caught up in horsing around with them, risking injury. Therefore weighted balls shouldn't be left laying around, but should only be brought out to do specific drills. It is also advisable to work with weighted balls no more than every other day. You can alternate or mix in their use with long toss.

Included in the chapter on drills are a Stride Drill and Wrist Drill that utilize weighted baseballs.

WEIGHTED BALLS come in the following colors:		
● RED	(7.5 oz)	for 10 - 12
● GREEN	(9 oz)	for 13 - 14
● BLUE	(10 oz)	for 15 - 16
● YELLOW	(11 oz)	for 17 yrs
● BLACK	(12 oz)	for 18 + yrs

Recently 6 & 8 oz balls have become available.
Regular Baseball is 5.25 oz

LONG TOSS

Every pitcher should have long toss as part of his routine both in the off-season as well as between starts during the season. I don't really consider it as an extra drill, but rather as a fundamental part of the serious pitcher's regular — even daily — regimen. Long toss loosens and strengthens the arm and also provides a way to work on mechanics. In long toss, the intent shouldn't be to throw the ball as hard as possible, but rather to throw it in a straight line with as little arc as possible. While long tossing, one should go through the entire pitching motion from purchase to follow-through, working both in the full and the set position.

Without long toss you will lose arm strength over the course of a season.

Some pitchers will complain about long toss hurting their arms. If that's the case, you probably want to immediately reduce the throwing distance and take a real hard look at mechanics. If long toss produces pain, more often than not, a breakdown in mechanics is occurring which is causing the pitcher to throw with too much of his arm and too little of his body.

STANDARD LONG TOSS

(The first number of each pair is for Little Leaguers, the second for college and pro players. High-schoolers should fall somewhere between).

1. Ten throws at 45-60 feet apart
2. Ten at 60-90 ft.
3. Ten at 75-120 ft.
4. *Ten at 100-180 feet every other day*
5. Ten at 45-60 ft.

40 TO 50 THROWS TOTAL

Don't forget to practice long toss from the set position on a regular basis.

PART II

YOUR OFF-SEASON PROGRAM

While for fans, the baseball season starts with opening day in the spring, for ball players, the mindset has to be developed that the year starts right up again after the last out of the last game of the season has been recorded.

FALL PROGRAM

Take a few weeks off, catch up on your sleep and family matters; let the little nagging injuries calm down. Then get back to work in earnest while the problems of the past season are fresh in your mind. If you can get involved in a fall league, do so. Usually the pressure to succeed isn't as great; being less in the limelight, you have the opportunity to experiment.

> *Whether involved with a fall league or not, autumn is a good time to really work on making those fundamentals solid.*

WINTER PROGRAM

Winter's the time to break down and rebuild your mechanics. If you want to work on increasing strength, put in some concentrated effort in the weight room. Find a place to throw, engaging in Long Toss and Weighted Ball Drills. It's not important at this point to work from a mound. As spring approaches begin to throw some simulated innings; work on your borderline pitches. Now's the time to develop that change-up grip and work on locating your breaking stuff.

> *The more often you have a batter stand in when practicing the better. Simulate actual game situations to habituate yourself to the 1,001 decisions you will have to make in a game.*

It's a good idea to throw from a mound as often as possible. However, when working on fundamental mechanics, working on a flat surface can be preferable.

EARLY SPRING

Set your goals for the upcoming season. Really start to challenge yourself. Throw a lot of fastballs, work the weighted ball, do long toss. Make sure your arm is strong enough when spring training starts that you can handle situations that are no longer controlled. Work more simulated innings, keeping track of balls and strike and pitching patterns. Spend a good deal of time practicing from a set position. Fix your mind on the fact that you will be in peak physical condition by the first full-length exhibition game of the spring.

OTHER METHODS OF PRACTICE THROWING

SHADOW PITCHING (DRY MECHANICS) Performed with either a real or imaginary ball in your hand, you go through the motion of your delivery without actually releasing the ball, repeating it over and over until the motion feels smooth and definitive. Once you become intensely involved with the art of pitching, you'll do it without thinking, but it's also good on a daily basis to consciously perform the routine numerous times from both a full stride and set position.

SOFT TOSSING This can be performed throwing into a net or to a partner. Again, here you go through your full mechanics in slow motion, right through the release and follow-through. This can be done from stride position and/or full motion.

With these two exercises or when working long toss or on your actual pitch, be on the look out for flaws, and make corrections before they become etched into your muscle memory.

BE ON THE WATCH FOR...
- Landing on heels
- Dropping elbow before ball is launched
- Improper follow-through
- Hesitation as arm accelerates
- Rushing
    Opening early
    Moving before weight shifts
    Breaking hands harshly
    Shortening pitching circle

PART III

THROWING BETWEEN STARTS

As I mentioned earlier, at one point in my career, I was required to pitch batting practice the day after I pitched a game. This I believe led to some significant arm problems. After I got over my arm trouble and got on a balanced throwing program, I was able to return to consistently strong pitching.

What a starting pitcher does between his starts regarding throwing is as important as pitching the game itself. Any successful baseball program must incorporate a consistent regular throwing regimen for its pitching staff. Idiosyncrasies do exist from pitcher to pitcher, with some thriving on extra throwing and others doing better with minimal work between outings. Below, I've outlined what a typical program should look like for various pitching levels. Any such plan should be modified to meet individual needs.

STARTING PITCHERS AT THE PROFESSIONAL & COLLEGIATE LEVEL

Day 1 — Game day. PITCH!

Day 2 — Give your arm the day off. Don't touch a baseball. Do some shagging and maybe some running. For those who feel they absolutely need to throw, try a very light game of catch.

Day 3 & 4 — Work off the bullpen mound for 10-12 minutes at 60% velocity. Feel free to run or ride the stationary bike. Some pitchers will employ work with the elastic cord at this point (but not to muscle failure).

Day 5 — Work off a mound with concentration on rotation at about 70% of velocity for 12-15 minutes.

Day 6 — Game day. PITCH!

HIGH SCHOOL AND SENIOR BABE RUTH

In high school where inning limits are utilized — some as strict as seven innings a week — coaches will have to be creative with between game routines as some pitchers will use up their inning allotment in one game and others will spread it out. Also one must factor in the fact that the pitcher will typically play other positions as well. Use the outline below as a starting point.

Day 1 — PITCH!

Day 2 — Play catch.

Day 3 & 4 — Throw off a mound for 12 minutes at 70% velocity. Work on mechanics, control and rhythm.

Day 5 — Play catch and a little long toss.

Day 6 — PITCH!

The more often you have a batter stand in when practicing the better. Simulate actual game situations whenever possible to habituate yourself to the hundreds of decisions you will have to make in a game.

LITTLE LEAGUE

For Little Leaguers where six innings per week is the standard limit, game schedules are erratic and practices are rare, creating a throwing program is almost impossible without the assistance of parents and buy-in from the kids. Often times there can be more than a week between assignments. The trick here is to make sure that the pitcher works either in a game or a simulated situation every four or five days.

Day 1 — PITCH!

Day 2 — Play catch.

Day 3 — Throw off mound — work on control.

Day 4 & 5 — Play catch. Throw a little long toss.

Day 6 — PITCH!

The underlying theme for in-season throwing is regular and disciplined throwing with attention to mechanics, rotation and location.

IN-SEASON THROWING FOR RELIEF PITCHERS

Relievers should get the same amount of attention as starters. This doesn't always happen. A reliever can go unused for prolonged periods of time and suddenly their talents are called upon, with no room for error. Firemen that they are, they must always be ready to answer the bell.

A relief pitcher should never go two days in a row without throwing off a mound. Every other day he should either pitch in a game, or warm up with the intent of going into a game. If he doesn't pitch that night, the next day he should work on rotation and changing speeds for five minutes or so. This is the method used by the Atlanta Braves with their relievers and one that I completely subscribe to.

However, each reliever is going to have different requirements. For the most part power relievers will have an easier time staying sharp than finesse pitchers who may have to continually adjust their routines.

DON'T IGNORE PAIN & SWELLING

For cutting down on inflammation, ice is the best tool, especially if it's applied immediately after a game. A usual icing routine might be alternating five to ten minutes on with five to ten minutes off, for an hour. You do not want the arm to go numb with cold. Don't reapply ice until the skin returns to room temperature. If swelling is significant, another hour might be required.

Keep disposable self-cooling ice packs in your equipment bag. At home earmark a bag of frozen peas for the purpose. They shape nicely to the shoulder and arm.

If every time that you pitch, you swell up a few hours after your game, short circuit the process and apply ice before swelling sets in. Whirlpools and heat should be used with caution and only sparingly for ten or fifteen minutes max, as too much heat will actually cause tissue to break down.

Avoid the regular use of anti-inflammatories such as aspirin, Advil, and Motrin, as your body will grow to depend upon them to curb swelling. Their over-the-counter status makes us think of them as benign, but rather they are quite toxic. Over the long haul they can cause stomach ulceration and kidney failure. According to the New England Journal of Medicine they cause more deaths every year in the U.S. than AIDS.

IF YOU EXPERIENCE PAIN, USE COMMON SENSE. STOP THROWING UNTIL THE PAIN HAS ABATED FOR AT LEAST 24 HOURS.

Arm injuries do not heal without rest! If you throw while your arm is experiencing swelling, you are just asking for tendonitis which takes as long to heal and can be just as painful as a broken bone. Swelling is Mother Nature's way to immobilize an injured area; sometimes she just gets a little carried away. Swelling that doesn't abate should always be addressed by a doctor.

Spend some time studying a sports medicine book (See Suggested Reading at the back of this book) so that you will understand just how complicated the human arm and shoulder are. Learn just how the thing works and you will be better able to take care of it.

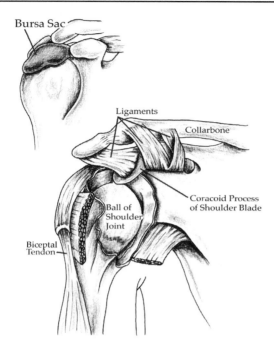

Bursa Sac

Ligaments

Collarbone

Coracoid Process
of Shoulder Blade

Ball of
Shoulder
Joint

Biceptal
Tendon

The channel through which the biceps tendon passes to the muscle is narrow — in some people it's very narrow. All it takes is just a small trauma to cause inflammation — that when active will cause the swollen tendon to constantly abrade itself against the channel, leading to a very painful and debilitating injury.

The shoulder is a very busy piece of anatomy; inflame a muscle and the swelling makes for a very crowded environment where nothing moves free of friction. Arthritis and swelling of the bursa can result which will further crowd the situation and lead to more abrasion and erosion.

A FINAL WORD ON TRAINING

Intelligence can be the determining factor as to whether one makes it or not as a pitcher. This doesn't necessarily mean having academic intelligence, but rather having the wherewithal to sort out truth from myth, the wisdom to properly prepare for the work at hand, the good sense to not mistake luck — good or bad — as an indicator of achievement, and the mindfulness to be able to differentiate between success and failure, with the capacity to learn from the former and not repeat the latter. It means the careful utilization of acquired knowledge in making one's self better. A well-conditioned, mentally prepared, mechanically efficient pitcher who has removed himself from the shadow of self-doubt becomes both artist and art personified. He is a beautiful sight to behold. Rarely does such a level of artistry come about by accident, or through occasional effort. What is required is relentless constant effort that never gives in to compromise or shortcuts of convenience.

GETTING GOOD:
PITCHING DRILLS & EXERCISES

It's a matter of repetition
and more repetition...

In this chapter, I've laid out many drills and exercises designed to help a pitcher develop and maintain his craft. Drills are not just for beginners and rookies, but should be part of every pitcher's regimen.

- Drills serve as a valuable diagnostic tool. They give the pitcher the opportunity to slow down and really take a look at what he is doing right and wrong, especially with regard to fundamentals. When things aren't going well and you don't know why, if you go back to your drills, you most likely will discover where the breakdown is occurring.

- Drills allow you to isolate specific parts of your delivery, not just to fix them, but also to enhance them.

- Through repetition, drills help you to develop muscle memory so that come game time you can focus on the batter before you and the game situation, rather than your mechanics.

- Drills can help you stay sharp without an excess of heavy throwing. In coming back from an injury, drills are a safe and smart way to start throwing again.

- Drills help to keep daily practice from becoming rote and mundane.

- Drills allow for practice in a completely non-competitive atmosphere.

For any specific problem, a drill can be developed to resolve it.
You are limited only by your own creativity when developing drills. I could have easily included another hundred in this chapter; probably over the years I've practiced and developed four or five times that many.

Drills are done as a **complement to long toss,** never as a replacement. Long Toss should always be the heart of your training session. It is the number one drill.

THINGS TO KEEP IN MIND AS YOU PRACTICE ANY DRILL

1. **DON'T EXPECT THE DRILL TO DO ALL THE WORK.** Your goal is to improve through your drills, not merely get through them. If your body is going to be putting in the time, make sure your head shows up as well. Mindless repetition is a waste of time.

2. **GIVE IT A FAIR SHOT.** Put in the time. Don't give up on something right away just because you can't get the hang of it. If you had that kind of attitude as a baby, you would never have learned how to walk.

3. **BE EXACT.** When doing drills, you are a scientist; the field is your laboratory. Don't accept mediocrity. Doing something almost right is never good enough.

4. **MAKE IT INTO A GAME.** Otto Bismarck, the great German leader once said, *you can teach a child anything if you make it into a game.* That truth can be extended to big kids as well. Set goals that force you to be precise. When throwing, set up targets and reward yourself a few points for getting close to the target and even more for nailing it.

> If you don't stay focused, instead of being alleviated, your bad habit may become even more deeply entrenched, or you may end up exchanging it for another that is just as bad.

5. **HAVE OTHERS WORK WITH YOU.** Do your drills with a buddy or have a coach keep an eye on you. The perspective from inside our body isn't always the best. Be open to people's suggestions and comments; if you're not, others will hesitate to give you advice — some of which might be the exact tonic you need. Your baseball life is too short to have to learn everything the hard way. The first step to achieving wisdom is getting smart enough to learn from those that have gone down the road before you.

6. **WORK ON STRENGTHENING YOUR WEAKNESSES**. Don't just do the drills you are good at. Give especial focus to those drills that challenge you.

7. **WHEN WORKING TO FIX A PARTICULAR FLAW, ISOLATE THE MOVEMENT.** Don't make things overly complicated. Work to fix one thing at a time.

8. **DON'T ABUSE YOUR MECHANICS BY BEING OVERLY EXTREME IN YOUR ADJUSTMENTS.** Keep in mind the *Seven to One Rule*. Every inch of adjustment on the mound will result in a seven-inch change at the plate.

9. **PLAY SAFE.** *A no pain, no gain* mindset serves no purpose with mechanics.

10. **APPROACH DRILL TIME WITH A POSITIVE ATTITUDE.** Typically, the resistance we feel at the thought of doing a task dissipates as we become more and more involved in that task. Watch out for self-fulfilling prophecies. If we don't think something is going to help us, then it probably won't.

11. **BE A LEADER, NOT A HOTSHOT.** Those teams are the most successful where the superstar is the one who works the hardest and longest, and approaches all endeavors with a positive attitude.

PART I

THE BASICS

1. FASTBALL WRIST DRILL

To increase wrist speed and improve rotation by properly engaging the fingertips on release

This drill can be performed standing or with one knee on the ground. Move about fifteen feet away from your throwing partner. Cradle the elbow of the throwing arm in your glove. Make sure to keep the elbow as high as your shoulder! Flex your wrist back so that it is parallel to the ground. Grip the ball with either a two or four-seam fastball grip. Later on you can experiment with other grips.

Forcefully snap the wrist forward on a downward trajectory aiming for your partner's chest. Keep the forearm as stationary as possible, isolating the movement to the wrist and the fingertips. Allow the hand to turn slightly clockwise (rhp). Attempt to impart as much 12/6 spin (1/7 rhp) on the ball as possible. You should feel a burn on your fingertips as the ball spins from your release.

THE WRIST CAN BE FURTHER STRENGTHENED BY USING A WEIGHTED BALL.

One way to work this drill is to do a set of ten reps with the weighted ball and then a set of ten reps with the weighted ball. Always start with the weighted ball and end with the regular ball.

For help in choosing the right size ball see page 291.

2. CURVEBALL WRIST DRILL
To maximize curveball spin

This drill is fundamentally the same as the Fastball Wrist Drill. The difference is with the grip. Hold the ball with a curveball grip. As the hand snaps forward to release, utilize pressure from the middle finger and the thumb to impart spin. End up after release with the index finger pointing to the target like a pistol. Emphasize tight quick spin by snapping the fingers hard enough to get good burn in the middle finger and thumb tips. This should not cause any discomfort in the forearm or the elbow. If you are experiencing any, try to make the snap of the wrist a little less violent and the wrist rotation a little less extreme.

An experienced coach should supervise your efforts to manufacture a curveball. Beginning pitchers should always make the development of fastball rotation their prime directive!

Just as important as developing wrist-action, Drills 1 & 2 should train the elbow to stay high.

3. SQUARE UP DRILL
To accelerate forearm & wrist and improve fingertip action

This is a natural progression from the Wrist Drill, as now we add arm movement to the snap of the wrist. Face a partner from about 25 -30 feet away. Place feet shoulder-width apart, neither foot forward. Bring your arm back and throw forward without any body movement. Focus on creating extreme wrist action so as to pop the ball. Spin the ball hard enough that you can hear it whir. As the ball is released from the fingers, you should also be able to hear a sharp tick or click; that indicates good fingertip action.

This drill can also be done starting with a closed shoulder. ▶

4. INDIAN DRILL
Isolating torso rotation and developing the high elbow

Line up a partner about 15-20 feet away. Take a squatting position. Bring the pitching arm up to a high launch position. Hold the glove up just below the face with the elbow bent (covering the box). Go through your throwing motion, leading with a high elbow. Throw with crisp rotation, pulling back the off-arm to maximize the twist of the torso as a source of power.

5. DOUBLE KNEE DRILL
To lead with high elbow

A good continuation from the Indian Drill. This time set down on both knees. When throwing, be conscious of leading with the high elbow. Use the off-arm as in the Indian Drill. Don't forget to give the throw good wrist action.

Note the high elbow of the pitching arm in Drills 3, 4 & 5.

6. WRIST FLEX EXERCISE
To increase velocity with improved wrist snap

Bring your pitching arm up with the elbow as high as the shoulder. Bend the forearm back towards the shoulder. Using your other hand flex the wrist back until it tightens significantly. Release the pressure, snapping the wrist forward at the same time. Don't go overboard; work this exercise gradually and you will find your range of motion improving with each rep.

7. HIP LOAD DRILL

Increasing power by using lead leg lift to fully load the hips

Take a set position with the hand, ball and glove in loop. Align the crown of the head over the back leg (keep it there through the drill).

1. **Slowly lift the front leg, bringing the knee as high as the belt, and hold for five seconds.** Keep the toe of the foot on the lead leg pointing straight out or slightly down; keep the chin straight out over the shoulder, focusing your eyes on the plate or another distant target. Always keep your weight centered on the balls of the feet as opposed to settling back on the heels.

2. **Bring the knee one inch above the belt and hold for a count of seven.**

3. **Now bring the knee as high as possible up and towards the rear shoulder and hold for a count of ten.** Don't allow the front shoulder to close more than a few inches; keep the chin forward. Slowly, let the leg down. Repeat three times and every fourth time bring the knee all the way up in one slow smooth motion, *On that fourth rep, don't count but rather focus all of your mind on the target.*

The idea here is to load the hips as much as possible. If you have trouble with balance, try slightly bending your supporting knee. Think in terms of bringing your balance up with you from the ground, rather than trying to gain it once you've lifted the leg. Keep the knee of the supporting leg bent from the start; bending the knee after you come up will move the weight off the ball of the foot – where it belongs – and onto the heel.

THIS DRILL SHOULD BE REPEATED EVERY DAY.

8. DOUBLE BALL DRILL
To stretch and strengthen grip

Take two baseballs and fit them snugly into your hand, holding them between your fingertips and thumb. Once secured, press the balls deeper into your palm and hold for a few seconds, maximizing stretch. Repeat the press five to ten times. After doing this drill, when you take one ball, it should feel like you can just about swallow it in your grip.

9. CURVE FLIP DRILL
To maximize use of thumb in imparting ball spin

Hold the baseball with a curveball grip. Place your thumb under the ball. Flip thumb straight up, giving the ball a 6/12-type spin. Repeat until it becomes easy.

Coaching TIP

Teaching should be one idea at a time.

PART II

THE STRIDE DRILL & ITS VARIATIONS
THE ONE DRILL THAT NEEDS TO BE IN THE TOOLBOX OF EVERY PITCHER AND PITCHING COACH

10. BASIC STRIDE DRILL
To get all parts of the body coordinated for the launch phase, while also providing a tool to self-correct mechanical flaws

The drill will help you coordinate your lead arm, your throwing arm and both your legs to maximize the launch phase of your delivery. In an instant, the potential energy created by the initial coiling of the hip and the shoulder, the reaching back of the arm, and the loading of the back leg, will explode forth into kinetic energy. How successfully that energy is transferred into the ball is strictly determined by the timing, mechanical precision and fluidity expressed at launch . . . and practiced here in the Stride Drill.

PREPARATION
Create a *Double Bar T* on the pitching area. This *T* can be scratched into the ground or pitcher's mound or marked off with lime. On an indoor mound, tape can be used. The back part of the *T* approximates the pitcher's plate. The long leg of the *T* is a line — that were it to continue would go directly to home plate. A second bar represents the wall as previously covered (page 64). This second bar will need to be adjusted to accommodate each pitcher's stride.

This line represents the wall.

The drill can be practiced with or without a ball. If using a ball, it can be released or held onto as in a dry run.

READY POSITION

◆ Place your back foot (right foot for a rhp) against the rubber at the back intersection of the *T*.

◆ Place the front foot on the long leg of the *T* with the toe slightly closed or turned in. This leg must never be stiff; always allow the knee to flex so that it might serve as a shock absorber.

◆ The power arm should be placed into the high-cock position (about ten o'clock) — behind the ear with thumb facing toward second base. If you turn your head, you should be able to see the back of your throwing hand. The elbow should be even with the shoulder or slightly higher.

◆ The lead arm (glove side) has the elbow pointing to the plate, the glove held palm down with the idea of covering the box (obscuring the batter's view of the throwing hand).

◆ Keep your chin over the front shoulder as much as possible.

LAUNCH

Action should be initiated with push-off coming from back leg — lifting the heel so as to pivot on the ball of the foot.

- Arm action commences with ten to three o'clock movement. The release point will always be imagined just beneath the bill of the hat.
- Shoulder starts to open as upper body begins to pass over the wall.
- Wrist should snap through release point with thumb being slightly to right (rhp). Here the pitcher can either release the ball or carry it through.

FOLLOW-THROUGH

- Pitching hand should pass into an imaginary bucket, seven or eight inches to the left of the lead leg with fingers pointing down.
- Pitching arm shoulder should be pointing directly to the target.
- Chest should be over the bent front knee and the knee should be over the ball of the front foot.
- The face or chin should be over or past the front foot; this should insure proper balance.

FINISH

◆ Action of the hips should pull the back leg off the pitcher's plate after the pitch is made.

◆ Back leg should come around as if stepping over a log or a bucket.

◆ The toe of the back leg gently lands even with, or slightly ahead of the lead leg.

IN EXECUTING THE STRIDE DRILL AND ITS VARIATIONS, CERTAIN ABSOLUTES SHOULD BE EMPHASIZED.

1. Use the off-arm to help accelerate the torso and maintain balance (For more detail about this look at the Off-arm Drill.)
2. Cover the box (for a better understanding see the Cover the Box Drill)
3. Always finish your movement by placing your hand in the bucket.
4. Always go over the wall.
5. Attempt to make your movement as smooth and continuous as possible.
6. Initiate your movement by turning the waist as this will get the upper half and the lower half working simultaneously.
7. Always be thinking in terms of unifying forces to achieve the maximum at release. Don't let one body part get ahead of another.

This drill should be practiced religiously in the off-season and whenever there appears to be a mechanical problem as indicated by loss of control, velocity or balance. Even when things are going well, you should occasionally come back to this drill so as to keep slight flaws from developing into significant ones. Whenever possible, have a knowledgeable person watch you. Have them check your elbow height, stride length, proper shoulder closure, and your going over the wall. *Make sure one part of your body is not getting ahead of or behind the other parts.*

11. STRIDE DRILL WITH WEIGHTED BALLS
Immediately improves arm speed and velocity

◆ **Make sure that you use the correctly weighted balls. More is not better. Mild overload is the goal. Be conservative in your choice of balls.**

◆ **Get the arm loose and well warmed before starting.**

◆ **Always throw the weighted ball less than standard pitching distances.**

◆ **Stress excellent mechanics from Stride Drill position with the weighted ball rather than accuracy.**

◆ **Focus on throwing the weighted ball *crisply* rather than hard.**

Make a half a dozen throws from about thirty-five feet to make sure the arm is well-warmed, about twenty-five feet for Little Leaguers.

Then set yourself fifty feet from a partner or a screen. Little Leaguers should stand about thirty feet. Adjust the distance accordingly, again being conservative.

In choosing a ball, start light.

This table shows the suggested weights.
Throwing the ball should not cause you to feel strain.

9-12 years	RED BALL	(7.5 oz)
13-14 years	GREEN	(9 oz)
15-16 years	BLUE	(10 oz)
17-18 years	YELLOW	(11 oz)
18+ years	BLACK	(12 oz)

Recently 6 and 8 oz balls have become available.
Regular Baseball is 5.25 oz

On every other pitch put a little something on the ball. With the regular ball, that means harder with more spin. With the weighted ball, it means crisply — not hard — with good spin.

When switching from the weighted ball to the regulation ball, it's not uncommon to start throwing the ball into the ground. Don't worry; your trajectory will self-adjust by the third throw.

Throughout this drill: DO NOT BRING THE LEG FORWARD FOLLOWING THE THROW, except for the last set.

Follow this order:

I. Fifteen throws with the weighted ball; every other one crisp
II. Ten throws with regular ball; every other one hard
III. Ten throws with weighted ball; every other one crisp
IV. Ten throws with regular ball; every other one hard, bringing back leg forward

THIS IS A GOOD TIME TO CHECK-IN WITH THE RADAR GUN AS THERE WILL ALWAYS BE A PICK UP IN VELOCITY HERE. However, this is a quick fix. To maintain the velocity gain, one should **do the above drill every other day,** pre and post season. This is an overload exercise and overload exercises shouldn't be done two days in a rows as without that day off, the muscle will not have time to rebuild. Some will use the weighted ball in season; I don't encourage this, although I have allowed my pitchers to do so.

This is a good time to check-in with the radar gun as there will always be a pick up in velocity here.

12. SET STRIDE DRILL
Improved launch from set position

Follow the same directions as the Stride Drill, only use the set position and to begin with start a few steps earlier with the hand-break, until you are solid with getting into proper launch position.

Once you are capable of achieving the strong launch position, you can start directly from there, but do notice the position of the back foot. A full ninety degree pivot will be required.

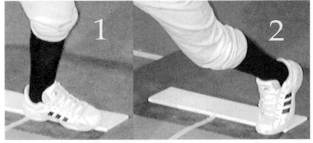

13. PIVOT DRILL
Getting the feet involved with the power equation

Get in your stride position with hands on hips. Keep the front foot closed 45 degrees. Lift heels a half inch off the ground, transferring weight to the balls of the feet. Pivot rapidly to the left so that your hips turn a full ninety degrees. Do at least a half dozen times, then switch forward legs and do it again, turning in the opposite direction. This exercise will develop explosiveness in the calves and keeps stiff feet from disrupting the power flow.

14. ONE-KNEE LAUNCH DRILL
To focus on upper body synchronization

This is the Stride Drill minus the striding, which allows one to focus on upper body mechanics.

Start by kneeling down with the knee of the throwing hand at rest on the ground. Raise the pitching arm to launch position with the fingers on top, being sure to keep the elbow up as high as the shoulder.

Put the lead arm forward in the *cover the box* position. Your chin should be out over the lead shoulder pointing toward the plate. Action begins by extending the forearm and wrist in throwing motion to the release point. Stop here and be sure the chest has been brought over the knee. Then continue through, finishing the pitch so that the arm swings around the lead knee with the shoulder pointing to the plate as the head and shoulders as well as upper back pass over the *wall*.

Once both parts of the motion are patterned, do the entire action with one smooth movement. This drill too can be done with or without a ball.

15. COVER THE BOX — KNEE DRILL
Isolates most essential component of covering the box

← THE BOX

Kneel down with the knee of your throwing side set on the ground. Bring the hand and ball up to launch phase. Close the front shoulder and bring up your glove, palm down, so that it obscures the would-be batter's view of the ball and your wrist position. Throw the ball to a kneeling partner who evaluates your success at covering the box.

IT'S NEVER TOO EARLY TO START THE DEVELOPMENT OF GOOD HABITS THAT CAN GIVE YOU AN EDGE.

Covering the box will add sneaky quickness to your pitch.

This is not so much a drill, but rather a practice to apply to all your drills. When the pitching arm is in the launch position, the batter gets a good view of the pitcher's hand.

Good hitters focus on an imaginary seven-inch box in which the ball is centered. Therefore, when the pitcher raises his lead arm — palm down — he can obscure the batter's view with his glove. This takes a fraction of a second off the batter's decision and reaction time, making the pitch seem a shade quicker.

Getting the right position with the right timing requires continual practice. You should experiment with this from the mound while having someone stand in the batter's box to help fine-tune your glove position for maximum covertness. Once you achieve the optimum positioning, practice it whenever the opportunity arises in your other drills.

16. OFF-ARM DRILL
Using the off-arm to generate power

This drill is to help utilize the *Captain's Wheel* in the throwing of a ball (see page 60). It can be done from the standing Stride Drill, the mound or the Knee Drill position.

Start from the position of the off-arm covering the box, with the throwing hand poised overhead. Leading with the elbow, pull the off-arm back, the glove hand rotating palm up; allow it to rotate the waist which subsequently drives the throwing arm forward. Imagine poking someone behind you in the gut with the off-arm elbow.

One of the most common mistakes is to forfeit power by bringing the lead elbow back with the stride. This can cause the upper body to open too early, and even if one stays closed the *Captain's Wheel* will only have the strength of one hand on it rather than two.

It's important to pull that lead arm back strongly, not letting it fly out. The final resting point of the elbow can be up high or down lower, just as long as it is tight to the body. The glove hand can come to rest anywhere from under the armpit to the side of the hip or slightly behind the back. Get the timing down so that the off arm comes to a stop at exactly the same time as the throwing hand hits the release point.

Make that coordinated timing of the two arms an absolute in all your drills.

17. BACK POCKET DRILL
To get proper deceleration when throwing the curveball

Get into stride position. Go through Curveball Drill and finish off the follow-through by bringing your throwing hand (rhp) to the left back pocket. A variation on this drill is to end up as though you were stabbing yourself in the lower left abdomen.

18. SHOULDER BURY & BUCKET DRILL
To take stress off pitching arm and enhance control

This is a variation on the Stride Drill, emphasizing finish as opposed to release. Often times when pitchers are having challenges with their control, it has to do with improper and inconsistent front shoulder alignment. This can be fixed by focusing specifically on the shoulder, something we don't typically do while throwing. Burying the shoulder also creates a little more *give* so that the throwing arm won't come to a sharp stop and jerk on the shoulder carriage as it comes across the body. This will take stress off both the arm and the shoulder.

Start from the Stride Drill position. Complete the throwing motion bringing the arm through the release point.

Rotate the torso enough to position the throwing arm shoulder to the plate, as if one were throwing the shoulder at the target. Bring the hand at least two to three inches into a bucket on the outside of the lead leg. As mentioned in the Chapter on Control, think of having a big eye on that shoulder and stare with it at the plate.

Count to six with your chin pointing to the target, before bringing the back leg forward.

19. BACK FOOT RELEASE DRILL

To keep the back foot from dragging on release

Assume the finish position on your stride. Position your back foot on a bucket or bench as shown. Finish your movement with back leg up. Work slowly with the purpose of transferring all of your weight to the front foot while maintaining balance.

Make sure to go over the wall and continue your follow-through.

After several reps, remove the bucket and work your mechanics through release (it's not necessary to throw the ball), achieving the same leg lift that you did while using the bucket. Getting the leg up must become an unconscious natural action, as come game time, you need your focus to be on the batter and the situation.

20. OVER THE BUCKET DRILL
To further reinforce the idea of not dragging the back foot

Place bucket to the side and front of pitching rubber. Take position with back foot against rubber. Go through pitching motion with leg releasing and coming up over bucket and touching down.

To get a better feel for lifting the back leg, turn the bucket up and place the back foot atop, and then continue the motion to completion. Repeat this several times.

21. CURVE STRIDE DRILL
To master breaking pitch release and follow-through

Start from the stride position. In this drill the idea is to keep the arm in a right angle position so downward trajectory is emphasized. Lead with the elbow and keep it high.

Turn hand at ear into breaking pitch position. Release the ball, the hand shaped like a pistol. Follow-through with the lead arm to either reach for your back pocket or stab yourself in the gut as in the Back Pocket Drill (#17).

OTHER PATTERNING DRILLS

Isolating parts of delivery to fine-tune and make proper movement and alignment instinctive

22. STARTING WITH A STRONG CONNECTION

Going from the stillness of the purchase into the motion of the wind-up, a pitcher can be his own worst distraction. Depending on how you start your delivery, your arms going over your head, or your glove coming up to your chin can break your focus. Your concentration on the plate must be a continuous thread, not something to be broken and then reasserted. As we've previously stated the same is true of balance. In order for your balance to be the strongest it must be brought from the ground in a continuous fashion, rather than regained after the leg-lift. Utilize one of the two options below according to whether you lift the arms overhead after the purchase or go directly to the chest.

OPTION ONE: BRINGING THE HANDS OVERHEAD

After taking the signal in the purchase position, bring the hands up high over head. Make a wide enough window with your arms, so that you needn't move your head to maintain your view. Keep your elbows high and your chin on the target. Your belt buckle should point to the hitter. The back of your glove should be to the hitter, hiding the ball and the wrist of your throwing hand. Bring your lead leg up as the hands come down to the chest, and hold for a count of two, keeping your eyes fixed on the plate.

If you make the window too narrow as shown here, you will have to drop your chin to get a good look at the target. Also anytime the knee gets stiff, the center of balance rises and good balance becomes more difficult.

Don't hold your breath. In fact, find a breathing pattern that works for your motion. What tends to work best is steadily breathing in as you go from the purchase through the loading and cocking, and then breathing out as you unload, release, and follow-through.

OPTION TWO:
HANDS BENEATH THE CHIN

For those that prefer to bring the hands directly to the chest, rather than overhead first, don't allow the glove to come up high enough to impede your vision. The same points apply as with the overhead approach. Keep the back of the glove to the plate, keep the belt buckle facing the plate, and don't allow your chin to turn away as your leg comes up.

FROM THE SET

When doing this exercise in the set position, the belt buckle should face towards the baseline. Efficiency must be factored in when runners are on base, consequently in the set, it is preferable to keep the hands under the chin rather than overhead. Also it's advisable to keep the front leg light so as to allow for a quicker move to the bases.

23. MOVING INTO ANGLE OF PRONATION

This should be done after the Stride Drill has been practiced enough that the basic mechanics of your delivery are as efficient and smooth as possible. About halfway through the Stride Drill, as the throwing hand approaches the ear, the hand changes from *thumb behind* to *thumb in front*.

Now is the time to achieve the proper pronation for whatever pitch you are throwing. Work at developing consistency with your various pitches. Even in the little things, muscle memory needs to take over so that your focus can remain on the plate and the batter.

24. BACK FOOT ACTION

Take the stride position. Focus on the back foot setting it up against the rubber. And as the body moves forward, the back foot will pivot on the ball of the foot and PUSH OFF.

Coaching TIP

Negative thoughts can eat you up — the art form is not to repress them, but rather to keep them from becoming all of who you are. It can be done and is done by successful people.

25. STEP TO A PARTLY CLOSED TOE

From the set position lift the lead leg and start forward, leading with the hip. Land the foot — the ball of foot touching down first — with a 45-degree angle inward. Don't bring the back leg forward. Work it again and again until you feel strong and balanced right through landing. This helps to keep the body closed so that the power is not dissipated early.

26. CHEST OVER KNEE DRILL

Starting from full stride or set position, move into follow-through with chest directly over the lead knee and the lead knee directly over the foot. The face or at least the nose should be in front of foot. The throwing shoulder should point to the plate. Repeat without releasing the ball until the alignment occurs without your having to correct your position as an afterthought.

THE GOOD COACH
COACHING IS TEACHING

No one should be in the coaching business if he or she is doing it for any other reason besides the fact that he or she loves the game and receives satisfaction from teaching. People who get into it for any other reason will not be successful at it nor have a positive impact on those young folks desiring to improve their game. And making a player into a better player must always be the primary directive.

A coach is often accused of playing vicariously through his or her charges. Such a statement is usually leveled as a criticism, but it doesn't have to be a bad thing. All parents want their children to realize their own dreams and so it is with the best of coaches.

What's important is that a coach has to recognize each player as his own person. And while it is quite natural to project our own wishes upon our players, we must also be objective enough to step back and recognize when our own desires are

not in accord with the desires of our players. Projecting our own desire for excellence onto our players is quite natural. But not everyone wants to be a superstar; some are satisfied with being just good enough to go along for the ride. Not everyone sees becoming an excellent ballplayer as a top priority in his or her life.

Certainly, part of our job is to motivate our players to be the best they can be. We should never stop encouraging them to learn how to reach down into themselves to get a little more, to go beyond their perceived limits, because that is a skill that will serve them well with whatever they choose to do in life. But we also have to remember that strength of will is simply another tool that players possess. And like running, throwing, and thinking, players possess various shades of it in different quantities.

A coach may be able to motivate a team while keeping his distance, but to improve an individual player is a labor of one-on-one love. Those who are unwilling to put in the time working hands-on with individuals, should find themselves another occupation or avocation. In order to help the player, the coach must have a solid knowledge of the absolutes of baseball and its fundamentals. There is nothing wrong with a coach and a player entering into an exploration together, but it's impossible to know if you are headed down the right path if you as the coach don't have a grasp of the absolutes.

Good coaching invites change and challenge; it requires a constant perusal of facts and an awareness of changing landscapes. An ideal coaching arrangement would be where the teacher is not only revealing useful information, but is always in a learning mode as well. Too often coaches stagnate. Typically, the more insecure they feel about what they know, the less willing they are to open themselves to learning, as any additional knowledge threatens their own sense of credibility.

COACHING SHOULD ALWAYS BETTER THE PLAYER

This is difficult to accomplish all the time, but it's what we should strive for. I commend all those great, dedicated coaches at all levels who attempt to do this. It is to them that coaching and instructional manuals such as this are dedicated.

I for one garner as much satisfaction in taking a non-talent and making him fundamentally sound, as I do in getting a great talent to realize his full potential. Although great talents are so rare that having the opportunity to mold and shape one is a true gift.

A great coach is before anything else a very skillful teacher. In successfully teaching the fundamentals as well as the more advanced concepts of throwing a baseball, the pitching coach must be able to identify flaws and then be able to employ an approach that will correct them. Many are able to handle the former, but few are those who can successfully find solutions. This is what separates the master coach from the pack.

FIRST RULE: DO NO HARM!

I've talked with professional pitching coaches — some of whom I played with during my professional days. So I know their background well, and in discussing pitching with them, I find that they feel they have to *unwrap* today's college pitchers. I have problems with this because in many instances, it's merely that the pro coach wants things his way.

What I find troubling is that in actuality, many college pitchers have been taught well and are quite ready for pro ball *as is*. To undo them is to hold back their progress. By the time a young pitcher hits his twenties, any attempts at drastic change will probably do more harm than good. Some fine-tuning is probably required. I don't argue that, but when a kid is throwing well and throwing successfully without doing harm to his body, then a hands-off policy is wisest. Obviously this doesn't apply to all. Some actually need to be *unwrapped*. But a great coach is one who understands the concept of physical diversity and doesn't feel a compulsion to put his brand on every horse in the stable. We all might have a tendency to over-coach, because we really want to feel useful. So then again it becomes a question of feeling secure enough to know that sometimes it's okay to just back off.

At the opposite extreme, some coaches are so afraid of messing up a young hurler, they hesitate to make any change even when the pitcher is having trouble. They think if you change a pitcher, you'll mess him up — even when he's having problems. Making the right decisions about when and how much to intercede is an art that is developed from years and years of situational experience. Making the right choices is as much a matter of instinct as it is expertise. No coach is right a hundred percent of the time, but the best ones know that there are no one-size-fits-all solutions. For those coaches who have been around a while — if they are able to recognize and set aside the influence of their own needs — their instincts will guide them well when it comes to making-over a pitcher; they will know when *to* and just as important know when *not to*.

PARENTS AND COACHES

We've all seen those articles in recent years or heard those stories on the news. *Parent of Benched Player Sues Coach. Spectators Inflict Beating on Losing Manager.* While those absurd occurrences are fortunately rare, they are indicative of what seems to be the increasingly volatile nature of the relationship between parents and coaches.

At the lower levels, the vast majority of coaches are volunteers who are there for love of the game and because of a willingness to spend their time directing youngsters in developing their skills, learning sportsmanship, and having fun. Few of these coaches are experts with any sort of experience beyond their own scholastic experiences. Some make it a point to know as much as they can by going to clinics, reading books and magazines and exploring the Internet for baseball forums. While this is positive, it doesn't necessarily make them good coaches. . . although it surely helps.

For some, the old adage — *a little knowledge is a dangerous thing* — becomes all too true. Some folks will assume because they know something they know everything. There are articles I wrote ten years ago that I now question; and there are solutions to problems that I will come up with today, that I will question tomorrow. I've come to know that's a fact. Ultimately, there is no such thing as an infallible expert, but there are folks with expertise. These are the ones to seek out. You can usually tell who they are by the fact that they have confidence in what they say, but enjoy being challenged, and actually don't mind being shown another way that might work better.

When you get into a scenario where the parents in the stands feel they know more than the coach on the field does — whether they do or they don't — trouble is just around the corner. Oftentimes a parent tries to make him or herself look important or the player perfect, at the expense of the coach. Oftentimes fur will fly over the question of how a player is used or not used. Such arguments rarely produce winners; nobody walks away feeling good, least of all the player in question.

Coaches can help avoid this pitfall as much as possible by recruiting parents to help with the team. From the stands it's easy to forget about someone else's Johnny while pulling for your Tommy. Down on the field, with twelve to twenty-five players to watch out for instead of just one, the view is always different. Parents aren't privy to the discussions between player and coach during a game, nor do they have a clue as to what happened in practice the day before. Chances are if they knew all the variables involved — which is impossible from the stands — they'd have a greater appreciation for the decisions being made. To keep peace, a coach should attempt to involve parents as much as possible, listen to their concerns with an open mind, and keep them as informed as possible, laying out the ground rules from the start. And most importantly, coaches need to avoid a *because I said so* mentality.

And parents could do their part by taking an oath of silence during a game, with regard to criticism of the coach. Many leagues these days have a 24-hour rule which states that a parent must not approach a coach with a complaint until the day after a game. And even if they have a legitimate beef, they should refrain from expressing it to their children.

As a coach I've learned that it's important to appreciate how people feel, but you can never make everyone happy. But then my job is not about making people happy. My ultimate responsibility is to make sure that the young players trusted to my charge learn the right lessons and have the opportunity to develop their talents to their fullest potential.

RULES FOR TEACHING

If you're a good coach, you're probably already doing most, if not all of these things instinctively.

1. Make everything into a game — Every drill, every exercise can be made into a game. If you tell a kid to go pick up the equipment on the other side of the field, he'll moan and groan. Tell him, *I bet you can't get all that stuff together in thirty seconds* and he'll sprint to get it done. Even older players will respond when you turn a drill into a challenge. *You think you can hit that outside corner four out of the next five pitches?*
2. Repeat yourself — Don't be afraid of saying something more than once. Supposedly, something has to be repeated at least seven times before it sinks into the human brain. Explain something, then explain it again in a different way and then explain it a third way. By doing this you're giving someone different ways to grasp the material, and you're also buying a little time for those who are slower in processing information.
3. One idea at a time — A teacher's main job is to reduce information to the simplest most understandable level. Let your players go home each day focused on one important idea.
4. No bad questions — Dialogue is always valuable. Even if the questions are just repeats, that's okay, because dialogue is how some people learn. Never chide someone for asking a question.
5. Avoid sarcasm — While some players can handle a little joking, others are hypersensitive to anything resembling criticism. Don't dwell on mistakes; emphasis should always be on how to do something better the next time.
6. Peer models work best — Your showing it a dozen times is not as valuable as teammates showing each other once.
7. People like structure — Even if they rebel against it, people for the most part appreciate structure. In our especially lax world, many crave it. Make your expectations clear and design a concrete plan for achieving them with each player.

8. Avoid no-win situations and setting up for failure — Don't put players into situations where they have no chance.

9. Be honest — Certainly accentuate the positive, but don't tell a player he did good when he did poorly; your credibility will be shot.

10. Fair and equal are two different things — Some people need more guidance than others, and they should receive it without any concerns about fairness.

11. **Fun**damentals, **fun**damentals, **fun**damentals — Basics are everything, but if you make their practice tedious, they won't get mastered.

12. Teach your players how to practice on their own — The ones who learn the most, learn most of what they know on their own. Help your players develop the ability to think and problem solve on their own. Instill in them the attitude that they have to take charge of making themselves better. Make sure they know the difference between practice and practicing *right things*.

13. Don't blame a player for his parents — Treat everyone as a blank slate; don't over-concern yourself with whatever tree the apple fell from.

14. Mistakes and discipline should be forgotten immediately — Any player that hangs onto his mistakes in a game will surely make more. It may not be over until it's over, but when it's over, it has to be over. When offering criticism, be sure to offer a solution as well.

15. Teach your players how to be teachers — Everyone learns best from his peers and teaching something is the best way to learn that thing inside-out.

16. Respond to a player's needs rather than react to his or her behavior—

When a player, especially a young one, exhibits a maladaptive behavior, chances are he isn't any happier about it than you are. Acting-out behaviors are indicative of needs not being met. Rather than retaliate against a behavior, ask yourself *what is it that this person really needs?* Does he need more attention? Does he need to feel more productive? Make the person a partner in dealing with his behavior rather than setting yourself up in opposition.

THE WINDOW OF OPPORTUNITY

It's hard to convince an eighteen year-old with still green bones and a baby face that needs shaving once every third day, that life is a quick short affair and that its path is not paved from beginning to end with golden opportunities.

Even if a young pitcher has a 90 + mph fastball and a bionic arm, he needs to acknowledge that this life will hand him a limited number of opportunities and that each needs to be recognized, appreciated, and acted upon. Young people can't be expected to understand this and consequently, unless they have guidance, they will tend to let life just happen to them rather than become active participants in shaping and deciding their futures.

The dream of becoming a Major Leaguer resides in all players from tee-ball to Triple A. For some, the dream is a driving vision; for others it is just a passing fancy. But while it can be easy to decide what we want, making the right decisions to get us to our goal is no simple matter.

A young man today with a golden arm has different roads open to him. Is he best off going to college and building up his value, his life experience and talent; or is he best off taking the money while it's available and make baseball the entire focus of his being? No formula exists that can make that decision. Each case is unique. And the only chance that a young man has of making the right choice — besides depending upon luck— is depending upon the wisdom of his elders and the instincts of his heart.

With hitters there is much more pressure to develop sooner rather than later, because if one does not develop a capacity to hit big league pitching by ones early 20's, the statistics tell us it just isn't going to happen. But while hitters tend to reach their peak at the age of 27, pitchers might not reach theirs until after they turn 30. However, there is a trade-off, as pitchers are far more susceptible to career-altering injuries.

> We can never be certain whether a decision — even as it plays itself out — is right or wrong, but we can be certain that those decisions that a young pitcher makes will often have a dramatic impact on the course of his future.

Coaching TIP

A good coach gives someone a reason to think he can make it and contributes nothing that would make him think otherwise.

YOUR DAY IN THE SUN

Before we look at this further, we should once again remind ourselves that it's a very small percentage of college players or minor leaguers who end up in the big show. For every hundred high school pitching prodigies, less than one will ever play in a Major League All Star Game (and only then if we use the word prodigy in a very strict sense). But you don't have to make it to the big leagues to be a successful player.

Being the best pitcher you can possibly be might mean that you'll earn a varsity letter in high school, or a scholarship to college. What it definitely means is that you'll be blessed with a thousand great memories and have learned dozens of life lessons that can give strength, character, and meaning to your day-to-day life.

Throw a no-hitter in a big high school game and you will discover just how high the human spirit can soar. Strike out the side in the last inning of your last college game with a proverbial fastball that can't break glass and you will have a well you can go to every time you need a drink of courage. Hear the Legion fans cheer your effort as you leave the mound trailing 1-0 and you will never forget that ultimately it's by how you play the game that the people who matter will judge you.

Even though the closest you might ever get to a big league field is a box seat, if having played baseball allows you to look back at high school fondly, if it earns you a college education, if it teaches you something about the synergy of mind, heart and body, you have had a successful baseball career.

IS COLLEGE THE BEST PLACE TO MAJOR IN PITCHING?

If a young pitcher can go through four years of college, and then sign a professional baseball contract of some financial worth, we might speak of that player as having his cake and eating it too. We might also think of it as the player covering his bets — if he was wise enough to use his college tenure to develop the skills for a career outside of baseball.

Playing high level baseball (Division 1) under a good coach, supplemented by competitive summer league ball is an excellent way to develop as a pitcher, especially if the individual is scholastically oriented and perhaps even has interests in other sports. With a diploma in hand at the age of twenty-one, a young pitcher still has plenty of time to develop a career in professional baseball — providing he's maintained his health, his fire and his love for the game.

The pitcher who goes through college is apt to be more mature, better rounded, and much wiser in the ways of the world. Having that college diploma gives a young man the confidence to deal with the business side of baseball and chances are by having a degree, he will be treated with more respect — by his peers, by those in the front office, as well as by the press and the public. Studies have shown that when a college player makes it into the big leagues, he's more apt to have a longer sports career than his less educated peers. And though I can't conclusively prove this, I believe that those players taking the college route are less susceptible to our modern society's worst habits, especially alcohol and drug use. Professional players of all educational levels have gone on to prolific second careers, but those with a college background seem to fare a better — even if it is just because the world expects them to.

By the time a young man puts on his cap and gown, it is expected of him that he be prepared to leave childish things behind. For the young man who has gone right from high school to the minors, that delineation — where one exits childhood and enters into adulthood — is far less clear, and in fact many who travel that route never do completely cross the line into adulthood. Some of them end up being among baseball's most colorful characters, but a far greater number end up as lost souls whose only experience with intact relationships are the ones they have with their vices.

The better college programs could be considered to be at the level of Class A professional baseball, although one should not deceive himself into thinking that college or even semi-pro baseball, where the competition can be quite substantial, is on a par with professional ball. In the pros, every player is out there fighting to become a Major Leaguer. There are no slow bats in professional baseball, no second basemen more concerned with their grade point average than their batting average, no center fielders more suited for understanding the physics of a rocket than interacting with the physics of a baseball. In the pros, every player digs in at the plate as if tomorrow's meal money depends on it, which in fact it does.

On the other hand, most college players have likely had good coaches and good guidance and are quite well prepared for the professional game, if they have the talent and drive to take them that far.

> *I would advise almost every high school*
> *player to attend college if he has the capacity*
> *to succeed in an academic environment.*

Are there exceptions to this? Of course there are. Some folks just aren't cut out for college and putting them into an environment where they are going to fail is foolish. And once in a long while, a player comes along with such overwhelming talent that he can name his price. I don't think I would ever advise a young man to walk away from a six or seven figure contract that could provide his family with security for life.

Also in some instances if his career potential has reached its maximum economic value, a young man might want to opt out of finishing college for the time. It happens in other fields of high talent. Programming wizards and graphic designers are often recruited as underclassman. The window on educational opportunity is quite large compared to pitching. The ability to throw a baseball with velocity and accuracy is very subject to genetic and situational randomness. Career-ending injuries are too close to commonplace in the world of baseball. There is no guarantee that the money laid on the table one year will be offered the next. Another real factor to consider is that a Major League team may be willing to pay a college sophomore or junior more money than a graduating senior, as the team knows that the underclassman has the option to return to college if the money isn't good enough.

MAKING THE JUMP FROM HIGH SCHOOL

No matter how many games he has won in high school, unless a pitcher possesses a fastball in the upper eighties, has decent control, and has the start on a breaking pitch and/or a change-up — skipping college for the pros is unquestionably a bad choice. However, for a young man with a live arm, it may be quite advantageous to accelerate his career with an immediate jump into pro ball. In

the pros he will see an increased level of competition, learn the nuances of the professional game more quickly, and have longer to establish himself.

Another thing to consider when weighing such a choice is the quality of coaching that the young hurler has received. Making the jump can be a lot easier if the pitcher has the advantage of having his development attended to by a quality high school coach with professional experience. Chances are that a coach who has gone the course himself will know a little bit about what it takes, and understands the importance of laying down a proper foundation, both physically and mentally.

No set formula exists and there are no guarantees that one will ever make the right choice, even though there will always be journalists, friends, relations, and agents who believe they know what is truly best. In the end, the young man and his parents will have to weigh all the factors of situation and personality. And once a decision is made, they must be strong enough not to fall victim to futile second-guessing.

THE TRICKY BUSINESS OF MAINTAINING ELIGIBILITY
YOU'D BEST KNOW THE RULES.

It is very important that amateur athletes, their families and their coaches are familiar with the complex guidelines governing the maintenance of ones amateur status. Ignorance of the rules doesn't preclude one from having the responsibility to follow them. While the rules for maintaining ones amateur status are not as harsh as back when Jim Thorpe was stripped of his Olympic medals for taking meal money, they are far more complicated. If a student athlete intends to participate in Division I or II athletics, he or she must register with and be certified as eligible by the NCAA Initial-Eligibility Clearinghouse. The student should apply for certification after his or her junior year in high school.

To order a copy of the NCAA Guide for the College-Bound Student-Athlete, which contains a copy of the student release form as well as an informational brochure, call 800/638-3731 or write to:

> Initial-Eligibility Clearinghouse
> 2255 N. Dubuque Road
> P.O. Box 4044
> Iowa City, IA 52243-4044

Further information can be found by visiting the NCAA's website at http://www.ncaa.org/eligibility/

TROUBLE SHOOTING

Sometimes there isn't much to say. You can walk out to the mound and tell the young hurler to keep the ball down, but it's not as if he just served up that hip high change-up because he thought it was a good idea.

Or you can tell him to throw strikes, as if he didn't understand that's what he's supposed to be doing. Or you can tell him to throw harder, although throwing as hard as he can doesn't seem to make the ball go any faster.

Every coach has a laundry list of cliches designed to give his pitchers a little bit of encouragement when there's really nothing to say. The pitcher is doing all he can, but whether it's due to luck, the prowess of the other team, or simply that he doesn't have that little edge on this particular day, nothing seems to be working as it should. At such a time the cliches are really all there is. But more often than not, a little bit of advice is what's needed — right then and there on the spot. And at such a time what separates a good coach from the pack is the ability to perform a little triage and come up with a way to stop the bleeding.

Ultimately, to be a good troubleshooter, to be able to fix problems, you need to have a solid understanding of the mechanics of pitching and appreciate how even the most subtle deviations can have the greatest impact. You must understand the

Seven to One Rule: that for most deviations in mechanics of one inch, there will be a resulting difference of seven inches at the plate. What that means is that if your release point is an inch higher than normal, the pitch will end up being seven inches higher than anticipated. It also means that if your stride is an inch longer, your release will be an inch higher, etc. It also means that just a slight seemingly insignificant change in the turn of your wrist will mean a big difference in the flight of your breaking ball. If your legs are just a scarcely noticeable fraction of a second ahead of your upper body, there will be a very noticeable drop in velocity. Troubleshooting then, is about the little things. It's also about knowing the situation and knowing just who it is you are dealing with — knowing how much frustration he can handle, knowing how he best takes in information.

A coach who knows his pitcher from working with him day in and day out will sense something is wrong before he can even analyze it. He will be able to look beyond the results and see trouble lurking down the road. The coach holds a mental picture of what his pitcher looks like when all the cylinders are firing, when his mechanics are fluid and solid. And an alarm will go off in his head when the real life pitcher's motion is discordant with that mental picture. Paying closer attention, he will notice an elbow dropping, a shorter stride, or shoulders that open too soon, and he will begin to work backwards from there, seeing where along the motion the problem originates.

This section of The Act of Pitching is not designed for the seasoned pitching coach who knows his stuff. It is intended for those rookie coaches who may not know what advice to give their young pitchers when the wheels are starting to come off the cart. It's also intended to help those pitchers who are eager to analyze their own problems (an attitude that most good pitchers should have. One word of advice though: Before you start troubleshooting, make sure you have a strong grounding in mechanics. Read through that chapter with a fine-tooth comb, and you will discover that most of the advice offered here will become quite self-evident.

STAVING OFF THOSE FIRST INNING DISASTERS

Many an excellent pitcher has had problems with first inning demons on a continual basis. Much of it I believe, is psychological. It can become a self-fulfilling prophecy. *I usually have trouble in the first inning,* the pitcher thinks, therefore he starts out tentatively — and being tentative never works to a pitcher's favor. With some good pitchers, it may be a psychological thing on the part of the opposition. The hitters think, *I'm not going to get this guy unless I get him early,* so they increase their own intensity. For control pitchers like Glavine and Maddux, it can be about learning what the limits of the strikezone are on that given day and then subtly adjusting the umpire to their version. In such a case there probably isn't much to do but encourage the pitcher not to lose his cool and keep the damage to a minimum. Being overly cautious and walking in a run is far preferable to getting impatient and allowing a three-run homer. A coach can't afford to have a short fuse in such cases either. Glavine and Maddux would never win their fifteen to twenty every year if their manager was yanking them out every time they have trouble in the first.

PROPER PREPARATION

First inning problems can also be caused by improper and unfocused bullpen work. Many pitchers simply do not adequately warm up. With such a focus on watching pitch counts, a lot of pitchers have come to erroneously believe that if they spend too much time warming up, they are going to leave some of their best stuff in the pen. A pitcher needs to enter a game with his body fully warmed-up, and he must have also thrown enough serious pitches that he knows which of them is working well. If his curve is flat, he better have found out about it before the opposing team does.

Sometimes the atmosphere in the bullpen can be a problem. The bullpen catcher might not be serious about his job, and when you get six or seven guys hanging around with little to do, the task at hand can lose its sense of priority.

A pitcher must learn what it takes for him to get ready. And what works for one doesn't work for all. I always found that throwing curve balls was the way to get my arm warmed up in a hurry. Maybe you need eighteen minutes to warm up instead of fifteen. If you pitch much more strongly in the second inning maybe you need to pitch that first inning in the bullpen. Lee Smith, one of the finest closers ever, threw just as hard, if not harder, as he was warming up in the pen. Airing it out in the pen isn't a bad idea, as you need to know just how fast you can throw that day without losing control. Fans witnessed some of the most powerful pitches ever thrown with catbird seats over the bullpen.

Go through a mental checklist as you warm-up; make sure your stride length is where you want it; give a fair allotment of time and concentration to each of your pitches.

Made sure that your coach also understands what it takes to get you ready to enter a game. Tell him the truth and not what he wants to hear. The best managers have players knowing what role is expected of them. With that kind of management, a pitcher will know when he needs to start getting himself ready mentally and physically even before the phone rings.

KNOW THE SITUATION

Pitchers will get pounded simply because they haven't done their basic homework. You should know the hitters and should have spent some time deciding how you will pitch to each. And of course. you should also be following the game so that you know who is hitting the ball well and what kind of pitches he's nailing.

GET ADJUSTED TO THE MOUND

Part of every pitcher's pre-game routine should include scoping out the mound, paying attention to both height and slope. Even in pro ball they can vary quite a bit; it's all part of the home field advantage. If at all possible, see that the bullpen mound bears a good resemblance to the game mound. And when you first arrive on the mound, take time to set up shop, even if there are forty thousand pairs of eyes on you.

Rather than adjusting your stride to the mound, whenever possible adjust the mound to your stride. Make sure that the dirt is well packed where your strike foot is going to land and that the edge of the rubber isn't buried. At your home field, make friends with the groundskeeper and take him into your confidence. Chances are he'll be more than happy to become a factor in your team's success.

TROUBLE WITH KEEPING THE BALL DOWN

If one throws consistently high all the time, then some kind of mechanical adjustment needs to be made. The stride might need to be adjusted. The pitcher may not be leading with his elbow. But when a pitcher is going along
fine and has solid mechanics, throwing high is probably an indicator of fatigue. Jim Palmer was a prime example of this. He would be pitching brilliantly, and then without seeming to lose anything, he would begin to throw high. For Palmer those high pitches were a good *early warning device*. Because Palmer threw a high fastball as his bread and butter, *up* for him was shoulder high which could be adjusted for before any real damage occurred.However, for a pitcher who lives around the knees, throwing high will bring his pitch up around the thighs, which can be instantly lethal.

When one's energy begins to fade, it usually starts with the legs. As the pitcher is focused on the game before he notices that fatigue it's apt to show up in a shortened stride. Also, when the legs are tired the front knee is apt to get a little stiff which will also result in a higher release point. One should be able to pick up this difficulty with keeping the ball down while warming up between innings. Lengthening the stride a fraction of an inch at a time will often solve the problem. If not, it may be time to hit the showers.

Landing on the heel rather than on the ball of the foot can be an old habit that pitchers fall back into during the middle of a game. This will result in the knee bending less, thus raising the release point.

Other bad habits that pitchers fall into is failing to bring their head and shoulders over the imaginary wall (see page 64), and shortchanging the follow-though so that one is no longer reaching through the release point.

WILDNESS ON THE HORIZONTAL

Pitchers will more typically suffer control problems with the inside corner (too far to the right for the righthanded hurler) rather than the outside of the plate. This will typically happen because of improper body alignment or because the movement that usually carried the pitch on a trajectory from right to left (rhp) has decreased.

Poor control along the horizontal plane also can be caused by improper alignment to the target (check out the use of supplemental eyeballs in Chapter Two). Timing could also be a factor. The shoulders and hips might be opening too soon or the body may not be driving to the target, which will make the ball have a tendency towards the outside. This is a tough thing to adjust for in the middle of a game and often times the pitcher can create a temporary fix by stepping slightly to one direction of the other with the lead foot. To correct throwing inside, step slightly to the glove-side.

When the problem is occurring with one pitch, be it the slider or tailing fastball — grip, hand and arm angle, and amount of snap can all be factors. Or it may simply be an issue of atmospheric conditions. Even the best of pitchers sometimes have to scuttle a particular pitch during a game, which is why a pitcher must have at least three quality pitches in his toolbox.

CURVE PROBLEMS

Fixing a curve with an anemic break is a pretty risky business in the middle of an inning. In the majority of cases this is indicative of a pitch that is still in its embryonic stages and not ready for prime time. The fact of the matter is that you probably shouldn't be using a curve unless it's behaving properly seventy to eighty percent of the time in practice and warm-up.

Dryness, extremes in air pressure (ask Darryl Kile what it was like to pitch in Colorado) and cold weather all influence the Magnus Force, and can really wreak havoc with the best breaking pitch.

It is not uncommon for a pitcher under stress to grip the ball too tightly thus reducing its rotation. Tightness in the wrist will limit ones ability to snap it with authority. In such cases, the curve will seem to tumble about, rather than dart. Reminding one's self to finish the pitch can help, as can visualizing the pistol-like finish with the throwing hand talked about in Chapter Four. The thumb should snap upward with release, with the middle finger firing the trigger, and the index finger pointing to the target like a gun barrel. Every curveball pitcher has days when the pitch is not behaving properly. Don't be stubborn; if it's not working while warming up, it won't suddenly improve on the mound. But that's not to say it won't be there for you that second time through the order, when you're apt to be better relaxed. This happens quite often with curveball pitchers.

THROWING TOO LOW

Normally this isn't a major concern. One shouldn't be too quick to change anything as the problem might be a random one. Being too low is not usually dangerous, as long as you don't start loading the bases with walks, and aren't throwing in the dirt with runners on. If an adjustment needs to be made, start by shortening the stride in very small increments. Half to three-quarters of an inch should make all the difference. Actively visualizing a higher pitch helps also.

THROWING HIGH INSIDE

Usually caused by throwing against your body, this will happen when the lead leg goes across the stride line to the pitching arm side. Quite often it also involves a stiff front leg. In addition to causing the ball to go high and inside (rhp against right hand batter), it also prevents the pitcher from properly uniting the energy of rotating hips and shoulders into the pitch. In extreme cases, the pitcher won't be able to open the hips and shoulder hardly at all. This is indicative of not putting in enough time practicing ones mechanics, or it might be the result of rushing, especially while throwing from the set position. You must remind yourself to always lead with the hip while driving forward, and to step to the stride line (with a closed front foot). Sometimes you may have to step slightly to the glove-side of the stride line. Just be careful that in stepping further over, you remain closed until foot plant.

FINGER BLISTERS

If the blisters are on the ends of the fingers this may be indicative of the fact that one is getting a lot of rotation on the ball. Soaking the fingers in brine periodically may toughen the skin. If blisters come on the side of the fingers then ethyl chloride can be used. It's important to get the fingers well conditioned early on in the spring. Early blisters will ultimately give way to calluses. Don't hide your blisters but seek help from the team trainer. If properly tended they will not impact your season.

SITUATIONAL DO'S AND DON'TS

I believe strongly in being very aggressive and going after the hitter. The initiative is yours to take. Hitters must react to your decisions. They can't dictate how you should pitch. Establishing yourself as the Overlord should be the goal as soon as you take the mound. Yes, you must give some consideration to the strengths of the hitter, but in match-ups of strengths against strengths, you should always assume that you have the upper hand.

LOW-BALL PITCHER TO LOW-BALL HITTER

Most good hitters are low-ball hitters. That's a fact — which is why I especially like the North/South style of pitching; but unless you have a fastball or a cutter that can overpower a hitter upstairs, North/South might not be the best. You need to stick with your strength. Most good hitters have their bats tuned in at slider speed, so saving your best change-up to use against a quick bat is most advisable. The deeper you get in the count, the more dangerous the situation becomes. Know the hitter; know what he likes to sit on for the first pitch. Don't challenge him with a fastball if that's what he likes to look for. The advantage is all yours the first time through the order, so don't give the batter a ton of stuff to look at. Without men on, your goal should be to get him to hit the ball on the first or second pitch, preferably throwing something with good sinking action on the inside of the plate so he can't extend his arms. If he's a lethal pull hitter he may however, be looking for the ball inside on that first pitch.

You of course need to use a little more caution with men on base. Don't allow the baserunners to distract you and cause you to rush. In today's game, baserunners seldom get the green light when the best hitter is batting. They don't want to open the base and give you the option of walking him, nor do they want to distract the batter or force him to swing at bad pitches to protect the runner. The concept of clutch hitting is largely a myth. Very rare are those hitters who actually hit significantly better with men on base. However, certain hitters do perform better with certain counts. Be aware of this, as the hitter certainly is. Avoid self-fulfilling prophecies by being overly cautious. Don't get caught up in visualizing what you don't want to happen.

PITCHING INSIDE TO A PULL HITTER

Here I definitely would match power against power. If you are a power pitcher then you can't be afraid to throw to a batter's assumed strength. Saw off his bat. We really are talking about degrees. With a Ted Williams, I might think twice and stay on the outside. It really depends on how good a power pitcher you are. Power hitters often are weak on pitches outside, particularly breaking pitches — so a mixture of power in and off-speed outside should be a viable mix to the power hitter. Power pitchers should not try to be too fine, as this is not their forte. Ultimately, as long as you're not surrendering walks to the weaker bats, a good power hitter isn't going to be able to destroy you with a single swing.

INTENTIONAL WALK TO GOOD HITTER

I've lost games both as a pitcher and a coach by refusing to either pitch around or intentionally walk a good hitter at a critical time in the game. Walking a hitter with the tying or winning run on second base makes good sense. Not only is a force play set up, but a chance perhaps to pitch to a lesser hitter is created. Pitching around a tough hitter can be a smart move, because in his anxiousness to deliver, he may chase some bad pitches thereby giving an advantage to the pitcher and the defense. Raw ego should not get in the way of logic and good sense, when it comes to pitching around a hitter or giving an intentional walk.

STOPPING THE BUNT AND THE HIT & RUN

Wherever there is an obvious bunt situation, the pitcher should always throw the ball high and hard. This will quite often result in a pop-up, which renders the bunt attempt meaningless. On a hit and run, the ball should also be thrown high as the batter is trying to hit a ground ball in the vacated infield position. The high pitch, if missed, will give the catcher a better chance to nail the baserunner.

TO ENCOURAGE A DOUBLE PLAY

To elicit a doubleplay, the pitcher needs to keep the ball low. A sinking fastball is the ideal pitch, but a curveball or slider down in the strikezone can also be effective. The ball must be kept at the knees or lower.

FACILITATING THE MOVE FROM LITTLE LEAGUE TO BABE RUTH

Many twelve year-olds who are superstars at the Little League level have their egos substantially deflated when they trade up to a full-sized diamond and begin pitching from 60 feet 6 inches after three or four years of throwing from 46 feet. They inevitably find their pitches running out of gas or arching and hanging over the plate. A Little League flame-thrower firing the ball at 65 mph from 46 feet possesses the equivalent of an 85-mph fastball thrown from 60' 6" in terms of batter reaction time. And no matter how much a kid grows, he is not going to make up that 20 mph differential over the course of a single year. Previously dependent on blowing the ball by hitters, he suddenly finds that even the slower bats can tune right into his best stuff. Rather than eat crow while waiting for his body to catch up, he will often quit the game altogether.

Going from sixth to seventh grade is a major challenge for all kids; as in addition to being introduced to tougher academic requirements and a more sophisticated social order — in which they find themselves at the bottom — the hormones begin to kick in as well. Nothing is simple anymore, and in order to regain some success with pitching, a young hurler will be forced to think about what he is doing and develop a strategy to beat the hitters that goes beyond throwing the ball harder. If the thirteen-year old happens to be small for his age, the dilemma becomes even greater.

I've had serious talks with thirteen year-old hurlers who have given up baseball because the distance frightens them and they can't cope with the idea of being overmatched for the time being. Taking solace in the fact that every pitching star goes through this tortuous maturation phase helps some, but the real solution to this problem lies with preparation.

My own son was particularly big for his age, so he did not fully experience this frightening dilemma. But even more important to his success than his size, was that we had him throwing from Babe Ruth distance when he was twelve. Long toss is an especially effective drill to employ. Throwing from a long distance with no concern for strikes, the prospect's arm will be strengthened, as will his basic mechanics.

With long toss, the young pitcher should be encouraged to throw the ball with as little arc as possible. This will force him to employ strong mechanics and to get his entire body into the action. He can also spend some time doing long toss from the set position. Let him start at around sixty feet than gradually, over the course of several weeks, increase the distance to between 75 and 90 feet.

Typically, Little League season ends around early summer, so that after competitive ball is finished, a boy can begin to work more arduously at establishing himself from the longer distance. And if the boy is serious enough about what he is doing, sending him off to baseball camp might be the best thing to do. It's far better to face the early-on and develop a positive attitude, rather than to wait all winter in fear of what spring might bring.

Back in the days before youth baseball became so organized most of our playing time was garnered playing pick-up games on full sized diamonds. Not aware of any alternative, as grammar school kids we always threw from 60´6˝. So when the time came to throw in high school, we were more than adequately prepared. And quite contrary to modern day notions, we didn't do any damage to our arms whatsoever. Nowadays it would be frightening to see a twelve year-old weaned on 60´6˝ throwing at 46 feet.

Many youth leagues are considering the implementation of a transition distance such as the old Pony League once utilized. There is talk of moving the pitching distance back five or six feet and increasing the length of the basepaths for the Major League divisions of youth baseball. Such an idea would probably have already been implemented except for the expense of having to build and maintain two sets of ball fields for the kids. The summer-long tournaments being run at the Cooperstown Dreams Park for twelve-and-unders uses fields where the pitchers throw from fifty feet and the basepaths are longer. This allows for base runners to lead and steal which then necessitates that pitchers learn to throw from the set. Most youngsters are very excited to play the game in the same fashion as their big league heroes.

VARIABLES
THERE'S MORE TO IT THAN JUST TALENT — MUCH MORE . . .

15

PART I

THE MAGNIFICENT SEVEN

We've all heard the stories: This unknown kid who drives a truck or bags groceries, just happens to pitch the game of his life in some locals league on the very day that a big time scout pops up to check out some other rising star, and before you know it, fame and fortune is his.

Though such a story may delight us, it probably doesn't surprise us; we always assume that talent will rise like cream to the top. We always assume that in our just world, the better man never goes unrecognized. However, the truth of the matter is that there are guys today behind the wheels of big rigs or stuffing produce in plastic bags who have better stuff than some fellows earning six and seven figure paychecks in the big show. At first glance, such a curiosity seems to defy explanation, but the fact is there are almost always reasons for things ending up as they do.

As a long time coach, I've seen it again and again, and fallen in the trap myself of wanting to believe that every great talent is a *can't miss* prospect. And no matter how often it happens, it's always tragic to see pitchers that seem to have all the physical equipment necessary to be outstanding at any level, who never fulfill their potential. But there does seem to be a balance: for every surefire golden boy that doesn't make it, there's a fellow with seemingly average stuff, that somehow makes it to the top of the heap.

What is it then that determines who will make it and who won't?

The formula is clearly much more complicated than that of Physical Talent = Success. In fact there are at least seven variables involved in the mathematics of success. And while every pitcher has more of some and less of others, if any of those variables at the front of the equation equal zero, then it doesn't matter how much of the others one possesses, as zero times anything is always zero.

$$\frac{(\text{talent})(\text{attitude})(\text{motivation}^2) +/- \text{luck}(\text{opportunity} + \text{support})}{X} = \text{YOUR CAREER}$$

where X = THE UNKNOWN FACTOR

THE SEVEN VARIABLES

I. TALENT Made to pitch

Talent has always been to me a very overrated quality. Probably, because when we talk about talent, what we usually mean is physical talent. Applied to pitchers, physical talent would include natural velocity, movement on the ball, rhythmic agility, size to some extent, and flexibility— particularly in the wrist.

If I were ordering a pitcher from Dr. Frankenstein, I'd want him to build me one with furiously powerful legs and hips. I would want this prototype to be rangy, on the taller side, with especially long arms to improve leverage, and long exceptionally strong fingers designed for imparting spin. He'd have great balance and coordination, a finely tuned neural system and the perfect balance of accelerating and decelerating muscles to produce great arm speed.

For every great pitcher who fits this physical description there are probably a dozen great ones who don't — which of course lends credence to the fact that a lot more goes into pitching than physical make-up.

II. MOTIVATION How bad do you want it?

Do you want it bad enough to put thousands of hours of practice into the perfection of your craft. Do you want it bad enough to dig down deep when you've got nothing left to give? Do you want it bad enough to swallow your pride, to admit to your faults, to keep trying again and again when the results seem to be lagging behind the effort? Do you want it bad enough to keep going when others around you give up the quest and tell you it can't be done?

The motivated spirit can be manifested in many ways. It can be packaged in braggadocio, or burn like a fire behind quiet cool reserve. The motivated soul can approach his craft like a savage warrior, or a cerebral intellectual, or an obsessive-compulsive technician. But in any approach, the motivation must be omnipresent, relentless and well honed. It can never be fully satisfied by yesterday's accomplishment. Without drive. . . everything falls short.

Motivation can be initiated by external forces, but it can only be maintained by one's own inner fire. It's amazing how much you can do when you believe you can. The record books are full of folks with average talent who parlayed their great motivation into momentous accomplishments. Conversely, the gutters on the road to success are littered with the carcasses of great talents who developed very slowly or not at all because they could not convince themselves of the need to do so.

The sincere pitcher needs to continually set goals for himself that are barely reachable, and along the way, stop every now and again to take an honest accounting of just how well those goals are being met. Close scrutiny of the main theme will serve to keep the motivational fires alive.

Players often go astray when they reach a goal they have aimed for and then only attempt to maintain themselves rather than move forward with further improvement.

III. MENTAL FACTOR Are you tough enough to embrace success? Are you smart enough, aware enough?

My concern for all young men is that they become aware enough and wise enough and brave enough to recognize, develop, and master their own positive potential.

When we talk about the mental factor involved in success, not all of our discussion should center exclusively on mental toughness. Many other qualities of mind are required, such as perceptiveness, discipline, attention to detail, adaptability, and of course intelligence. Not just what Ted Williams refers to as *baseballic intelligence,* but also the kind of people smarts that is necessary for dealing with coaches, players, management and media. Many people are naïve in this area and it retards their development and can even stymie their climb up the professional ladder.

Even when we talk about mental toughness, we need to get beyond the obvious in understanding just what that means. While talent might buy us opportunity, and motivation will inspire us, it's mental toughness that will determine just how far we'll get when the path through the woods is overgrown with brambles and thorns and the woods themselves are full of lions and tiger and bears. You can model mental toughness, you can encourage it, but I don't think you can teach it.

People make the mistake of thinking that dealing with adversity is what purely defines our capacity for mental toughness. The real question that begs to be answered is the one that asks, *Are we tough enough to handle success?* The human spirit is geared towards coping with disaster; embracing success is another matter all together.

Being successful carries a burden that few of us are willing to even recognize. I think most of us are afraid to let ourselves get good. With success comes heightened expectations, from others and ourselves. Success requires a greater level of responsibility and it also obligates us to let go of the habits of our resentments.

Taking to the field as a champion is equally if not more challenging than performing as an underdog with nothing at all to lose. When we are successful, no longer can we join in the common 'moan' that *the world is an unfair place.* We no longer have the excuse to fall back on of having to fight all our battles uphill. Once you realize that about human nature, you start to understand the real battle that has to be fought is with one's self.

If you are afraid to succeed, you'd best get over it.

You have to feel that you deserve to win, that your winning is the right thing. While we can imagine perhaps one or two scenarios of success, we can usually imagine a hundred different ways to fail and they can be very distracting if we allow them. A soldier who goes into war best not be preoccupied with dying, so too a pitcher entering a game must not be preoccupied with losing.

Being successful at anything requires a measure of mental toughness, being the best requires a bushel. The kind of mental toughness we're talking about here isn't always visible and it doesn't necessarily represent some kind of hardened and selfish approach to this world. Giving and receiving compliments can require a kind of toughness, so too it is with taking criticism and making your needs known.

Pitchers who win games when everything suggests they should lose, are those that I consider to possess the ultimate in mental toughness.

There are certain pitchers who can rise to the occasion again and again, who can make their stuff — however good it is — good enough to win. Such pitchers seem able to will a game to victory. They seem able to defy the odds, snatching victory when the odds indicate it would be perfectly understandable to lose. They are rare and at their best, they inspire awe in even the most casual fan.

Pitching a good game almost always requires a certain approach to perfection. Yet, keeping your mistakes to a minimum requires that you can't be paralyzed by a fear of making mistakes. Nor for that matter can you afford to be crippled by a fear of being afraid, as fear becomes even more dangerous when we pretend it doesn't exist. Recognizing fear is a good thing as long as we don't allow it to become all of whom we are.

The keenness of mind and heightened level of performance that manifests itself in pressure situations is a natural human condition. It is no coincidence that many pitchers are at their best when everything is on the line. We all have the capacity to rise to the occasion and we all at least occasionally do. But few are those who know how to tap that wellspring often and continuously. Not willing to be the victims of circumstance and randomness, they have the ability to seize the moment and hammer it into victory.

A Dave Stewart or a Jack Morris leaves us not just with the vision of a well-pitched game and a gutsy performance. They also remind us how when it matters the most, we all have the power to be more than what we seem, providing that we are willing to make that conscious choice to prevail.

To be aware of our internal resolve, and evoke it, is to develop it. However, for most of us it is a latent option, one that is used occasionally, if at all.

IV. SUPPORT SYSTEM Sometimes it's more about who knows you, rather than who you know

While many pitchers tend to dance to the beat of a different drummer, I will venture to guess that no pitcher has ever made it very far without the support of others. It is startling how many players have poor or no support systems. In fact, for some kids, baseball provides them with the only support system they've ever known.

Everyone, from the Little Leaguer to the grizzled veteran, needs someone who can be there to provide guidance and encouragement. Parents, spouses, grandparents, friends, fraternity brothers, agents, advisors, scouts, coaches, teachers and even one's children, can all in their varied roles provide the fabric that makes up a support network. They can provide us with guidance at all levels and motivation, as well as the security and stability that allows us to concentrate on the task at hand.

Good advice at the right time is priceless, especially the sage and often definitive advice of someone who has traveled the road before. This type of advice should be very much valued.

A boost in confidence can also be a priceless event, whether it comes by way of a boot in the pants, or through unconditional love. Some people need such boosts on a continual basis, but all of us now and again need to be reassured of our goodness and our capabilities by those that are dearly trusted and whose opinions are cherished.

Most every successful pitcher has a person or two in his life who has known him since his goals were fresh and his talent raw. Such a person can act as a touchstone to keep one from losing sight of ones goals and straying too far from ones most honorable intentions. For pitchers, that person is often an old coach who remains available to help fix a mechanical flaw or add an extra pitch.

Ultimately, that support has to become internalized, because people eventually get tired of providing support to those who are unwilling to believe in themselves.

V. LUCK Plain and not always simple

Nobody survives in baseball merely by luck, but on the other hand, very few ever make it to the big show without at least the occasional blessing of good fortune. While much with regard to luck is out of our hands, there is some truth to the old adage that you make your own luck. And while I tend to subscribe to this notion, I also tend to think the magical quality of luck is often overestimated and overrated.

Certainly, one has a hand in ones destiny, but I've seen too many fluke injuries, too many guys make it who were no better than guys that didn't, to doubt that some randomness is involved. However, luck can also be a matter of perspective. Having the rotten luck to be overlooked when going out for a team becomes a big break, if the rejected pitcher allows the cut to motivate him to achieve a level of excellence that can't be overlooked. It might seem like bad luck when a pitcher doesn't make it into a big time college program. But then maybe if he did make it, he would have ended up rotting on the bench, rather than going to a small program where a terrific coach takes him on as a pet project.

Chalking things up to luck can sometimes blind us if we're not careful. How many times does the opposition have to blast us before we realize it's our mechanics rather than our luck that is doing us in? And how many undisciplined pitchers blame injuries on bad luck, when good conditioning and proper mechanics would have prevented those injuries from being so disastrous or even from occurring at all?

There is also the element of luck when it comes to being at the right place at the right time. Being the pitcher most available to fill a team's need is often a serendipitous event. But while luck may bring a knock at our door, we must be awake enough to hear it.

VI. OPPORTUNITY Prepping for serendipity

When we're young and opportunity comes knocking, we don't think of it as that big a deal; we assume that other opportunities will come along as surely as Monday or Wednesday show up every week. As we mature, we begin to understand that opportunity isn't a yearly crop, especially in a highly competitive field. Great opportunities often come as a surprise. For many this surprise catches them unprepared to capitalize. For those that are prepared, events such as getting moved into the starting rotation, or getting called up to the next level, provide them with the necessary exhilaration and stimulus to capitalize on the opportunity and achieve the dream.

What a crime it is when a young player has not kept himself ready and the serendipitous moment is missed. Who knows when such a moment will arrive again, if at all? When the band starts playing, we'd better be ready to dance and not make excuses. When opportunity comes knocking, we had better be at home to answer it.

VII. THE X-FACTOR

I can't tell you exactly what it is, but I've been around long enough to know that things will come up for which one has no way of preparing. Sometimes it shows up as our friend Mr. Murphy, and then everything that could possibly go wrong, does. This can happen in both the small and the large sense. The tough situation that gets out of hand! The apparently good situation that suddenly goes sour! Some people are experts at handling Murphy. Some are completely overpowered by him.

Great pitchers, while they may not be able to avoid him, seem to have an instinct with regard to Mr. Murphy's arrival. Those are the fellows we look at as having a knack for damage control.

Things Happen: A defense that goes porous in the ninth inning. The capacity for a batted baseball to find the weakest link on the field. The disappearance of reliable run support for weeks at a time. The blister that trashes your curveball. A favorite glove stolen before a big series.

It happens off the field too. A wife who runs off with the flower delivery guy you send around every week when you're on the road. Ending up as the player named later in a trade to Minnesota. Life throws an awful lot of Uncle Charlie's. Anyone involved in athletics or any other competitive scenario knows this. It bodes well to be constantly prepared for these moments without becoming paranoid about them.

And you have to be smart enough to know which battles *can* be fought. When its pouring rain, birds have sense enough to find a solid branch and tuck their heads under their wings until the storm passes. People rarely possess enough sense to recognize that often all we have to do is wait out the hard times, rather than take desperate action. Are we patient enough to rest an injury rather than play through it? When even the umpires seem against us, are we smart enough to walk in a run with the bases loaded rather than grove a pitch to a clean-up hitter?

Successful people are very intimate with disaster control. When trouble occurs, they don't beat their breasts and say, "Why me?" Often this is why they are successful.

THE FINAL CHOICE

> *Our deepest fear is not that we are inadequate;*
> *our deepest fear is that we are powerful beyond measure.*
> *It is our light, not our darkness that most frightens us.*
>
> — NELSON MANDELA

As I said in the introduction, I believe that if you do enough right things, you can get good at pitching, very good. In these 300 some pages I've tried to provide information enough to give the aspiring pitcher and his coach a strong foundation in the art and craft of pitching. And I've tried to present it in a systematic enough way so that not only will you have the material but also a blueprint for developing that foundation and refining it in such a way that you might begin to develop an appreciation of pitching's inner sanctum.

But I would be remiss if I didn't tell you that none of it matters if you aren't willing to let yourself get good.

All the coaching and information in the world, even when added to a lifetime of practice; all the right equipment, right exercise, right diet, right lifestyle, won't buy you that proverbial cup of coffee in the big leagues if you aren't willing to let yourself get good.

One of the great enigmas I've witnessed over the years is the large number of young pitchers who have balked at entering through the door of success. It's especially frustrating to watch a talented young man invest his time and energy in the pursuit of excellence and then negate all that effort through some pattern of self-destruction. And not just the *talented* young men either. . . .

When one starts by practicing the right things and stays with it in a consistent fashion, dramatic improvement will inevitably follow, while confidence builds up along the way. No one has to give a person permission to get good for it to happen. That's part of the scheme. Practice right things and it happens. It can be subtle, and suddenly one is good.

One of the especially satisfying events in coaching is to oversee the skinny kid with the weak fastball, as he becomes the efficient, even domineering pitcher, because he has worked at it and allowed himself to develop. Contrast this with the apparently talented star who, enamored with his early success, remains at a static level, not attempting to learn anything new. Gradually, he is surpassed by others with lesser physical talent. It happens all the time! Obviously choices have been made.

It impresses me seriously as a coach when I notice the pitcher who is opting for improvement regardless of his physical prowess. I will do all I can to help this person along.

But too often whether the pitcher starts off with great talent or not, somewhere along the way he too often stops making the right choices and begins to stagnate or regress. This kind of self-destruction can manifest itself in many ways.

THEY TEACH THEMSELVES BAD HABITS. It's just as easy to learn right things as it is wrong things, but some will insist in practicing the wrong things. Perhaps because of laziness, perhaps because of stubbornness, some young men will put in the time practicing, but they will practice the wrong things; they will teach themselves improper timing or develop mechanical hitches that they practice over and over again until they are imbedded in muscle memory.

THEY BECOME IRRESPONSIBLE. Sometimes a young man who has always proven himself dependable will begin missing practices. He'll fail to honor his word and start showing up late before games. He might stop taking care of his body. He might choose to eat the wrong things or eat too much of everything. Others will put themselves on the injured list as a result of risky behavior whether it be in a car or on a bike or at horseplay with friends.

THEY FAIL TO KEEP THEMSELVES READY. Some players will take the attitude that throwing between assignments, doing bullpen work isn't needed once you have your game together.

THEY SUFFER AN ACADEMIC COLLAPSE. Even though the scholar-athlete knows that that he must keep his grades up to keep playing, he lets it all slide. Others will allow romantic endeavors to supersede their schoolwork and their baseball work.

THEY BECOME SLOPPY. They stop paying attention to detail. Their mechanics become a little off. An off-hand starts to wander or the head turns away from the batter, or the elbow gets a little behind. They fail to keep the runner close at first or take too long to the plate.

THEY FREEZE UP. The message to fire the muscles comes from the brain but another message preempts it. The once fluid arm goes stiff and what was once an autonomic response becomes waylaid by hesitation.

THEY BECOME COCKY. There is now no one who knows more about pitching than they do. They will sometime pretend that they listen, but they know better and when they do fail, it's because they happened to follow your advice that day.

THEY FAIL TO THINK. The brain puts out the *Gone Fishing* sign and the mistakes made are painfully obvious on hindsight. You tried to sneak a cutter by him in the fifth and he put it in the bleachers so *Why in Christy Matthewson's name would you come right back with that cutter again?*

The preceding isn't a list of why pitchers fail, but a list of the means they utilize to keep themselves from getting good. It would probably take an entire book to fully explore the reasons why people won't give themselves permission to get good at pitching, or for that matter, anything else in life.

A good coach might not be able to articulate those reasons anymore than could those young men whom they guide. But they should understand that it's not just the appearance of willfulness or stubbornness or spite that keeps a player from progressing. And while the player may not admit he is unhappy about failing to fulfill his potential, deep down he is not any more happy with himself than those who would support him.

If a pitcher could have the insight to articulate the reasons why he is reluctant to give himself permission to succeed, he might express one or more of the following.

- ◆ I'M NOT DESERVING OF IT.
- ◆ I'M AFRAID OF INCREASED EXPECTATIONS.
- ◆ I DON'T WANT TO BE NOTICED.
- ◆ I ABHOR CONFLICT AND COMPETITION.
- ◆ I DON'T KNOW HOW TO HANDLE FAILURE.

These sorts of thoughts are those that would occur at the core of an individual's personality and more than likely would have been with the individual since he entered elementary school. To develop the capacity to look at them takes a huge step in maturation, the step that moves one from being reactive to being reflective and responsive.

> **The diamond is a school where we will face every challenge that life could hand us. For the developing pitcher, he has the chance to learn just what he is made of and the chance to go beyond the limitations that life will hand him, the first of which are the ones he has placed on himself.**

When the pitcher says to himself, *I am willing to give myself permission to get good,* he is acting on life, rather than merely reacting to it. He is learning how to dominate. To dominate the hitter and the game is easy; to dominate himself is the larger challenge. But he must overcome this greater challenge to become the overlord of those smaller challenges that define the game. So consciously and quite loudly, he must tell himself, *I am willing to give myself permission to get good.* And be ready to reassert that permission whenever he hesitates in the face of progress. *I am willing to give myself permission to get good.*

Working hard to become good, he will then find it easy to say *I give myself permission to get very good.* And if he...if YOU are genuine in giving yourself this permission and you DO ENOUGH THINGS RIGHT, *you will get very very good at this act of pitching.*

About the Author

The Act of Pitching is the work of Dr. John Bagonzi, one of the foremost authorities on the techniques of pitching a baseball. Coach Bagonzi has written dozens of articles for among others, *Coaching Management, Junior Baseball, Hardball Magazine, Scholastic Coach,* and *Collegiate Baseball.* As a pitcher he spent time in both the Boston Red Sox and Chicago Cubs organizations. Before his professional career began, he attended the University of New Hampshire where he set many pitching records that still stand today, including the most no-hitters, of which he threw five. Over the course of his pitching career he won 117 games and pitched a total of nine no-hitters.

Leaving baseball as a player, he continued to coach and earned a doctorate at Indiana University doing his thesis on "Improving Pitching Velocity and Accuracy through Resistive Exercises."

Coach Bagonzi spent many years teaching and coaching at Woodsville High School in New Hampshire, where his baseball and basketball teams won thirteen state championships. He coached Woodsville to over 700 victories with a winning percentage of .830. He also worked as baseball coach of Plymouth State College from 1982 through 1985, taking the team to the ECAC PLAYOFFS in 1984 and 1985.

Pitchers working under him have thrown an amazing 25 no-hitters. He has coached numerous outstanding college pitchers as well as several professional pitchers: Jim MacDonald, Houston Astros; Steve Blood, Minnesota Twins; Dennis Paronto, Atlanta Braves; Todd Brill, New York Yankees; Rich Gale, Kansas City Royals; and Chad Paronto, Cleveland Indians.

Former director of the Major League Scouting Bureau, Lennie Merullo, now with the New England Scouting Bureau, says, "John is probably the finest pitching coach in the east, a pro's pro." For the last twenty years Coach Bagonzi has operated his Championship Pitching Camps, working with over 600 pitching prospects each year.

Coach Bagonzi is in the New Hampshire Coaches Hall of Fame. In 1988, he was selected as one of New Hampshire's all time coaches. In 2000 he was chosen as one of 50 top sports achievers in New Hampshire for the past century (Boston Globe). He was recently elected to the first class of the NH Athletic Association Hall of Fame. He is also a member of the University of New Hampshire Hall of Fame and the Manchester Union Leader Hall of Fame.

Our Pitchers

Between all of them, our models have probably won close to a thousand ball games at various levels of play. First and foremost they are real pitchers, not models, each with his own little idiosyncrasies and unique personality as evidenced in the photos. While each exhibits strong mechanics, every one of them, from third grader to pro, will tell you, one way or another, that he is a work in progress with room for improvement. Each knows that excellence will always require nothing less than his hardest and smartest effort.

Coach John Bagonzi, Matt Simula, Marcus Levin, Jacob Holden, Jeff Locke and Bill McLane *(l to r)*

Bill McLane This lefty with good movement on his fastball and a Bagonzi-tutored curveball led his Plymouth Area High School team to the Class I state championship as a sophomore. Boasting a phenomenal strikeout to walk ratio, this intense competitor has earned himself a college scholarship.

Matt Simula This class of 2003 Plymouth Area High School pitcher and catcher promises to keep his school at the top of the pack for another two years. Having grown tremendously over the last two years, this righthander is starting to maximize the great leverage system he has inherited. A baseball purist, he is now adding a curve to his stinging fastball.

Jacob Holden An all-around athlete, Jacob is a prime example of how hard work and conscientious training can turn an athlete into a pitcher. He continues a tradition of great ballplayers coming out of tiny Woodsville High School.

Scott Blood Scott just completed his senior year as a starting pitcher at a Division I college. This righthander with picture-perfect mechanics has a strong pedigree. His father, Steve, won 50 games at Woodsville High for Coach Bagonzi and spent some time with the Minnesota Twins.

Chad Paronto Another pitcher with a strong Woodsville bloodline. His father and uncles were stars at Woodsville High, with one of his uncles getting signed by the Atlanta Braves. At this writing, Chad is a rookie with the Cleveland Indians and has been cited by Roger Clemens among others as having great mechanics. Throws in the mid-nineties with a bat-breaking sinking fastball. He is one pitch away from becoming a genuine Major League star.

Dave Soroka A Bagonzi clinic award winner for his great mechanics, this small-sized righthander from Conway, NH proves that mechanics is just as important as size when it comes to generating power. He was picked as an All-Star this past year and will be going on to play college ball.

Marcus Levin During 2001 this twelve year-old righty led his team to the Mt. Washington Valley Cal Ripken Major League Championship. Giving up only two runs, both unearned, over 32 innings, he flirted with a perfect game every time out. With fielding mechanics to match his pitching mechanics, he mishandled just two balls over three years while leading his team in assists.

Jeff Locke Last year as a rangy twelve year-old, this lefty mowed down batters with a 70 mph fastball with terrific second stage movement. A great hitter, when pitching, he frequently out-hit the opposition. This season he has moved up to Babe Ruth where he is becoming an instant star, both on the mound and at the plate.

Other models used include Ryan Ackerman, Garret Chambers, Matt Bray, Alex Jacobine, Chris Foss, Brian Comeau, Sam Glynn, Nick Kevlin and Keith Trombley.

GLOSSARY OF PITCHING TERMS

BURYING THE SHOULDER When a pitch is delivered to the plate and chest is brought over the front knee, the pitching shoulder ends up pointing to the plate with the pitching hand coming to the left of the lead leg (rhp).

CAPTAIN'S WHEEL Where one visualizes both arms and the entire shoulder girdle as a large wheel. Helpful when trying to get the off-arm (a second hand on the wheel) involved in turning the upper body to add extra power.

COVER THE BOX This is positioning of the glove hand so that the imaginary box (a seven-inch square around the pitching hand) is obscured to keep the batter from seeing the ball until as late as possible. Pitchers who are good at this are often referred to as sneaky-quick.

FADE Action of the ball that moves away from the hitter (to the left for rhp).

FOOT PLANT When the foot of the lead leg touches down — ideally just as the throwing hand reaches the high-cock position. Landing on the ball of the foot helps in trunk rotation.

FORWARD WRIST This is the direction of the wrist from the high-cock position to the release point. The arm must rapidly accelerate after reaching high-cock position. As the hand passes the ear with thumb in front, the elbow should be leading. This is essentially the Magic Moment.

HAND-BREAK The instant where the pitching hand brings the ball out of the glove. This occurs when lift leg begins to stride forward. Proper timing here along with leading with the hip avoids rushing.

HIGH-COCK POSITION The position of the pitching hand when it reaches the height of the pitching circle. At this point the fingers should be on top of the ball and the thumb should face generally towards the outfield. This is position seven in a ten step approach to full mechanics. Also referred to as launch position.

HIP ROLL Positioning of the hip in a leading manner by brining the lead knee toward the back shoulder on wind-up. This also loads the hips.

LOADING THE HIPS This maximizes power like the coiling of a spring. With the knee coming up towards the back shoulder, the lead hip should be aligned towards the plate.

OFF-ARM This is the glove side or directional side. The tuning of this part in pitching helps accelerate the pitching arm. The correct use of this side also helps in balance.

PITCHER'S LOOP This is the position of the hand, ball, and glove, in anticipation of the pitcher beginning his wind-up. Usually somewhere behind the body's mid-line. Loop can be held high (chin level), medium (chest) or low (just above waist).

POWER SINKER A sinker fastball thrown with a lot of velocity — it has bite to it and works best when low. Will typically result in groundballs

POWER SLIDER A quick hard breaking slider thrown with velocity. A very good pitch used together with a high velocity fastball.

PRONATION Turning the thumb outward on release of the fastball and other pitches. For a RHP the thumb would go to the right in pronation. The opposite of supination. Lefties tend to have a more natural pronation.

PURCHASE This is the preliminary position when pitcher is taking sign from catcher and is addressing the batter. The pitcher's front foot is on pitching plate at this time as required by the rules of baseball.

PUSH-OFF An absolute required for hard throwing, where the back foot engages the front edge of the rubber and helps drive the body forward.

RISER A fastball that goes up (it probably doesn't go up — but because it doesn't go down as quickly as the brain expects, it gives the impression of going up). This is thrown straight through the heart of the ball utilizing a four-seam grip with a 12/6 rotation.

RUSHING When the action of the body gets ahead of the pitching arm. Caused by various mechanical problems, it will result in the hips opening too early.

SCROOGIE The screwball thrown with an extreme pronation of the hand. It is essentially a reverse curveball. It breaks in and down from a righthand player to a righthand batter.

SECOND STAGE FASTBALL A fastball that acts in the last 5 to 10 ft. of its flight. Usually due to a lot of rotation. Best type of fastball there is.

STAYING ON TOP This is set up by the pitcher lifting the ball to the top of the pitching circle. Through the launch phase the pitcher should keep his hand over the ball to keep from pushing the ball forward.

TAILER This is the veer on a fastball generally a 1/7 (rhp) or 11/5 (lhp) type spin. For a righthand player the ball moves toward a righthand batter. For a lefthand player it moves towards a lefthand batter — sometimes called a runner.

TIGHT SPIN An extra amount of rotation applied to the baseball by the fingertips. This makes the ball act.

UNCLE CHARLIE Another name for a good, big breaking curveball. The precursor to a yellow hammer.

THE WALL An imaginary barrier midway through one's pitching stride. The head and shoulders always pass over this wall in delivering a pitch. Visualizing this will help a pitcher get his chest over his knee upon release.

YELLOW HAMMER The epitome of the majestic curveball. A quick, sharp breaking downward curveball. Named after a bird that dives suddenly for an insect in flight.

Official Rules of Pitching Major League Baseball

8.00 The Pitcher.

8.01 Legal pitching delivery. There are two legal pitching positions, the Windup Position and the Set Position, and either position may be used at any time. Pitchers shall take signs from the catcher while standing on the rubber. Pitchers may disengage the rubber after taking their signs but may not step quickly onto the rubber and pitch. This may be judged a quick pitch by the umpire. When the pitcher disengages the rubber, he must drop his hands to his sides. Pitchers will not be allowed to disengage the rubber after taking each sign.

(a) The Windup Position. The pitcher shall stand facing the batter, his entire pivot foot on, or in front of and touching and not off the end of the pitcher's plate, and the other foot free. From this position any natural movement associated with his delivery of the ball to the batter commits him to the pitch without interruption or alteration. He shall not raise either foot from the ground, except that in his actual delivery of the ball to the batter, he may take one step backward, and one step forward with his free foot. When a pitcher holds the ball with both hands in front of his body, with his entire pivot foot on, or in front of and touching but not off the end of the pitcher's plate, and his other foot free, he will be considered in the Windup Position. The pitcher may have one foot, not the pivot foot, off the rubber and any distance he may desire back of a line which is an extension to the back edge of the pitcher's plate, but not at either side of the pitcher's plate. With his "free" foot the pitcher may take one step backward and one step forward, but under no circumstances, to either side, that is to either the first base or third base side of the pitcher's rubber. If a pitcher holds the ball with both hands in front of his body, with his entire pivot foot on or in front of and touching but not off the end of the pitcher's plate, and his other foot free, he will be considered in a windup position. From this position he may: (1) deliver the ball to the batter, or (2) step and throw to a base in an attempt to pick off a runner, or (3) disengage the rubber (if he does he must drop his hand to his sides). In disengaging the rubber the pitcher must step off with his pivot foot and not his free foot first. He may not go into a set or stretch position_if he does it is a balk.

(b) The Set Position. Set Position shall be indicated by the pitcher when he stands facing the batter with his entire pivot foot on, or in front of, and in contact with, and not off the end of the pitcher's plate, and his other foot in front of the pitcher's plate, holding the ball in both hands in front of his body and coming to a complete stop. From such Set Position he may deliver the ball to the batter, throw to a base or step backward off the pitcher's plate with his pivot foot. Before assuming Set Position, the pitcher may elect to make any natural preliminary motion such as that known as "the stretch." But if he so elects, he shall come to Set Position before delivering the ball to the batter. After assuming Set Position, any natural motion associated with his delivery of the ball to the batter commits him to the pitch without alteration or interruption. Preparatory to coming to a set position, the pitcher shall have one hand on his side; from this position he shall go to his set position as defined in Rule 8.01 (b) without interruption and in one continuous motion. The whole width of the foot in contact with the rubber must be on the rubber. A pitcher cannot pitch from off the end of the rubber with just the side of his foot touching the rubber. The pitcher, following his stretch, must (a) hold the ball in both hands in front of his body and (b) come to a complete stop. This must be enforced. Umpires should watch this closely. Pitchers are constantly attempting to "beat the rule" in their efforts to hold runners on bases and in cases where the pitcher fails to make a complete "stop" called for in the rules, the umpire should immediately call a "Balk."

(c) At any time during the pitcher's preliminary movements and until his natural pitching motion commits him to the pitch, he may throw to any base provided he steps directly toward such base before making the throw. The pitcher shall step "ahead of the throw." A snap throw followed by the step directly toward the base is a balk.

(d) If the pitcher makes an illegal pitch with the bases unoccupied, it shall be called a ball unless the batter reaches first base on a hit, an error, a base on balls, a hit batter or otherwise. A ball which slips out of a pitcher's hand and crosses the foul line shall be called a ball; otherwise it will be called no pitch. This would be a balk with men on base.

(e) If the pitcher removes his pivot foot from contact with the pitcher's plate by stepping backward with that foot, he thereby becomes an infielder and if he makes a wild throw from that position, it shall be considered the same as a wild throw by any other infielder. The pitcher, while off the rubber, may throw to any base. If he makes a wild throw, such throw is the throw of an infielder and what follows is governed by the rules covering a ball thrown by a fielder.

8.02 The pitcher shall not—

(a)

(1) Bring his pitching hand in contact with his mouth or lips while in the 18 foot circle surrounding the pitching rubber. EXCEPTION: Provided it is agreed to by both managers, the umpire prior to the start of a game played in cold weather, may permit the pitcher to blow on his hand.
PENALTY: For violation of this part of this rule the umpires shall immediately call a ball. However, if the pitch is made and a batter reaches first base on a hit, an error, a hit batsman or otherwise, and no other runner is put out before advancing at least one base, the play shall proceed without reference to the violation. Repeated offenders shall be subject to a fine by the league president.
(2) Apply a foreign substance of any kind to the ball;
(3) expectorate on the ball, either hand or his glove;
(4) rub the ball on his glove, person or clothing;
(5) deface the ball in any manner;
(6) deliver what is called the "shine" ball, "spit" ball, "mud" ball or "emery"
ball. The pitcher, of course, is allowed to rub the ball between his bare hands.
PENALTY: For violation of any part of this rule 8.02 (a) (2 to 6) the umpire shall:
(a) Call the pitch a ball, warn the pitcher and have announced on the public address system the reason for the action.
(b) In the case of a second offense by the same pitcher in the same game, the pitcher shall be disqualified from the game.
(c) If a play follows the violation called by the umpire, the manager of the offense   may advise the plate umpire that he elects to accept the play. Such election shall be made immediately at the end of the play. However, if the batter reaches first base on a hit, an error, a base on balls, a hit batsman, or otherwise, and no other runner is put out before advancing at least one base, the play shall proceed without reference to the violation.
(d) Even though the offense elects to take the play, the violation shall be recognized and the penalties in (a) and (b) will still be in effect.
(e) The umpire shall be sole judge on whether any portion of this rule has been violated. All umpires shall carry with them one official rosin bag. The umpire in chief is responsible for placing the rosin bag on the ground back of the pitcher's plate. If at any time the ball hits the rosin bag it is in play. In the case of rain or wet field, the umpire may instruct the pitcher to carry the rosin bag in his hip pocket. A pitcher may use the rosin bag for the purpose of applying rosin to his bare hand or hands. Neither the pitcher nor any other player shall dust the ball with the rosin bag; neither shall the pitcher nor any other player be permitted to apply rosin from the bag to his glove or dust any part of his uniform with the rosin bag.
(b) Have on his person, or in his possession, any foreign substance. For such infraction of this section (b) the penalty shall be immediate ejection from the game.
(c) Intentionally delay the game by throwing the ball to players other than the catcher, when the batter is in position, except in an attempt to retire a runner.
PENALTY: If, after warning by the umpire, such delaying action is repeated, the pitcher shall be removed from the game.
(d) Intentionally Pitch at the Batter. If, in the umpire's judgment, such a violation occurs, the umpire may elect either to: 1. Expel the pitcher, or the manager and the pitcher, from the game, or 2. may warn the pitcher and the manager of both teams that another such pitch will result in the immediate expulsion of that pitcher (or a replacement) and the manager. If, in the umpire's judgment, circumstances warrant, both teams may be officially "warned" prior to the game or at any time during the game. (League Presidents may take additional action under authority provided in Rule 9.05) To pitch at a batter's head is unsportsmanlike

and highly dangerous. It should be-and is-condemned by everybody. Umpires should act without hesitation in enforcement of this rule.

8.03 When a pitcher takes his position at the beginning of each inning, or when he relieves another pitcher, he shall be permitted to pitch not to exceed eight preparatory pitches to his catcher during which play shall be suspended. A league by its own action may limit the number of preparatory pitches to less than eight preparatory pitches. Such preparatory pitches shall not consume more than one minute of time. If a sudden emergency causes a pitcher to be summoned into the game without any opportunity to warm up, the umpire in chief shall allow him as many pitches as the umpire deems necessary.

8.04 When the bases are unoccupied, the pitcher shall deliver the ball to the batter within 20 seconds after he receives the ball. Each time the pitcher delays the game by violating this rule, the umpire shall call "Ball." The intent of this rule is to avoid unnecessary delays. The umpire shall insist that the catcher return the ball promptly to the pitcher, and that the pitcher take his position on the rubber promptly. Obvious delay by the pitcher should instantly be penalized by the umpire.

8.05 If there is a runner, or runners, it is a balk when–

(a) The pitcher, while touching his plate, makes any motion naturally associated with his pitch and fails to make such delivery; If a lefthanded or righthanded pitcher swings his free foot past the back edge of the pitcher's rubber, he is required to pitch to the batter except to throw to second base on a pick off play.

(b) The pitcher, while touching his plate, feints a throw to first base and fails to complete the throw;

(c) The pitcher, while touching his plate, fails to step directly toward a base before throwing to that base; Requires the pitcher, while touching his plate, to step directly toward a base before throwing to that base. If a pitcher turns or spins off of his free foot without actually stepping or if he turns his body and throws before stepping, it is a balk. A pitcher is to step directly toward a base before throwing to that base but does not require him to throw (except to first base only) because he steps. It is possible, with runners on first and third, for the pitcher to step toward third and not throw, merely to bluff the runner back to third; then seeing the runner on first start for second, turn and step toward and throw to first base. This is legal. However, if, with runners on first and third, the pitcher, while in contact with the rubber, steps toward third and then immediately and in practically the same motion "wheels" and throws to first base, it is obviously an attempt to deceive the runner at first base, and in such a move it is practically impossible to step directly toward first base before the throw to first base, and such a move shall be called a balk. Of course, if the pitcher steps off the rubber and then makes such a move, it is not a balk.

(d) The pitcher, while touching his plate, throws, or feints a throw to an unoccupied base, except for the purpose of making a play;

(e) The pitcher makes an illegal pitch; A quick pitch is an illegal pitch. Umpires will judge a quick pitch as one delivered before the batter is reasonably set in the batter's box. With runners on base the penalty is a balk; with no runners on base, it is a ball. The quick pitch is dangerous and should not be permitted.

(f) The pitcher delivers the ball to the batter while he is not facing the batter;

(g) The pitcher makes any motion naturally associated with his pitch while he is not touching the pitcher's plate;

(h) The pitcher unnecessarily delays the game;

(i) The pitcher, without having the ball, stands on or astride the pitcher's plate or while off the plate, he feints a pitch;

(j) The pitcher, after coming to a legal pitching position, removes one hand from the ball other than in an actual pitch, or in throwing to a base;

(k) The pitcher, while touching his plate, accidentally or intentionally drops the ball;

(l) The pitcher, while giving an intentional base on balls, pitches when the catcher is not in the catcher's box;

(m) The pitcher delivers the pitch from Set Position without coming to a stop.

PENALTY: The ball is dead, and each runner shall advance one base without liability to be put out, unless the batter reaches first on a hit, an error, a base on balls, a hit batter, or otherwise, and all other runners advance at least one base, in which case the play proceeds without reference to the balk.

APPROVED RULING: In cases where a pitcher balks and throws wild, either to a base or to home plate, a runner or runners may advance beyond the base to which he is entitled at his own risk.

APPROVED RULING: A runner who misses the first base to which he is advancing and who is called out on appeal shall be considered as having advanced one base for the purpose of this rule. Umpires should bear in mind that the purpose of the balk rule is to prevent the pitcher from deliberately deceiving the base runner. If there is doubt in the umpire's mind, the "intent" of the pitcher should govern. However, certain specifics should be borne in mind:

    (a) Straddling the pitcher's rubber without the ball is to be interpreted as intent to deceive and ruled a balk.

    (b) With a runner on first base the pitcher may make a complete turn, without hesitating toward first, and throw to second. This is not to be interpreted as throwing to an unoccupied base.

8.06 A professional league shall adopt the following rule pertaining to the visit of the manager or coach to the pitcher:

    (a) This rule limits the number of trips a manager or coach may make to any one pitcher in any one inning; (b) A second trip to the same pitcher in the same inning will cause this pitcher's automatic removal; (c) The manager or coach is prohibited from making a second visit to the mound while the same batter is at bat, but (d) if a pinch hitter is substituted for this batter, the manager or coach may make a second visit to the mound, but must remove the pitcher. A manager or coach is considered to have concluded his visit to the mound when he leaves the 18 foot circle surrounding the pitcher's rubber. If the manager or coach goes to the catcher or infielder and that player then goes to the mound or the pitcher comes to him at his position before there is an intervening play (a pitch or other play) that will be the same as the manager or coach going to the mound. Any attempt to evade or circumvent this rule by the manager or coach going to the catcher or an infielder and then that player going to the mound to confer with the pitcher shall constitute a trip to the mound. If the coach goes to the mound and removes a pitcher and then the manager goes to the mound to talk with the new pitcher, that will constitute one trip to that new pitcher that inning. In a case where a manager has made his first trip to the mound and then returns the second time to the mound in the same inning with the same pitcher in the game and the same batter at bat, after being warned by the umpire that he cannot return to the mound, the manager shall be removed from the game and the pitcher required to pitch to the batter until he is retired or gets on base. After the batter is retired, or becomes a base runner, then this pitcher must be removed from the game. The manager should be notified that his pitcher will be removed from the game after he pitches to one hitter, so he can have a substitute pitcher warmed up. The substitute pitcher will be allowed eight preparatory pitches or more if in the umpire's judgment circumstances justify.

—The rules here are published, courtesy of Major League Baseball.

Recommended Reading

OPTIMUM SPORTS NUTRITION, Dr. Michael Colgan
Advanced Research Press
Absolutely the finest book on sports nutrition for those disciplined enough to gain a further competitive edge through proper nutrition. Great practical advice on how to properly fuel the body, backed up by intense research and numerous practical studies. Also addresses supplements and includes discussion on the use of steroids and alternatives for building strength and endurance.

POWER, A SCIENTIFIC APPROACH, Dr. Frederick C. Hatfield
NTC/Contemporary Publishing
Dr. Hatfield has written several books worth looking at that include excellent information on developing power through weight training as well as the use of supplements. For the pitcher, his training programs are excellent for building lower body strength. He is known as Dr. Squat for setting world records in the squat. His methods will maximize and streamline your time in the gym. But as we state elsewhere in the book, power-lifting for the upper body is not a smart way to go for pitchers.

THE PHYSICS OF BASEBALL, Professor Robert Adair, HarperCollins
This Sterling Professor of Physics from Yale provides ample food for thought for those curious about why a baseball behaves the way it does. Will give a deeper understanding to those interested in the hows and whys of getting a pitched baseball to move.

SPORTS HEALTH. THE COMPLETE BOOK OF ATHLETIC INJURIES
William Southmayd, MD and Marshall Hoffman, Perigee Books
Over the years this has been the bible of sports injury and rehabilitation. Currently, out of print, the book can still be found on store shelves and purchased used. Covering the entire muscular-skeletal system, the book offers one the opportunity to self-diagnose injuries and help with determining whether professional treatment should be sought. It also covers treatment, both what can be done at home and what a doctor and physical therapist might prescribe. Excellent drawings and clear cut explanations will give the layman a better understanding of how various joints and muscle systems function.

Professional Ballplayers of America
"One of the greatest books ever written on pitching called "The Act of Pitching" has just been released. Written by a coaches' coach, Dr. John Bagonzi, he synthesizes over 40 years of coaching experience in creating a master textbook on pitching. The book features over 400 photos in 15 chapters that show in minute detail how to become an accomplished pitcher. Dr Bagonzi's writing style is brilliant as he offers a new dimension to pitching instruction from youth players to pitchers in the Big Leagues. If you choose to purchase only one book on pitching this year, this is the one to look at. I had a difficult time putting it down until all 350 pages were devoured."*

**— Lou Pavlovich, Jr.
editor, Collegiate Baseball,**

Bert Blyleven, 287 game winner, Minnesota Twins great pitcher, and future Hall of Famer, with Coach Bagonzi admiring "The Act of Pitching."

Bagonzi's book shows AND tells. His 400 photos (chosen from nearly 7,000 snapped) illuminate his crisp, clear and concise writing style. Is the book just for professional pitchers? Not even close. **Bagonzi covers the craft for players from Little League to The Show.**

**— Joe Sullivan, sports writer
Manchester Union Leader,
New Hampshire**

"The Act of Pitching" details more grips, more pitches, more strategies than any one pitcher could use. Pitchers come in all sizes, shapes, and make-ups, and the Bagonzi way is not about creating robots, it's about developing great mechanics and a head for the game.

**— The Berlin Daily Sun,
Berlin, New Hampshire**

This one is different. It's a great read. *Bagonzi has found a way to spin the tale so that the book gets the message across without seeming like instruction.*

**— Tom Haley,
Rutland Herald, Vermont**

This is an in-depth, scientific study on the act of pitching. Like it's author, this book has a no-nonsense approach to the subject matter. **This is an in-your-face, drum-banging lesson on the act of pitching.**

**— Don Mahler, sports editor
Valley News, W. Lebanon, NH**

For more information on

The Act of Pitching

visit **pitchingprofessor.com**

Pitching Professor Publications
19 Pine Street, Woodsville, New Hampshire 03785

Book Reviews

The best book on pitching that I have ever read.

—Bob Feller, Cleveland Indians Great and Major League Hall of Fame Immortal

"*The Act of Pitching*" offers concise pictures and diagrams, and very readable instructions on how to become a better pitcher. **Any player can enhance his skills at pitching by reading your book.**

Many years of research and hard work has produced a great book for the sport of baseball.

**— Richard Seko,
20 year professional scout,
Texas Rangers**

I have known John Bagonzi since we entered the first grade together. It didn't take too long to realize that John was special and I feel very fortunate for the friendship that we have maintained throughout our lives.

John's special abilities have been demonstrated as an athlete, coach, writer, husband, father, and friend to name a few.

Now he has delivered big time with what I feel without a doubt is the best and most complete tutorial ever published — "The Act of Pitching."

Cover to cover this is a masterpiece in it's field that will appeal to anyone even slightly interested in the pitching aspect of baseball. A must for the libraries of those who teach pitching. Thanks for sharing this marvelous teaching tool with others.

— Bob Smith, former pitcher, Boston Red Sox, Detroit Tigers and Pittsburgh Pirates
Lifetime member, Association of Professional Ballplayers of America

BASEBALL

THE ACT OF PITCHING
By John Bagonzi.
Edited by Alex Levin.
Pp. 344. Photos.
Hedgehoghill Press, Madison NH
(paperback).

One of the exceptional veteran pitching instructors in the great Northeast, John Bagonzi was a great college pitcher who developed his playing and teaching skills in the Boston Red Sox chain before settling down to a lifetime of specialized teaching.

Blessed with an inexhaustible fund of knowledge, he has been producing outstanding pitchers on every level of the game.

The Act of Pitching offers an outstanding example of his teaching skills. He uses hundreds of special

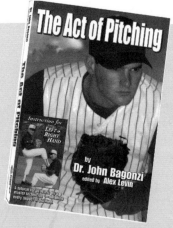

photographs to illustrate and articulate every facet of the pitching art. Dr. Bagonzi has been exhibiting it in *Scholastic Coach* over the past several years.

Coaches on every level of the game, from Little to Big League, will find the book extremely useful.

Featured article from ***Scholastic Coach and Athletic Director***,
March, 2002. Herman Masin, editor

—continued